HISTORIC
WOLFVILLE
GRAND PRÉ
AND COUNTRYSIDE

TOM SHEPPARD

NIMBUS
PUBLISHING

Nimbus Publishing Limited
PO Box 9166, Halifax, NS   B3K 5M8
(902) 455-4286

Printed and bound in Canada
Design:Terri Strickland
Author Photo: Peter Barss

Cover: Tea in the garden at Fred Brown's house, c. 1885
Title page: A schooner enters Wolfville harbour, c. 1884

National Library of Canada Cataloguing in Publication

   Sheppard, Tom
   Historic Wolfville, Grand Pré and countryside / Tom Sheppard.

   (Images of our past)
   Includes bibliographical references.
   ISBN 1-55109-469-X

1. Wolfville (N.S.)--History. 2. Grand Pré (N.S.)--History. I. Title. II. Series.

FC2349.W64S44 2003   971.6'34   C2003-905406-3

We acknowledge the financial support of the Government of Canada through the Book Publishing Industry Development Program (BPIDP) and the Canada Council for our publishing activities.

In memory of my parents,
Barbara Eaton
and
T.M. (Tony) Sheppard

Acknowledgements

I would like to acknowledge my wife, Sheila, who travelled with me during the preparation of this book, cheerfully undertaking research assignments, carefully reading the final copy and making many useful suggestions. Her friendship and support have been invaluable.

I received an enormous amount of help from the Esther Clark Wright Archives at Acadia University and from the Randall House Museum. At the archives, University Archivist Pat Townsend became a part of the project, digging out materials, consulting on photographs and reading the manuscript. She and the others in the archives—Rhianna Edwards, Greg Brown and Winnie Bodden—were always welcoming and provided needed assistance. At the Randall House Museum, curator Heather Davidson opened the museum and its resources to this project. She and the Wolfville Historical Society, whose president is John Whidden, have collected a treasure trove of history about Wolfville and its countryside and have been generous in sharing it. I thank people like Glen Hancock, Gordon Haliburton and Eileen Bishop for the work they have done, and for the conversations we had. I also want to acknowledge the work done by James Doyle Davidson and his team of researchers, who in 1985 collected their work in the book *Mud Creek*.

The Nova Scotia Archives and Records Management, Halifax, was also very helpful to me. My thanks to Philip Hartling and Garry Shutlak for their expertise and assistance. Likewise, Bria Stokesbury and the Kings County Museum, Kentville, were of assistance.

I was given access to Tony Kalkman's valuable collection of Edson Graham photographs, for which I am extremely grateful. Tony, who lives in Kentville, found pictures needed for this book and shared them with me. I likewise want to thank my brother, David Sheppard, whose interest in history and genealogy have led him to collect a number of photographs important to the history of the area. He also made available the Jack Marriott photographs for use in this book. I would acknowledge too the help of Elizabeth Goodstein, who spent a good deal of time talking with me about the history of various families and who provided some important photographs. I thank Joan Eaton, who dug out photo albums and made pictures available.

I thank Susan Haley, who provided photographs and stories of her parents for this book, and Warren Peck, who gave me some of his father Ron Peck's photographs. I am grateful to the many others who contributed in some manner, including Sandra Atwell Tennyson, David Burton, King and Ruth Butler, Rhoda and Alex Colville, Sandy VanZoost Dyer, Marcia Merrett Elliott, Robbins Elliott, Shirley Elliott, Robert Harvey, Andria Hill, Larry Keddy, Bill Pearman, Ron Porter, Garth Regan, Peter and Brenda Sheppard, Mayor Robert Stead, Brodie Thomas, Jim Tillotson, Alan Wilson, Jeff Wilson, and Gertrude Phinney Beattie, who appears in this book and with whom I had a conversation about her family's role in Wolfville's history. I also want to acknowledge the assistance given by Dan Soucoup, Sandra McIntyre and Dorothy Blythe, at Nimbus Publishing. As always, I thank my sister, Sandra, for her insights, and my children, Anne-Marie and Jonathan, for their continuing support.

Contents

Introduction

A Land of Legend

This is a land of legend; every mount
A story has, would hoary shades recount.
There is no valley, marsh, or misty shore,
Without the charm of mystery and lore—
Where rivers mute with wonder yet might tell
The whole to him who waits and questions well.

—John Frederic Herbin, 1893, Wolfville poet and merchant

Wolfville sits on the shores of the Minas Basin, with Blomidon providing a majestic backdrop to it and the surrounding communities. This book is its history, told through the enduring magic of old photographs. It focuses on Wolfville and Grand Pré, but touches as well on the places close to Wolfville and on those historically connected to it by the Cornwallis River and the Minas Basin—places like Gaspereau, Port Williams, Starr's Point, and Kingsport. It also looks to the shiretown of Kentville and to Canning, historically Kings County's other two major towns.

In January 1909, Wolfville mayor W. Marshall Black told his townspeople that from every standpoint they had one of the finest towns in the province: "You have churches of all denominations, unsurpassed educational facilities, good sewerage, superior water service, a good train service, an all-night telephone system and an all-night electric service within your reach, and the lowest [...] tax rate in the Province taking into consideration the services at your command."

There have been some changes in nearly a century: the electric lights operate all night now but the train service has declined. In many respects Wolfville is still one of the finest places to live in Nova Scotia. The town forms the heart of this book. Since this is a history told through photographs, there is a necessary historical framework bounded on the one side by the popular use of photography, which occurred from roughly the 1870s onward, and on the other by the 1950s, anything later being considered too recent for inclusion. Where there are no photographs, text fills the gap, particularly in the years before photography.

The human history of Wolfville and the communities that surround it belongs first to the native peoples, then follows from the great events occurring in Europe and North America. When the French arrived in the Minas Basin—to create an area described by John Frederic Herbin as being noted "both for the richness of its soil and the loveliness of its farms and orchards"—they formed an alliance with the Mi'kmaq, which brought them into conflict with the English, who eventually won

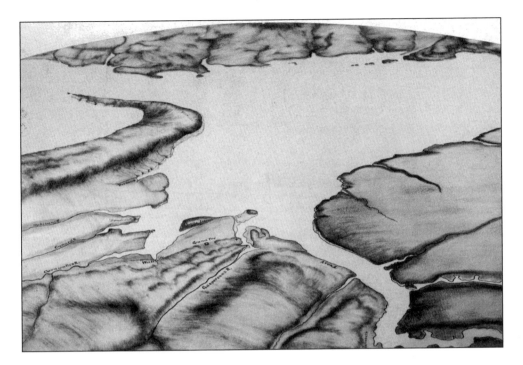

The Minas Basin, from the 1800s

This old map was acquired by the Nova Scotia Archives and Records Management from the Maine Historical Society. A label on the map indicates that it is from the 1700s, but since the name "Wolfville" shows (west of Grand Pré), it must be dated from around 1830, when the town was named. The curve of Blomidon is nicely depicted, as are the rivers flowing into the Minas Basin, ranging from the large Avon at the lower right centre, to the Pereau, close to Blomidon.

Nova Scotia. After the French were sent away, New England settlers, called Planters, were invited in to populate the vacant lands, which they named Horton and Cornwallis. Making use of dykelands built and lost by the Acadians, they and their descendants built prosperous farms and expanded their communities, many of them settling in what is now Wolfville. The way the area grew, and the pictures that survive from that time, are the subject of this book.

The Early People and Their Valley

The student publication at Wolfville High School was always called *The Glooscap*. Not many names from the native peoples survive in Kings County, unlike elsewhere in the province, but Glooscap—the mythological figure who made Blomidon his home—is one that does. Glooscap presided over the lands surrounding the Minas Basin and beyond, watching over his people. This was their land, and in it they lived, hunting, fishing and gathering food, establishing a sophisticated and fundamentally democratic society. It was a society that later welcomed, then came into conflict with, waves of European settlers who arrived to occupy their land.

In 1910, Arthur Wentworth Hamilton Eaton wrote *The History of Kings County: Heart of the Acadian Land*, which devoted a chapter to the "Micmacs"—now referred to as the Mi'kmaq (spelled "Mi'kmaw" when used as an adjective or when referring to an individual). Eaton said that the land in ancient times was full of moose, caribou and wild fowl, and that these furnished the Mi'kmaq with food. Groups moved from place to place as the seasons dictated, setting up homes in many parts of the lands dominated by Blomidon. He quoted an early witness who wrote of a Mi'kmaw encampment where food was being prepared in cauldrons suspended over a fire, containing stews of porcupine, caribou and duck: "Salmon were roasting before the fires, the fish being inserted, wedge fashion, into a split piece of ash some two feet in length, crossed by other splits, its end planted firmly into the earth at a convenient distance from the fire." These encampments might have been found to the middle of the nineteenth century, in many places familiar to people in Kings County today.

The ancestors of these Mi'kmaq inhabited the area eleven thousand years ago, moving in after the glaciers of the last ice age retreated. There is little evidence of their

Mi'kmaw at Evangeline Beach, c. 1906

The photograph identifies the Mi'kmaw woman in this photograph only as Mrs. Knockwood. The Mi'kmaq used to set up a camp at Evangeline Beach for the summer, where they would make and sell handcrafts, such as baskets.

life, perhaps because rising sea levels covered the places where they lived, but the *Natural History of Kings County*, edited by Merritt Gibson and published by the Blomidon Naturalists Society in 1992, notes that a site between two and five thousand years old was discovered near Gaspereau Lake. Archaeologists have discovered more recent sites, dating from between five hundred and twenty-five hundred years ago, on the western side of Long Island near Evangeline Beach, and in the Scots Bay area near Blomidon. The village of Melanson is believed to have been a summer base camp for the Mi'kmaq, where they fished salmon, smelt, gaspereaux, striped sea bass, eel and shad. They made use of what is now Wolfville, naming it *Mtaban*, a word translated as "mudcat fishing ground."

Mi'kmaw sites, from both before and after contact with the Europeans, have been found as well around Starr's Point, Canning, and the mouth of the Canard River. These areas were part of their natural world. *The Natural History* makes an important point when it says that the Mi'kmaq believed that every living thing had a spirit: "They protected their environment, communicated with plants and animals to show respect and to encourage abundance, and only took what was needed." Other histories have noted the sophistication of the Mi'kmaw culture. Naomi Griffiths, who gave the 1988 Winthrop Pickard Bell Lecture in Maritime Studies at Mount Allison University, said during her address that it is now acknowledged that the people indigenous to the Americas had a complex history, religions that were mystical and sophisticated, and cultural lives of intricate subtlety before Europeans ever reached their shores.

The arrival of the European settlers was difficult for the Mi'kmaq. They had befriended the first settlers, the French, by intermarrying, sharing food and converting to the Roman Catholic religion. When the English arrived and entered into a contest for control of the area, the Mi'kmaq were loyal to the French and fought beside them. Consequently, bounties were placed on Mi'kmaw' heads, their way of life was changed irrevocably, and their numbers declined; so much so, Eaton said, that in 1901 Kings County's share of the Mi'kmaw population numbered just twenty-eight.

The Acadian Land

John Frederic Herbin wrote *The History of Grand Pré* at the turn of the last century. In it he argued for a memorial to the Acadians, to stand among the few landmarks of the departed people that have come down to us from their day: "The row of willows they set out alongside the church road must in time fall into decay. The depression in the earth which was once a cellar will be filled up. The well may cease to exist. The site of the Acadian church is less plainly discernable every year. Not a trace remains of the cemetery. Time is obliterating the Acadian roads."

Herbin was a descendant of the Acadians, his mother's family having lived and farmed in Grand Pré for generations. Herbin was himself a poet, merchant, outdoorsman and mayor of Wolfville. He thought that Longfellow's celebrated epic poem, *Evangeline*, was a remarkably correct page of history, and devoted much of his life to preserving the story of the Acadians. In *The History of Grand Pré* he characterizes the Acadians as honest, sober and frugal, the women virtuous and industrious. Singing, dancing and open hospitality cheered their homes, and they lived as one large family. Herbin often visited the areas occupied by the Acadians, writing that their orchards still bore fruit, and that cellar walls marked the places where they lived and died. By some strange chance, he felt, he was the only Acadian he knew of living among the scenes that the Acadians once knew.

The Acadians arrived in the 1670s. Pierre Melanson and his wife, Margaret Mius d'Entremont, as well as Pierre Terriau and his wife, Celine Landry, moved there from the settlement at Port Royal. They were among the first of the Minas Basin Acadians. French explorers Samuel de Champlain, Jean Sieur de Poutrincourt and Pierre Sieur de Monts had sailed into the basin in 1604, looking for minerals, and had called the waters "Les Mines," from which the name Minas Basin evolved. When the settlers came from Port Royal they found a magnificent land stretching from Blomidon

EVANGELINE MONUMENT AND MEMORIAL CHAPEL GRAND PRE, N.S.

The Evangeline monument, Grand Pré, c.1929

This statue of the Acadian heroine of Longfellow's epic poem was unveiled in August of 1920, in what is now the Grand Pré National Historic Site. Among those speaking were Acadia University President George Cutten and Sir Gilbert Parker, MP.

around the basin to the mouth of the Avon River. It was protected on the north by the ridge of land terminated at its eastern end by Cape Blomidon, originally called "Blow-me-down" by sailors. It was protected on the south by the South Mountain, a term some feel overly generous when applied to the hills of the Southern Uplands. In between was a valley, its red soils a fertile mixture of loams, clays and sand. Its five rivers attracted settlers: Pierre Terriau went to the banks of the Cornwallis River, then called Rivière St. Antoine, and Pierre Melanson to not far from where the Gaspereau empties into the Minas Basin. The other rivers are the Pereau, closest to Blomidon; the Habitant, near Canning; and the Canard, in between. All five rivers flow into the Minas Basin.

Others soon followed Melanson and Terriau. By 1686 three or four families had settled near Melanson and seven near Terriau, for a total of fifty-seven people. By 1701 there were, according to A.W.H. Eaton, seventy-nine families, totaling 498 people—farmers, tailors, seafarers and a physician among them. Settlements were established at Canard, Piziquid (now Windsor), Cobequid (near Truro), and in what we now know as Grand Pré, Gaspereau, Wolfville, Port Williams, Kentville, Starr's Point, Canning and Pereau. There was a settlement at New Minas, with a chapel and a priest, where later English settlers found buried a set of blacksmith's tools. There was also what was understood to be an Acadian stone fort in New Minas.

Eaton wrote that the history of Acadian settlement in Kings County covered a period of exactly eighty-four years. In that time they built houses, churches and small forts. They cleared hundreds of acres of fields, and sent produce by schooner to Louisbourg, as well as to Port Royal and Canso. They spun and wove wool and flax. Building dykes was the most laborious industry of all: the Acadians who had originally come from the marshy west coast of France, where they had learned to keep out the sea, enclosed several thousand acres of marshland from the sea on the Grand Pré and

John Frederic and Minnie Herbin

Merchant, poet, author, geologist, politician and sportsman, John Frederic Herbin influenced not only the town of Wolfville but the way history has treated the Acadians. His wife was Minnie Rounsefell Simpson, of Grand Pré. They married in 1896.

along the five rivers. Herbin wrote that the dykelands were their chief support; on their natural meadows they raised wheat, rye, oats, peas and flax, along with hay in large quantities.

The Acadians around the Minas Basin grew to be the most prosperous of all the Acadians in Nova Scotia. Their settlements covered the area from the mouth of the Gaspereau River to close to what is now Kentville. They were proud and independent and not inclined to follow authority blindly. It was said of them by a fellow Frenchman employed by the British (and later the lieutenant-governor of Nova Scotia), Paul Mascarene, that they were less tractable and subject to command. "All the orders sent to them," Eaton quotes Mascarene as saying, "if not suiting to their humours, are scoffed and laughed at, and they put themselves on the footing of obeying no government." Yet where the British saw intractability, Herbin later described a land of beauty and peace.

International events were beyond the control of the Acadians at Minas, however. France and England had been jousting for control of North America. The Treaty of Utrecht in 1713 ceded Acadia—all of the lands that now are Nova Scotia and New Brunswick—to England, leaving France with Ile Royale, or Cape Breton, and Ile Saint-Jean, or Prince Edward Island. Louisbourg, the massive French fortress on Cape Breton Island, continued to be a threat to the English, and there was some resentment of the fact that the Acadians supplied it with food and goods. Nevertheless, the Acadians went on with life as usual under British rule. In 1744 hostilities broke out again between the French and the English, one result being the capture of Louisbourg by a fleet from the New England colonies. The Acadians attempted to remain neutral, hedging their bets: they would prefer it if France were able to regain control of their lands, but were prepared to live with the English. The English, for their part, assumed that if a conflict broke out again, the Acadians would side with the French. There was the question of the famous loyalty oath, which the Acadians were quite happy to take, as long as the oath did not obligate them to bear arms against their own people. While that had been good enough for earlier governors, for the current one, Governor Charles Lawrence, it was not. He came to believe, as Naomi Griffiths puts it, that his colony could not become a reliable outpost of the British Empire while the Acadians were among its people, and that the best solution was to send them to be assimilated among the populations of the other British North American colonies.

As the backdrop to this situation, the French were sending a force from France to attempt the recapture of Louisbourg, and were ordering a detachment of troops from Quebec to Nova Scotia to assist the French fleet. In 1747, Mascarene and Governor William Shirley of Massachusetts moved to protect Nova Scotia by sending New England volunteers to the province under the command of Lieutenant Colonel Arthur Noble. They landed in Annapolis and made their way to Grand Pré, where, since it was late in the year, they were forced to billet with Acadian families for the winter. Troops from France and Quebec were holed up in present-day Cumberland County. On hearing of the English forces in Grand Pré, they headed there in January 1748 for a sneak attack on the New England troops. It was, by all accounts, a massacre: Noble and his men were awakened in the middle of the night and forced to do battle in their nightshirts. He and a hundred of his men were killed, with fifty captured and many more wounded. The French lost just seven men. Partly owing to this defeat, Halifax was founded as a military post two years later.

What happened next is known to all. That the Acadians were sent away from their lands beginning in 1755 is a dark page in Nova Scotian history, and controversy over the events continues to this day. Some historians would have us consider the context of the times, ameliorating the enormity of the expulsion by weighing the dangers of leaving the Acadians in place at a time when Nova Scotia was worried about further wars with the French. Others believe that the Acadians—a peaceful people uprooted from their loved ones and their homes—were wronged completely. Wherever one stands on the issue, the act itself was without natural justice, a situation where leaders faced with a moral choice between right and wrong chose wrong. One may recognize the extenuating circumstances, yet condemn the decisions made. For Kings County, it changed the course of history.

On September 4, 1755, all male Acadians were ordered to assemble at three in the afternoon the next day at the church in Grand Pré. John Frederic Herbin writes that within less than twenty-four hours they came, from all of the villages around the Minas Basin—from Canard, Pereau, and the Habitant River area, from the Gaspereau Valley, from Minas in the west to Avonport in the east. Four hundred and eighteen men entered the church at the appointed time to find Colonel John Winslow at a table in the centre of the church, surrounded by his officers. When they were gathered, they were told that their homes, lands, poultry and livestock had been forfeited to the Crown, and that they would be taken away from Nova Scotia. They were allowed to retain their savings and household goods. According to Herbin, Colonel Winslow told the men that his words were "very disagreeable to my natural make and temper," but that he must obey orders. He said that he would do everything in his power to make certain that whole families would go in the same vessels, and he offered the hope that wherever they landed, they would be a peaceable and happy people.

Naomi Griffiths writes that there was no need for any measures of brutality to get the Acadians to do Winslow's bidding. They were stunned by what they had heard: "Even when gathered together on the shores, waiting to embark on the transports, the Acadians were not even then fully persuaded that they were actually to be removed." She says that within days the Acadians were turned from a free and flourishing people into a crowd of refugees, their settlements burned and their cattle driven off. Winslow himself described what happened, noting in his journal that when the Acadians began to leave on October 8, the women were in great distress, carrying their children in their arms, while others carried their decrepit parents in their carts, along with their goods. Herbin describes these as "scenes of great confusion, woe and distress." Some of the men had earlier been placed aboard ships in order to lessen the risk to English troops ashore, and Herbin writes of grief and anger, pleadings for mercy, and the calling of father to son, son to father. Yet when it came to the actual deportation, Herbin could not dwell on the closing scene of the Acadian occupation of Grand Pré and Minas. Harsh words, he said, were useless.

Close to six thousand Acadians were sent from Nova Scotia in 1755, most from the largest Acadian settlement, Grand Pré. They were dispersed among the populations of Massachusetts, Connecticut, New York, Pennsylvania, Maryland, Virginia,

North Carolina and South Carolina. As Sally Ross and Alphonse Deveau note in their book, *The Acadians of Nova Scotia: Past and Present,* they were not sent to Louisiana, as it was not a British colony, though many found their way there later. At the same time, some escaped deportation. They either hid, assisted by the Mi'kmaq, or moved to more distant locations, like the Restigouche and Miramichi areas.

It almost seems a genetic trait that even to this day Nova Scotians, wherever they are, want to come home. It was no less so for the Acadians. In 1764 they were given permission to return to Nova Scotia, providing they take an oath of allegiance. Many had harboured the desire to return to their own lands. One story of their return is told by William Coates Borrett as part of a series of talks for the Canadian Broadcasting Corporation in the late 1940s and early 1950s. Borrett describes how, in 1766, eight hundred Acadians met in Boston, determined to walk to Nova Scotia through Maine, along the Bay of Fundy, across Chignecto, and back to Grand Pré. Despite many hardships, they walked for four months. Some stayed near Saint John, but others pressed on to Grand Pré, "only to find that it…was now thoroughly English, with the English name of Horton." Unwelcome there, they walked in despair through the Annapolis Valley until at last they reached Annapolis Royal, where sympathetic garrison officers arranged for them to receive grants of land along the shores of St. Mary's Bay. Their descendants are there to this day.

The New England Planters: A Proclamation is Posted in Boston

The lands left by the Acadians stood idle for five years. Kings County was virtually empty of people, the homes destroyed and the farmlands falling into disuse. Thomas Chandler Haliburton's 1829 *History of Nova Scotia* notes that on the lands were found "the ruins of the houses, that had been burned by the Provincials, small gardens encircled by cherry trees and currant bushes, and inconsiderable orchards, or rather clumps of apple trees."

Louisbourg, which had been returned to the French in a deal with the English, fell for the last time in 1758. French power in Nova Scotia was at an end. With the province assuredly English, officials began thinking of how to settle the land and, after some prodding from Massachusetts, hit upon the idea of inviting New Englanders to come and take up the lands left by the Acadians. A proclamation was published in the *Boston Gazette* on October 12, 1758, which attracted considerable interest among farmers anxious for land. The proclamation, to quote A.W.H. Eaton, offered land that had been "cultivated for more than a hundred years past, and never fail of crops, nor need manuring." Each head of family would also be given a hundred acres of wild woodland, with fifty additional acres for each person in the family. The farmlands would be distributed with proportions of plow land, mowing land and pasture. Townships would be formed, with each township sending two representatives to the provincial assembly. The proclamations offered land across the province, but the people of Connecticut and Rhode Island were most interested in the Minas Basin area. Nova Scotia agreed to provide ships to bring their possessions and livestock to the province. The story of the Planters is continued in Chapter Seven.

Chapter 1

Town Scenes

The Town of Wolfville

Not long before he died, Canada's beloved broadcaster Peter Gzowski said he had fallen in love with Wolfville. He spoke of its stately elms, historic architecture and sense of belonging. "As pretty a town as I've ever seen," he wrote in *Friends, Moments, Countryside.* "Someday, I'm going to live here. There's the university in whose library I want to hole up and write. There's the house where I want to live. There's the restaurant…where I want to eat lunch every day. And there's the sidewalk I want to stroll." Sadly, he died before he could live that dream.

A century before, in 1898, a *Halifax Herald* writer spoke of the bewitching beauty of the "blossom-embowered town." The writer Margaret Graham described walking up towards the crest of the Ridge, behind Wolfville, turning frequently to view the enchanting scenes behind. A.W.H. Eaton, in his 1910 *History of Kings County*, wrote of the view from the same Ridge,

Wolfville orchard in bloom

Edson Graham took the picture of this apple orchard at full bloom in the town of Wolfville.

which he described as being among the loveliest views in the province, with the valley's tidal rivers in the distance looking like silver threads: "On the left may be seen the winding Cornwallis River, bordered by fertile fields and productive orchards; while in the middle distance, ten miles away, rises bold Blomidon, always majestic in his simple grandeur, but varying in beauty as the lights and shadows alternate upon his changeful brow."

The Ridge is part of the southern uplands, the slope of which is interrupted by the Gaspereau Valley, which is carved by the river that empties at the spot where the Acadians left their lands and the Planters came to take them up. On its northern side, a creek collects water and runs down the hill towards Wolfville and the Minas Basin, and it is this creek that provided the reason for Wolfville's early existence: a harbour could be set up at its mouth and the creek itself used for shipbuilding.

The original plan had been that the township of Horton, laid out with one edge touching Horton Landing, in Grand Pré, would be the centre of the community of Horton. That failed

The course of Mud Creek, in 1885

The creek so central to Wolfville's history flowed along this gully, curving towards the Minas Basin and emptying into a channel that snaked its way out to the mouth of the Cornwallis River. The photograph, taken by E. Sidney Crawley from Randall's Hill, shows Acadia Ladies Seminary and the second College Hall on the left, the old Baptist church in the centre, and the Methodist church on the right. The first school in the village, built in 1864, can be seen to the left of centre. The photograph was taken shortly after the Presbyterian church was moved in 1885 from what became Prospect Street down to Main Street. Marks left by the move can be seen to the left, leading from the house belonging to the Crawley family—originally the Presbyterian manse. The move followed the main road to Gaspereau along the Mud Creek gully.

to happen, the existence of the little creek emptying into the Minas Basin at what became Wolfville dictating otherwise. The centre of Horton's settlement thus drifted west, with the creek becoming the new heart of the region. Along its banks grew houses, blacksmith shops and yards where schooners were built. Large residences were built beside the old Acadian road that led to and around the creek, many of them occupied by families with the surname DeWolf, or DeWolfe, the spelling seeming to change with the whims of the owners.

According to A.W.H. Eaton, the DeWolf families were in all respects among the most notable families in Kings County. Originally from Connecticut, Simeon, Nathan and Jehiel DeWolf had been granted land in Horton. Nathan had a son, Elisha, born in 1756, who eventually occupied a house at the western edge of the community. The house, known as Kent Lodge, was built by the Planter John Atwell in 1761 and is still standing today. Heather Davidson, the curator of the Randall House Museum in Wolfville, says that the house may have been built on the site of an older Acadian house. She writes that Elisha DeWolf was a prominent citizen, having been high sheriff of Kings County, an assistant judge of the Court of Common Pleas, postmaster, collector of customs and a justice of the peace. He was also a farmer, merchant and father of thirteen children.

The keenly observant Planters had named the creek in question Mud Creek, and the bridge they had built across it came to be called Mud Bridge. Before long, the community itself was being called Mud Creek, a name that did little justice to the aspirations of its people for respectability. In a 1981 article in the *Atlantic Advocate*, James Doyle Davison tells the story of how this name was changed: Elisha DeWolf's son, Elisha Jr., had a niece, Mary Woodworth, who in 1830 was attending the Female School on Argyle Street in Halifax. She and her sister had been complaining to her uncle about the name of the village, which embarrassed them. Elisha, a member of the provincial parliament in Halifax and postmaster in the village, attended a meeting in the village called to discuss changing its name. It was agreed that the new name would be Wolfville. There has been disagreement over whether the name change was made in 1828 or 1830, and whether it was made in exactly this fashion, but the new name was appropriate, due to the number of DeWolfs in the village.

Edmund Crawley, grandson of Acadia founder Edmund A. Crawley, described the Mud Creek area in a letter. He wrote that the bridge over Mud Creek had been built on wooden piles, between which the tide ebbed and flowed. At high water the area now occupied by Willow Park was flooded for some distance along Willow Avenue, and when the tide left, he and his friends used to catch fish in the brook left behind. On the west side of the creek, separated by a narrow board sidewalk, was a row of old buildings standing on piles, one or two of them dwellings and one or two stores, plus a cobbler's shop "kept by a man named Kelly."

Bowman O. Davidson, one of the founders of the local newspaper, *The Acadian*, wrote a paper for the Wolfville Historical Society, published in 1945, in which he reminisced about Wolfville in 1869. In it he says that Mud Bridge was the slum district of that day, in striking contrast to conditions in the 1940s: "The roadway was crooked and narrow, lined on one side by a row of decrepit tenements and on the other by the waterfront. As a boy I recall when I had occasion to pass that way keeping to the centre of the road. It was Wolfville's seaport in the older days and the road from Gaspereau terminated there before 'Chapel Street,' now Gaspereau Avenue, was opened."

When the Windsor and Annapolis Railway built a bridge over Mud Creek in 1868, the harbour basin fell into disuse and began to fill in with mud. *The Acadian* agitated for people to hasten this process by dumping in whatever they could find, including furnace and stove ashes. The creek was then dammed and a duck pond was created, where children would feed the ducks and sail toy boats in the summer, and skate with their friends and families in the winter. The duck pond has been sanitized today; the ducks are gone and the bottom of the pond has been covered with cement, but the area remains the historic core of the town of Wolfville. It is now a park, where earlier it was a busy place of commerce.

In the 1985 history of Wolfville entitled *Mud Creek*, the Wolfville Historical Society tells us that from a purely physical perspective, Wolfville occupies about two thousand acres of land and runs two miles between its eastern and western boundaries. Its lands include the Beckwith and Wickwire dykes. Much of it is suitable for growing fruit trees; orchards have been in place on a large scale since the last quarter of the nineteenth century.

The Minas Basin defines Wolfville

In the early years of its history, Wolfville looked very much to the Minas Basin. As the name of the town was being changed, a debate was going on about Parrsboro, across the Minas Basin from Blomidon. Parrsboro was then part of Kings County, just a short distance by ferry. As time went on, the difficulty of travelling to Kentville for official county business led to the excision of Parrsboro from Kings County, but the fact that it remained a part of the county until 1840 was a clear indication of the importance of the water as a means of transport, and of the difficulties of travelling overland.

Mud Creek dammed and made into a duckpond

After its useful life as a centre of commerce for Wolfville, the little creek was dammed and made into a duck pond, with a fountain in the centre. This image is from a popular postcard.

Wolfville Harbour at the turn of the century, c.1900

The tide is fairly low in this sunrise photograph by A.L. Hardy. It is a peaceful scene: the Skoda plant, now a flour mill, had recently been moved to this spot on the waterfront from its original location just east of the railway station. A three-masted vessel sits mostly out of the water in what was said to be the world's smallest harbour, waiting for the world's highest tide to come in before it can leave. Just behind the ship are the tracks of the Dominion Atlantic Railway, which helped keep the port and the town an important shipping centre, despite the size of the harbour.

The time that elapses between high and low tides in Wolfville harbour is close to six hours. Due to the position of the moon in relation to the earth, the cycle of high and low tides is about fifty minutes later each day, according to the Acadia Centre for Estuarine Research. There is about a six-metre distance from the bottom of the harbour to the top of the wharf.

The daily difference in tide times meant that schedules for ferries and arrival times for ships were confusing to outsiders, but local residents understood the natural forces at work and followed the schedules carefully. In Esther Clark Wright's words, for people unused to the tides, the ferry schedules were "incomprehensible, irresponsible, impossible madness." She describes an early tourist who looked at the harbour at low tide and refused to believe that there would be a ferry. She said the tide would come in—it always had—and the *Kipawo* would nose in around the banks of Wolfville Creek just before high tide, take on its load as expeditiously as possible and leave as the tide began to drop. It was a juggling act faced by all captains who brought their vessels into Wolfville Harbour.

A schooner passes Wolfville, c.1884

E. Sidney Crawley took this photograph of Wolfville with the Minas Basin beyond, showing a schooner sailing down the river from Port Williams. On the original photograph, the large white house whose corner shows in the right foreground is marked in what appears to be Crawley's handwriting as that of Dr. Artemas W. Sawyer. The much-loved Dr. Sawyer, a native of Vermont, was forty-four when he became president of Acadia in 1869, and almost sixty when this picture was taken; he remained Acadia's president until 1896.

The big house third from the left and partly hidden by trees was the residence of merchant and farmer John L. Brown, who moved to Wolfville from Grand Pré in 1847. Five years later he built a store on the corner of Main Street and Highland Avenue, where the lawn of the Beveridge Arts Centre and Vaughan Library are now. Brown's house later became the university president's residence, and is today the headquarters of the University Alumni Association. The picture was taken from the roof of the Acadia Ladies Seminary.

Looking northeast from the roof of the Acadia Ladies Seminary, c.1884

Some of the important institutions in the town are visible in this photograph. The church at the left is the old Baptist church, erected in 1859 and demolished in 1910 to make way for the brick church which remains to this day. The Methodist church is in the right of the photograph, its roof and steeple showing clearly. This church, situated near Gaspereau Avenue, was taken down in 1925. At the far right the Church of England can just be made out, and below it at the edge of the photograph is the school.

The school was built in 1864 on the Highland Avenue edge of today's school grounds. The bell on top of the schoolhouse served as the town's fire bell, and the school contained primary, intermediate and advanced departments, as well as the town jail. At about the time this photograph was taken, *The Acadian* editorialized that it was pleased the school was doing so well: "There is a larger attendance this winter than usual—the register showing about 175 pupils enrolled." Work had been done over the previous fall: "The rooms are as snug and comfortable as parlours and not a day has been lost on account of smoking chimneys and uncomfortable rooms. We congratulate the Trustees on the new order of things and hope they will not stop even here at the changes so much desired."

Horses and wagons on Wolfville's busy Main Street, c.1890s

A woman on the left inspects the dresses at J.E. Hale's store and, on the right, horses and wagons are parked near Burpee Witter's store. Farther down the street there is almost a traffic jam. This is a perfect picture of life in Wolfville's business district toward the end of the 1800s, as horses and wagons jockey for position. Contemporary newspaper reports give the impression that the streets of Wolfville were sometimes in chaos. *The Acadian* noted in May 1884 that Mr. F.V.P. Rockwell "was thrown out of his express wagon while turning the corner of Church and Main Sts. and narrowly escaped serious injury." Later that month it was reported that "a horse, one of a pair attached to an express wagon, did a bear dance in the street one day this week smashing the pole but doing no other damage."

In July of that year "the wheel, of a wagon containing four men, broke down spilling the occupants out on Main Street Wednesday afternoon." It was no better with sleighs. *The Acadian* of March 27, 1885, said that on Tuesday evening "J.L. Brown was driving down near Church hill with a horse and sleigh, some person came up behind him driving at a furious rate and, before Mr. Brown could rein his horse out of the way the rear horse and sleigh, in which were two ladies and a driver, ran into his sleigh damaging it considerably and striking Mr. Brown in the back and cutting his horse in the leg. The occupants of the rear sleigh were thrown out but received no serious injury."

In May 1885, on a Saturday night, a light wagon driven by Fenwick Gertridge of Gaspereau and Rupert Prat's Express wagon collided on Main Street. Rupert's father, Samuel Prat, who was driving the express, and Samuel's brother George were thrown out, "the former lighting on his shoulders and back of his head and the latter on his hips. Both were badly shaken up. The occupants of the other team escaped without injury. Both horses went clear of the wagon. Prat's went down street, lively with the whiffletree gracefully slapping him on the back, but Gertridge's did not get away. The wagons were uninjured with the exception of the shafts. Mr. Gertridge had turned off to stop at Weston's tailoring establishment and was consequently on the wrong side of the street. He also says he did not see Mr. Prat coming as the night was dark and he had just come out of the glare of the shop lamps. Mr. Prat saw the other team coming and turned out to let it pass on his right and so collided. Who was to blame for the collision?"

High tide at Wolfville, showing the Beckwith dyke, c.1910s

West of the harbour in Wolfville is the Beckwith dyke; that to the east is the Wickwire dyke. In this photograph the effectiveness of the Beckwith dyke can be seen. "The dykes," writes Esther Clark Wright, "have had a share in making us what we are. They are a part of our inheritance from the past, a legacy from our fathers and grandfathers and great-grandfathers who laboured to build and preserve." In this photograph, taken by Edson Graham, the former Skoda plant can be seen clearly, and a three-masted schooner is in port.

The picture was taken from Randall's hill, above what is now the Wolfville Historical Society's museum, Randall House. The house in the right foreground is that of Mrs. Charles Borden, who in 1892 was a charter member of the Women's Christian Temperance Union. According to *Mud Creek*, her husband had come to Wolfville in 1881, and opened a store, which eventually became a familiar part of Wolfville. "Men and Firms of Wolfville," a *Halifax Herald* article from 1898, notes that "the C.H. Borden store sold boots, shoes, and clothing, and also men's furnishings, hats and caps, trunks, and valises. It is particularly well stocked with goods purchased only from the best houses and every effort is made to please customers with good quality and reasonable prices." The store had actually been started by Borden's brother, Alfred. After C.H. Borden sold it, the store became F.K. Bishop's, then Waterbury and Company. Borden was also a musician, playing the cornet and acting as band director for the Wolfville Harmony Band.

At the corner of Main Street and Central Avenue, c.1910s

The store on the corner of Main Street and Central Avenue, to the right in the photograph, is that of J.D. Chambers, while the one across Main Street and on the left belongs to J.E. Hales. Both Chambers and Hales were at one time mayors of Wolfville, Chambers from 1912 to 1914, then 1924 to 1925, and Hales from 1917 to 1919. The Chambers store today serves as C.H. Porter and Sons.

The *Halifax Herald* of June 27, 1898, reported that Chambers' store "does a general dry goods and millinery business; carries a fresh stock, including many of the latest novelties shown in larger towns. A roomy, attractive store, with handsome plate glass front, adds much to the appearance of Main Street. The dry goods business has been conducted at this stand continuously for over twenty-five years, which makes it very familiar with the surrounding country people, with whom a large trade has always been done." The J.E. Hales store had been built by Hales' uncle, O.D. Harris in 1884, and later sold to him. The same issue of the *Herald* describes the store as Harris had it: "an evidence of the faith in both the present and future of Wolfville is found in the commodious dry goods store on Main Street, where an up-to-date establishment, second to none in the country, is kept by O.D. Harris." The building is described as three storeys high with a pleasing exterior. The first floor carried staple and fancy dress goods, "including a varied assortment of ladies' dress goods, silks, laces, gloves etc. Upstairs are carpet and clothing rooms."

In this photograph, an old car and a horse and wagon both head west, while farther up the street another wagon and a person on a bicycle can be seen. Other evidence of life in Wolfville at this time includes fire hydrants, hitching posts, a bicycle leaning against a hitching post, and a sign pointing in the direction of public stables. A man can be seen looking in the windows of Herbin Jewellers, just across the entrance to Linden Avenue.

Looking towards the Cornwallis River from Randall's Hill, c.1885

The Cornwallis River is in the middle of this picture, taken by E. Sidney Crawley in 1885 from Randall's Hill, which is the rise of land behind what is now the Randall House Museum. The river was, and is, in use as the sea route to Port Williams, and a schooner can be seen making its way upriver. On June 27, 1898, this view was described in *The Halifax Herald*. In an article extolling "Lovely Wolfville," the author, Margaret Graham, describes the scene in all its glory: "To your left the Cornwallis River winds through emerald meadows, losing itself in the quaint inlets that Minas Basin stretches into the marshes; near its mouth the white homes of Port Williams are picturesquely grouped; beyond this is Starr's Point, a low ridge of fertile farms and splendid orchards...."

A Natural History of Kings County gives the source of the Cornwallis as the Caribou Bog, near Aylesford, which is also the source of the Annapolis River. The river is thirty-five kilometres long, meandering through extensive cattail marshes and grassy intervals. Originally, the waters of Black River flowed into the Cornwallis River along what is now the Deep Hollow Road, but eventually the Gaspereau River cut into Black River and captured its waters, adding them to its flow.

Winter scene, port of Wolfville, c.1886

E. Sidney Crawley took this fascinating photograph of the port of Wolfville in the winter of 1886. Several teams of horses and sleighs can be seen on the wharf. Four sailing vessels are in port, some with their sails drying. A year before, the *Canada Gazette* gave official notice that the port, up to then known as Horton, would be known as the "outport of Wolfville." *The Acadian* applauded the move, saying that "ever since we have been in the newspaper business we have been calling attention to the great trouble to business people caused by having the name of the port different from the name of the place. Goods intended for Wolfville were frequently bonded to Kentville or Port Williams and occasionally to Windsor and Halifax. Under the new name such mistakes need not occur and a great saving of time and inconvenience will be made."

Seven years after this picture was taken, *The Acadian* fretted about wharf conditions. It had heard a great many complaints concerning the condition of the wharf: "It is said that it is not safe to take teams on, and that trade is being driven from the port by its unsafe condition." The newspaper thought the town should buy the wharf and make the necessary repairs, then operate the facility.

Main Street, Wolfville, N.S.

The muddy streets of Wolfville, c.1900

On April 18, 1884, the local newspaper bemoaned the condition of the streets, remarking dryly that it was supposed that several small boys, the evidence from a forgery case, a prominent medicine man, and the cemetery trustees had all been lost in the mud of the village this spring, "as the boys did not get to school for some days, and the evidence, the medicine man, and the trustees cannot be found at all." A week earlier near Caldwell and Murray's store (an area just to the centre right of this picture), the streets were covered with mud some inches deep. The road to Gaspereau was in frightful condition, and in some places it was almost impossible for a loaded team to get along. The newspaper asked "an intelligent and long-suffering people if they intend to put up with this much longer."

"After every rainstorm," writes Harry Bruce in his biography of R.A. Jodrey, "Wolfville was still a mud hole. In the springtime, the country roads turned into quagmires. Wagonwheels sank like setting suns and, once submerged, held fast in the muck as though giant hands were gripping them."

Gaspereaux Avenue, Wolfville, N.S.

Gaspereau Avenue, the road to the Gaspereau Valley, c.1906

In 1895, councillors in the newly incorporated town of Wolfville decided to rationalize both the boundaries of the town and the names of its streets. A committee was set up to name the streets, and it was decided that the roads running east to west would be called streets, and those running north to south would be called avenues. Because this road ran to the village of Gaspereau, the Town Council decided to call it Gaspereau Avenue.

In earlier days, the route to the village of Gaspereau wound along Willow Avenue, following the brook, which emptied into what is now Willow Park. Gaspereau Avenue was called Chapel Street, Watson Kirkconnell tells us in his history of the streets of Wolfville, because a Methodist chapel was situated on it, south of Main Street. The chapel was taken down after the Methodists joined the Presbyterians to form the United Church of Canada in 1925. When the road advanced beyond Prospect Street, it joined with Willow Avenue and continued on to Gaspereau. Here, young trees line the avenue while two women talk on a front walk.

LINDEN AVE. Wolfville N.S.

Linden Avenue, c.1900s

Two schoolgirls walk down the sidewalk towards Main Street. Herbin's jewellery store is on the right, while above it is a sign pointing to the Acadia Villa Hotel on the corner of Linden Avenue and Acadia Street. A horse and wagon come down the street. Linden Avenue runs southward up from Main Street to Acadia Street, halfway between Gaspereau and Highland avenues. Kirkconnell's history of the streets of Wolfville says that George Valentine Rand gave the land—part of the open area in the centre of the community known as Rand's Field—to the town in 1894. For a time the street was called Rand Street, but when the town decided to rename its streets, Rand Street became Linden Avenue, the Rand name falling victim to "the ungrateful new Council's passion for trees."

There is a wealth of town history on this street. Going up the street, the large house on the left was built in 1851 by Thomas Barss, a carpenter. Acadia President John Mockett Cramp bought it in 1853. From 1856 to 1874 it was owned by William C. Blackadder, who had a furniture factory on the lot. Just above the house is the home built in 1894 for George Thompson, who was Wolfville's third mayor, and above that the house lived in by Robie W. Ford between 1911 and 1916. Ford was principal of the Wolfville school for twenty-four years, a president of the Nova Scotia Teachers Union, then town clerk for another twenty-one years. The house, on the corner of Linden and Summer Street, burned in the 1960s but an identical structure was rebuilt.

On the right, looking up the street, is the Louis Godfrey house, built in 1835 and moved from its original location on Main Street to the left of the Baptist Church. Above that is the house built in 1907 and used between 1924 and 1980 as the Baptist parsonage, while above that is a stucco house built in 1918 by the legendary builder Charles H. Wright.

Main Street
Wolfville, N.S.

A view east on Main Street in the 1910s

This photograph was taken before the changeover in 1920 to driving on the right side of the road, as shown by the cars driving and parking on what today would be the wrong side. The Evangeline Inn, earlier the Royal Hotel and still earlier Grand Pré Seminary, is on the left, with people on the verandah talking to two people on the street. This hotel was located where today is Founders'—or Clock—Park, opposite the Baptist Church.

Just ahead, with the Coca Cola sign on the side wall, is Arthur Young's bakery, today The Coffee Merchant. At right can be seen the small building that housed the J.W. Williams jewellery store, and next to it is the Godfrey House, built in the 1830s and moved in 1930 to Linden Avenue when the Irving company bought the land for a service station. Next to the Godfrey house is Rand's drugstore, which burned on New Year's Eve, 1937, in a spectacular fire that killed electrician Roy Pulsifer. Next to it is the building known first as the McKenna Block and later the Eaton Block.

Wolfville a decade later, in the 1920s

This view of Wolfville is taken from the middle of the road at the intersection of Main Street and Gaspereau Avenue in the 1920s, looking west. The elm tree on the right was removed in 2002, a victim of Dutch elm disease. Also dying are lovely elms on the lawn of Randall House, home of the Wolfville Historical Society museum, and on the lawns of Acadia University. The huge one on Elm Avenue beside A.M. Young's old bakery has recently been taken down, leaving only the odd elm on Elm Avenue.

The post office on the left side of the street can be identified by the light standards at its front. Just west of it in the 1920s was the J.E. Hales and Company store. The photo studio of Edson Graham is across the street. Other stores and businesses in operation in this decade include Caldwell-Yerxa Ltd., which sold groceries, including six cans of peas for a dollar; Hutchinson's taxi and bus service, which ran a bus between Wolfville and Kentville; Lewis W. Sleep's hardware store; the Evangeline Café, which promised "to give the best attention to ladies and gentlemen," located next to Bruce Spencer's taxi; A.V. Rand's drugstore; the D. Ross Cochrane pharmacy; W. Frank's, in the Eaton Block, seller of men's and women's clothing; Bishop's Men's Wear, in the Orpheum building; Waterbury's, west of the post office, which at one time had been C.H. Borden's, seller of shoes, boots and men's clothing; A.M. Young's, which sold wrapped bread for twelve cents a loaf; the J.D. Harris store, purveyor of meats and groceries; W.O. Pulsifer's, offering sweet oranges for thirty cents a dozen; J.C. Mitchell's electrical store; C.H. Porter's dry goods and men's wear; O.D. Porter's, dealer in good second-hand furniture and automobiles; A.W. Bleakney's paints; and H.E. Bleakney's book and novelty shop, opposite the post office, which had the franchise for Victor phonograph records.

Among the professionals in operation in the mid-1920s were doctors Malcolm R. Elliott, Allan Morton, H.V. Pearman, J.A.M. Hemmeon, W.S. Phinney, osteopath Grace M. Curry, and G.K. Smith in Hantsport and Grand Pré. For dental work there were the Eaton brothers dentists, Leslie and Eugene, as well as dentist V. Primrose. S.W. Crowell advertised as a professional engineer and land surveyor; H.E. Gates as an architect; George C. Nowlan, whose office was over the Orpheum Theatre, as a barrister and solicitor; and W.D. Withrow, also a lawyer. E.A. Crawley, son of E. Sidney Crawley and grandson of Acadia founder Edmund A. Crawley, advertised as a civil engineer and land surveyor.

GRAHAM
PHOTO.

East end of Main Street at the Anglican church hill, c.1910s

The east end of Wolfville is long-settled and quite lovely. This is the area where St. John's Anglican Church was built in 1817 on land bought from Stephen Brown DeWolfe. The church has been in use continuously since June 1818, the time of its consecration. Nearby is the Anglican rectory, built in 1864 by Andrew DeWolf Barss, a grandson of Judge Elisha DeWolf. Oak Avenue hill, which runs out to the dyke, separates the Anglican church property from Annandale, built in approximately 1802 and inhabited by Dr. Lewis Johnston. Other luminous names from different periods include Theodore Seth Harding, George Ann Prat, Sir Charles Townshend, Judge James Ritchie, Joseph Starr, C.R. Burgess, John Rounsfell, John Frederic Herbin, John W. Barss, and Zebediah Wickwire, whose name was given to one of the Wolfville dykes.

The road in this photograph was originally the old post road between Halifax and Annapolis, started by the Acadians and built after a warrant was issued in 1760. In his book *The Streets of Wolfville*, Dr. Watson Kirkconnell describes the meanderings the road took in order to avoid the worst boggy spots. A stagecoach line ran along this road beginning in 1829: the journey to Annapolis took two days, with an overnight in Kentville. A description of a stormy weather journey from Annapolis to Halifax in 1833 in a second-hand American coach describes "the canvas curtains hanging down in long shreds, and flapping to and fro in the wind. The horses, too, were poor specimens of the Nova Scotia steeds, three out of four being lame..." (quoted in *Mud Creek*).

GASPEREAU VALLEY FROM "THE STILE". GRAHAM PHOTO.

Looking at the Gaspereau Valley from "the Stile," c.1910s

Esther Clark Wright devoted a whole chapter of *Blomidon Rose* to "the Stile," which sat on top
of the ridge overlooking the Gaspereau Valley. It is a place locked in the hearts of generations
of people who grew up in Wolfville or attended Acadia. Wright described going up Highland
Avenue to the Stile and taking the farm road to the brow of the hill. The view is totally unex-
pected, she writes, almost as if the farm road was "a magic carpet transporting us to another
land. In the bottom of the valley a glint of water catches the eye, and we trace the winding
course of the Gaspereau River, outlined by trees. The white houses and the white roads and
paths, are all spread out before us." The view from the Stile was so compact, so contained and
so miniature "that it calls to mind English scenes, the Wye valley, perhaps, or one of the
Yorkshire dales."

Thousands had come over the brow of the hill to the Stile, "laden with kettles and pots,
with baskets and rugs, old Wolfville residents, summer visitors, lovers hand in hand, college
classes, high school classes, boy scouts, girl guides, strangers and sojourners, their laughter
echoing down the years, their songs lilting in the memory." According to Wright, no one had
determined the number of proposals which were made at the Stile, how many were accepted,
and how successful the resulting marriages had been. The Stile was very much a part of university life, from initiation corn boils to graduating class breakfasts. At the one-hundredth
anniversary of the founding of Acadia, in 1938, a service at the Stile was an important part of
the celebrations.

The Minas Basin from Vinegar Hill, c.1910s

Edson Graham took this photograph of the Minas Basin from Vinegar Hill, just above Prospect Street. Graham lived below on Acadia Street, in the smaller of the two houses at the centre of the photograph. Blomidon can be seen under heavy cloud cover, and just below it is Kingsport. The spit of land jutting out into the water at right is the western tip of Long Island; on the other side of it, to the east, is Evangeline Beach. Grand Pré can be imagined to the south of Long Island, out of the picture. A ferry at the mouth of the Cornwallis River can be seen about to enter Wolfville harbour. A three-masted schooner is already in port, its masts visible just to the right of the steeple of the Methodist church.

Blomidon and the Minas Basin were always there, sometimes peaceful, sometimes not. In August 1884, *The Acadian* reported a close call involving George DeWolf, of the Boot Island Fishing Company. DeWolf left Boot Island, just off the eastern side of Long Island, for Kentville in a boat that capsized near Wolfville after it caught on a sunken tree. The boat carried twenty-five half barrels of shad, which were thrown into the water, along with the occupants of the boat. The newspaper reported that "Mr. DeWolf's son, being able to swim, swam ashore and procuring a boat, rescued his father. Part of the cargo has been saved." Boot Island was not so long ago connected to the mainland: charts in the 1700s show it as a part of North Grand Pré. At one time people lived on it year-round, carrying on a fishery of shad, salmon, cod and smelts.

Winter in Wolfville, Cochrane's drugstore, 1926

These pictures show that Wolfville, so temperate in summer, had its moments in the winter. The snow is piled up in front of the drugstore of D. Ross Cochrane in February 1926. On February 4 of that year *The Acadian* advised its readers that Nova Scotia was experiencing a "real winter," with many snowstorms accompanied by fierce gales. The storm that had begun the previous Thursday raged for thirty-six hours, making country roads impassable. Trains were late, but managed to get through.

Then, on February 11, things got worse. *The Acadian* carried the news that "Nova Scotia was visited on Friday by the worst snow storm of the year, and some say the worst in twenty years. Throughout Thursday snow [fell] and during the afternoon the velocity of the wind increased until we were in the middle of an old fashioned blizzard. Business was practically at a standstill on Friday and snow shovelling was the order of the day." Again the trains were delayed, with the afternoon express from Yarmouth not reaching Wolfville until after seven, and the evening and midnight trains from Halifax being combined to get to Wolfville.

D. Ross Cochrane had opened his drugstore in Wolfville just two years before. Eileen Bishop, who wrote "Wolfville on a Saturday Night" in *Kings County Vignettes*, speaks of going into the drugstore for a quick hello to the quiet druggist, Ross Cochrane, and his helper, Wilf Reading. The store was built in 1878 by James S. Morse, and it was here that the first vote on incorporating the town was scheduled to be held in January 1893. On December 4, 1924, *The Acadian* noted that the new pharmacy presented a fine appearance and was a credit to its young proprietor, D. Ross Cochrane. The store was attractively fitted up and well stocked, and "Mr. Cochrane is a regularly qualified pharmacist, who has had considerable experience, and is cordially welcomed by *The Acadian* to citizenship in our town."

Looking east along Main Street, Wolfville, c.1940

The unidentified photographer who took this picture was standing on Main Street not far from the front of the Baptist Church. On the right was the Irving Oil station, built in 1930 after the Louis Payzant Godfrey house was moved to just behind Herbin's Jewellery, on Linden Avenue. On the left was the Arthur M. Young bakery. On the very left, just out of the picture, was the Evangeline Inn. The Nyal Drugstore just up the street on the right was owned by Dalton R. MacKinnon, who had taken over the drugstore business in 1929 from Aubrey V. Rand, while across and down the street was D. Ross Cochrane's Pharmacy. Opposite Herbin's was the Orpheum Theatre, which at the time this photo was taken was advertising *Sunset Trail*, starring William Boyd; *Midnight*, with Claudette Colbert and Don Ameche; and *U Boat 29*, with Conrad Veidt, Valerie Hobson and Sebastian Shaw.

The professional life of the town was equally busy. Medical doctors included Dr. Perry S. Cochrane, Malcolm R. Elliott and A.S. Cowie. Dr. J.H.B. MacIntosh practised dentistry across from the high school, on Acadia Street. Leslie R. Fairn had a storefront for his architecture practice, and insurance was sold by J.D. Vaughan, Fred C. Bishop, J.D. Harris, Edgar L. DeWolfe and H.P. Davidson.

North side of Main Street, Wolfville in the late 1940s

Eileen Bishop described Wolfville as a "quiet, happy place" in the 1940s. In *Kings County Vignettes*, Bishop imagines people strolling by the stores in this photograph. From the Iriving Station, "their first stop was MacKinnon's Drug Store," she writes, "where Ernie Walsh was the pharmacist." After stopping at Val Rand's bookstore, her strollers continued down the street, passing Jimmie Williams' store, where Don Williams inspected watches being repaired. Then "past Otto Porter's grocery store they would stroll, past Betty and Pete Jadis' restaurant and then a stop to look in Herbin's store window to choose the watch or ring they would like to own." On the other side of the Irving sign, across Highland Avenue, the store that used to be Porter Brothers is visible.

The Wolfville duck pond, c.1950s

A little stream sometimes called Mud Creek ran from the ridge down to the Minas Basin in the area central to the founding of Wolfville. The bridge over the stream was called Mud Bridge. In Esther Clark Wright's time, it was a popular spot for skating. At the bottom, the stream had been dammed before it ran out into Wolfville Harbour. "In the early days of its existence," notes Wright, "the centre of the little settlement was the creek on which the duck pond was made. The creek was, indeed, the reason for a village growing up in that area. The banks, further down, across the road and beyond the railroad bridge, provided a landing place for the little trading schooners of the time, and there were two or three sites for shipyards along the creek."

At one point it was a real pond, with ducks and ducklings making it their home. Children would come in the summer, sail boats and feed the ducks, and in the winter they would skate on the pond. The little cottage at the back, which belonged first to Frank Porter, then to George Zwicker, was removed in 1964, and in 1967 the duck pond itself was filled in, and the area landscaped.

At the corner of Linden Avenue and Main, 1940s

On the left, with the awning hanging over the sidewalk, is Weaver's, which sold fine English china cups and saucers, as well as Stanfield's Novasilk. A branch to the store in Kentville, the store opened in October 1924. Thomas Weaver was a member of Town Council and president of the town retail association. He did a strictly cash business, and said that "buying for cash and selling for cash I am able to offer you many lines at lower prices."

Slightly farther east is C.H. Porter's store, which Porter bought from J.D. Chambers in 1920, at which time he hired an architect to redesign the front, and engaged builder C.H. Wright to do the work, leading *The Acadian* in that year to call Porter "one of our Wolfville boys who has made good." On the right, its brick walls covered with ivy, is the Maritime Telegraph and Telephone Company building. Telephones have had a long history in Wolfville, beginning with a private line in full operation in the town by 1883. Wolfville resident C.R.H. Starr was involved in the early work of the Valley Telephone Company, which began in 1891 to establish telephone service throughout the valley. At that time subscribers were prohibited from allowing non-subscribers to use the telephone, and were asked not to use the phones during a thunderstorm. The Valley Telephone Company line started in Middleton and was extended through to Hantsport by 1892. By 1905 Wolfville had close to one hundred telephones. Among those subscribing were the Acadia Villa Hotel, the Dominion Atlantic Railway station, Kent Lodge, A.V. Rand's drugstore, Dr. Thomas Trotter, and Arthur Young's bakery.

Looking toward Summer Street, c.1940s

A bird perched on the steeple of the Baptist church might have had this view of Linden Avenue towards Acadia Street, with Summer Street going off to the east in the centre of the photograph. The post office can be seen at the left of the photograph, while the top of Linden Avenue is where the schools are located.

Summer Street is a relative newcomer to Wolfville. According to Kirkconnell, it was approved as a street in 1898, its developers being C.A. Patriquin and O.D. Harris. Patriquin offered to deed the land to the town, and the developers agreed tp remove all trees and roots if the town would upgrade the street and install water mains. On December 6, 1899, the name "Summer Street" was made official. Five years later C.A. Patriquin gave the town land for another street, this time to be called Winter Street, running from Gaspereau Avenue to Willow Avenue, just beside his house.

Chapter 2
Historic Homes and Buildings

The oldest homes of Wolfville and the surrounding countryside are essentially Planter homes. Most Acadian houses were destroyed after the deportation, with some Planter houses built over the Acadian stone foundations. John Frederic Herbin described the scene that met New England settlers who moved in to take up the Acadian lands five years after they had been vacated, saying in *The History of Grand Pré* that "everywhere they found the ruins of houses near the little orchards or garden plots."

Some of the houses built by the Planters and their descendants appear in photographs in this book. Among them are Randall House, now the Wolfville Historical Society museum; Kent Lodge, built by the Planter John Atwell, lived in by Judge Elisha DeWolf and considered the oldest house in Wolfville; the Thomas Andrew Strange DeWolf house, once the Historical Society's museum and now demolished; Annandale, built by Daniel DeWolf and later the home of Dr. Lewis Johnston; the Perry Borden house in Grand Pré; and the Planters' Barracks, in Cornwallis Town Plot, near Starr's Point. A further example of a Planter house restored to its early glory is the Jeremiah Calkin house, built before 1768. Before restoration, Elizabeth and Ed Goodstein had it moved from its original location south of Grand Pré to a central spot east of the old village crossroads.

A.W.H. Eaton says in his history of Kings County that Planter houses in Cornwallis and Horton had the characteristics of earlier New England houses, as they were "chiefly low, steep-roofed, story and a half dwellings (the roof, back and front, having the same pitch), containing two rooms on the ground floor and often a back porch or ell, the narrow entry leading directly to the chimney, which occupied the end of the house, but was not uncovered." For the most part these homes had central entries, with chimneys between each pair of rooms on the first and second floors. They were placed a short distance off the main roads, with small flower gardens in front and vegetable gardens at the side.

The curator of the Randall House Museum, Heather Davidson, has described the Planter houses as vernacular in style, which means that they were built "using local materials by local craftsmen who combined tradition, individuality and utility to produce a graceful house." She says the houses were built close to the ground, generally asymmetrical and freely adapted to meet the changing needs. With some houses, a massive chimney was the focal point of the interior, its functions being to heat the house and cook the meals. It was located in a large room or hall with a low ceiling: "In this 'great' room cooking, eating, entertaining and business dealings took place. The hall was the common shared space for family and visitors while the loft served as one large sleeping chamber" (Davidson).

The earliest Planter houses in Kings County were basic shelters that protected the settlers while they established their farms. More permanent structures came quickly. As self-confidence and income grew, the houses expressed changing fortunes. Says Davidson: "While one prosperous homeowner might have been content to enlarge his house, divide it into small rooms, and add a few decorative touches, another homeowner might decide that the traditional utilitarian style was inadequate in expressing his individuality and status. He would copy or borrow from the academic style which older members of the community remembered from Connecticut."

The first houses and buildings in this chapter are the Planter houses; others were built as the Wolfville area grew. Davidson sees houses as a primary source that historians can use to understand a way of life. "History," she writes, "is the study of humanity. In order to examine and understand this species, the study of homes—where people are born, sheltered and nursed; where they play, eat and sleep, and where they procreate, raise their young and finally rest before the grave—is an essential pursuit for the historian who is eager to understand the human species in general and individuals in particular."

Wolfville has lost many outstanding homes, foremost among them the T.A.S. DeWolf house, with its legendary wallpaper, described later in this chapter. Beyond homes, the historic buildings in Wolfville include those that are pleasing to the eye and those that are more utilitarian. Many important buildings have been lost to fires or to the short-sightedness of those responsible for them. The most significant of the remaining structures is the Acadia Seminary, designed by F.P. Dumaresq and built in 1878 by the firm of Rhodes, Curry and Company of Amherst. The building is now a National Historic Site. Among those lost is the majestic sandstone post office, erected in 1911 but demolished in 1971 to make way for a squat, modern post office. Parts of the historic streetscape of the town have also been demolished, including the area in front of what is now the Beveridge Arts Centre on the corner of Highland Avenue and Main, and the cluster of buildings that used to stand just east of the old Maritime Telegraph and Telephone Company building at the corner of Linden Avenue and Main.

Strong towns are always mixtures of the old and the new, and there is always a tug among those with differing visions for particular pieces of property. Wolfville has lost much, but still has many historic homes and buildings. These give character and substance to the town. Decisions about them should only be made after serious consultation among the people who live in the town, the people who represent them, and the people responsible for the buildings.

Randall House, home of the Wolfville Historical Society, c.1950s

There has been argument over whether a coach maker, Charles Randall, built this lovely old house in 1815, or whether it had been constructed earlier. The house eventually became Wolfville's museum; its curator, Heather Davidson, notes that as far back as 1769 the deeds to the property mention a dwelling. In 1809 "a house stood on the 30 acre lot of land on the easterly side of 'muddy Bridge Creek,' whose boundaries included the south side of the highway, a river bank, and a small brook." The house on the property was inhabited between 1808 and 1812 by Aaron Cleveland, a cooper. Davidson feels that he may have built the house. The style and the methods of construction resemble other houses of the late 1700s and early 1800s. Today it sits on the hill overlooking what used to be Wolfville's harbour, while across the front runs Main Street, part of the old road running between Halifax and Annapolis Royal. On the west was Mud Creek, the earliest harbour, today the community's Willow Park.

Charles Randall bought the property from Cleveland in 1812, married Sarah Dennison of Horton, and had a son, Charles D. Randall, who was born in August 1816. Sarah died a month later at the age of twenty-four, and Charles eventually found the house too large for him and his son. In 1838 he rented it to a widow, Margaret Best, who operated a boarding school for girls there until 1844. In that year Charles, later principal of Horton Academy, bought the house from his father, and a year later married Nancy Bill, of Billtown, whose father Caleb was a member of the provincial parliament. Charles and Nancy had five children—Sarah, Elizabeth, Charles, Anna Bill and Eardley. At the time of the 1891 census the house was lived in by Bessie, Anna and Eardley. Bessie and Anna are both described in census data as housekeepers and Eardley as a farmer. Heather Davidson's history of the Randall House quotes a letter from Vernita Murphy, who lived two houses away from the Randalls during World War One and who remembers Eardley as a tall, dignified gentleman, and his invalid sister, Anna, as just a pale face at a window. By the 1920s the property was becoming sadly run down, and in 1927 it was sold by Eardley and Elizabeth to Wolfville merchant William C.B. Harris for $1525. Harris sold the property to Charles Patriquin in the same year, and both the story and the house began anew.

The old house, c.1927

By 1927, the year that Randall House was sold to Charles Patriquin, the house was in very poor shape. Graham Patriquin, Charles's son, remembered years afterwards that until 1927 the property was totally unkempt, a tangle of neglected fruit and ornamental trees with high grasses and thistles. "The house, equally neglected, displayed virtually no signs of habitation save from occasional smoke from the chimney (the eastern one only) and a rare appearance of Eardley Randall at the door, answering a neighbour's knock for admission…. If any property in Wolfville was unproductive, it was the Randall house."

Charles A. Patriquin bought the house and put tremendous energy into making the property well kept again. Graham remembered the energy and devotion that his father and mother put into making it an attractive, hospitable residence. It became a veritable gathering place for people. The side hill that faced the creek was turned into a garden by Charles. Glen Hancock, long-time Wolfville resident and stalwart of the historical society, is quoted in *A History of The Randall House* as saying that Patriquin was a stocky man with strong hands: "He can be remembered pushing a wheelbarrow laden with fresh vegetables to the Wolfville grocery store. He managed a fertile slope of early land leading from the house down almost to the edge of the duck pond."

In 1946, Wolfville lost the Thomas Andrew Strange DeWolf house, which had been the museum of the Wolfville Historical Society since its inception in 1941. The next year Graham Patriquin, who was making a career in other parts of the country as a teacher and professor, sold the Randall-Patriquin house to the historical society for seven thousand dollars. He also donated furniture and household items, and the Randall House opened its doors as a museum in 1949. As Heather Davidson points out, the responsibility for the maintenance and preservation of the museum is in the hands of the volunteer members of the historical society, who raise money, lobby government for funds, greet visitors, clean the house and its contents, and even "clear dead raccoons out of the chimney."

Kent Lodge, Wolfville's oldest home, c.1906

Judge Elisha DeWolf lived in this home on the western side of Wolfville. It was built in 1761 by John Atwell, a Planter who came from Connecticut with his wife and children. It was named Kent Lodge because Judge DeWolf had a royal house guest in 1794, when Prince Edward, Duke of Kent, the father of Queen Victoria, stayed with him during a trip from Halifax to Annapolis. It is the oldest house in Wolfville and today has been carefully restored by Reg and Pat Moore.

The History of Kings County, by A.W.H. Eaton, describes Judge Elisha DeWolf as one of the leading citizens of the village of Wolfville in his time. He brought his bride, Margaret Ratchford, to this house, and in it they reared their large family of thirteen children. The famous visit by the Duke of Kent occurred when the duke set off on horseback from Halifax on Saturday, June 14, 1794, to meet the sloop *Zebra* at Annapolis Royal in order to cross the Bay of Fundy to New Brunswick. The only stop he made in Kings County, Eaton's history notes, occurred at Wolfville when Prince Edward was entertained at Judge DeWolf's.

Elisha DeWolf was born in 1756. From 1784 to 1789 he was high sheriff of Kings County, and a member of the provincial parliament from 1793 to 1799, and again from 1818 to 1820. He was called Judge DeWolf because he was an assistant judge of the Court of Common Pleas, and he was also postmaster, collector of customs, and a justice of the peace. Judge Elisha DeWolf was one of the richest men in Horton, his family's hospitality a part of the tradition of Horton. He died in 1837, Margaret DeWolf in 1852.

Part of the cellar of the house may have been Acadian, according to Heather Davidson. The house evolved over the years, as different owners put on additions. In the basement of the house was a massive chimney, its origins unknown; upstairs there was a central hallway and rooms on either side, replacing what originally was, Davidson surmises, a large open room that covered the whole lower storey. At one time Kent Lodge was used as an inn, then later as a residence by Acadia University. During this time a fire destroyed the extension on the house, seen to the right of the main house in the picture, and the university gave it up. It is today a provincially registered heritage property.

The Thomas Andrew Strange DeWolf house, c.1940s

This was one of the most famous of the houses of Wolfville, but sadly it no longer exists. It was built in 1817 by Judge Elisha DeWolf for his son, Thomas Andrew Strange DeWolf, when Thomas married his cousin Nancy Crane Ratchford. Originally located on the northeastern corner of the Main Street and Gaspereau Avenue intersection, it was later moved to a site near Front Street.

The first house had a circular driveway. On the left was a drawing room, and on the right a parlour. The dining room was located on the left side of the central hall, next to the drawing room, and a bedroom was located on the right at the back of the house, behind a middle room which was sometimes also used as a dining room. Gardens and an orchard were at the right of the house, a stable and carriage house were behind, and brick ovens were located near the stables.

There is evidence that this house was one of the first schools in the community. W.C. Milner, in charge of the Maritime section of the National Archives of Canada, wrote in the 1930s that every scholar who attended school in the basement of the T.A.S. DeWolf house had to pay his teacher. In 1943, Mrs. W.L. Hall, of the Antiquarian Club, prepared a paper on the house, describing the basement as a place where the DeWolf children were taught their lessons, and where neighbour children were welcome to join in. The children shared the basement with a room where hams were cured.

In the late 1930s, Wolfville people were upset when the Wolfville Fruit Company, which needed the land, proposed that the house be torn down. *The Acadian* editorialized in June of 1941 that the town should gain possession of the "aged dwelling and convert it into some community institution that would appropriately preserve it to future generations." That same year a group of Wolfville citizens, under the leadership of Rosamond DeWolf Archibald—who is celebrated elsewhere as a teacher and promoter of good English—formed the Wolfville Historical Society, assuming management of the house as a museum. The needs of the Wolfville Fruit Company proved persistent, however, and the company offered to give the house to the historical society providing the house was moved to another location. The society was unable to assume this expense, so it shifted its attention to the Randall House, opening it as a museum in 1949. The DeWolf house was moved and later demolished.

A prince's gift of wallpaper to the DeWolf family, c.1940

It is one of the abiding legends of Wolfville that the wallpaper seen in this photograph was given to Judge Elisha DeWolf by Edward, Duke of Kent, as a wedding gift for his son, Thomas Andrew Strange DeWolf. The wallpaper was in the front room on the left side of DeWolf House, in the room thereafter called the Memorial Room.

Mrs. W.L. Hall's 1943 paper on the house said the wallpaper's origins might be a mystery, but it delighted and intrigued all who saw it. She described the room as having each wall from the wainscoting to the ceiling covered with the wallpaper panels, no two of them alike. The panels depicted scenes set in old Italian and French gardens "with marvelous trees, castles and towers and summer houses with Lords and Ladies fair with their attendants forming groups in a most romantic setting." The colours were mellowed by time, with soft shades of green and brown predominating, and "the room," in her view, "as a whole, has a dignified grace with nothing ornate to detract from the pictorial story of the paper."

By the 1940s, the wallpaper needed restoration, a task that was carried out by Annie L. Prat, one of the talented Prat sisters mentioned in chapter six. Edson Graham, who took the picture, gave it to Annie. Annie, who did the work during the time her sister, May Rosina, lived in the house, wrote on the back of the photograph that the wallpaper was rapidly falling into decay and was restored by her in the summer of 1942. She noted also that the picture of the wallpaper was likely taken when the house was occupied by Caleb Bill, who was collector of customs in Wolfville.

Annandale, home of Dr. Lewis Johnston, c.1886

Daniel DeWolf built this house, which still stands, around 1802. DeWolf was the son of Jehiel DeWolf, one of the original Planters. At one time a member of the provincial legislature, Daniel DeWolf was also a justice of the peace and a coroner. He died in 1837. The house, according to Wolfville historians, was built to replace one lost to fire.

The house was bought by Dr. Lewis Johnston, who had returned to Nova Scotia in 1822 from Kingston, Jamaica, where he—like his father before him—had practised medicine. He moved to Wolfville about ten years later. Dr. Johnston's connections to Acadia were strong: he was married to Mary Anne Pryor, the sister of John Pryor, one of Acadia's founders and its first president. A daughter, Elizabeth, who had been born in Jamaica, married Edmund A. Crawley, another of Acadia's founders and its third president. One of Elizabeth and Edmund's daughters married Acadia president Artemas W. Sawyer's son, Everett W. Sawyer.

The picture above was taken by Edmund Sidney Crawley, son of Edmund and Elizabeth Johnston Crawley. In the background, the tower of College Hall can be seen, as can the Acadia Ladies Seminary. Both buildings were completed eight years before the picture was taken. Directly above the house can be seen the Methodist church, and to its right the Presbyterian church, which was moved to this spot just two years before. The steeple of the Baptist church can be seen between the house and the barn. A pair of two-masted schooners are at the town wharf at low tide. Later, the house, known as Annandale, was given bay windows and a tower at the front, features which can be seen today at its location on east Main Street. The name, incidentally, was the name of the Johnston ancestral home in Georgia, itself named after the valley of the Annan River in Scotland. Lewis Johnston's grandfather was a Scottish physician who had settled in Georgia.

The home of Fred Brown, Wolfville merchant, c.1880s

Fred Brown was born in 1827, son of Charles Brown and grandson of Nathaniel Brown, who moved to Horton to be near his brother, Jacob, one of the original Planters. Fred was one of thirteen children, another brother being Edward, a doctor in Wolfville and at one time a member of parliament in Ottawa. In 1858 Fred Brown married Lydia Wells, daughter of James Simpson Wells, who was educated at Eton and lived in Chester.

Some time in the 1850s, Brown opened a hardware store near Mud Creek. The store was located in what was the central part of the commercial area of Wolfville, on the north side of the main road not far from the wharves. Later, the store, called Fred Brown's Hardware and General Store, was located at 176 Main Street. In the 1890s Brown bought his brother's grocery store at Main and Highland. He was active in civic affairs, serving on the town committee to rename its streets in 1891. This photograph, from the Randall House Museum, shows the

Fred Brown house near the site where the Nova Scotia Light and Power building was constructed, close to the duck pond. Kirkconnell and Silver's *Wolfville Historic Homes* notes that, according to the church map, in 1864 Brown was living in the house at 176 Main. The photograph shows what was likely a later residence.

This picture, also in the Randall House Museum, is entitled "At Fred Brown's c.1885" and shows five women sitting in the back yard. One holds a device for catching balls; another is pouring tea.

The Charles S. Hamilton home on Main Street, c.1890s

Still sitting on Main Street at Earnscliffe Avenue, but barely recognizable because of additions, this home was built in 1888 for Charles S. Hamilton, a lawyer. James Fry, of the Wolfville Heritage Advisory Committee, wrote in *The Advertiser* that it was a three-storey house with fourteen rooms. In 1934 it was sold to the widow of H.H. Marshall, Jessie C. Marshall. Frank C. Welch bought it in 1940, then Eric W. Balcom in 1943, who opened it as a nursing home called The Birches. Balcom actually owned the first two nursing homes in the province. In 1956 he was elected to the legislative assembly for Kings North. Maura S. Furlong, R.N., bought the property in 1958 and renamed it the Wolfville Nursing Home.

The Hales house, on Acadia Street, c.1900s

This house still sits on the corner of Acadia Street and Linden Avenue, across from the elementary school and across Linden from the old Acadia Villa Hotel site. The house is newly built in the picture, as evidenced by freshly planted trees along its front. The gravel street, as well as an old fire hydrant, can be seen.

In 1897 George Valentine Rand, who owned most of the land between Main Street and Acadia Street, sold this lot of land to J. Edward Hales, at that time a clerk. Hales later bought his uncle's dry goods store next to the post office, and later became mayor of the town of Wolfville. In 1897 Hales built this house on the land he had bought from Rand. The structure is notable for its elegant touches. It is a two-and-a-half-storey house with an elegant sun porch and a stained-glass window. The Hales family owned the house from 1897 to 1977.

Professor Daniel M. Welton's house, Maplewood, c.1910s

Daniel M. Welton graduated from Acadia College in 1855. Ronald Longley's history of the university notes that he was its first tutor of English by 1858. In 1867 he was pastor of the Baptist Church in Windsor; in 1875 he rejoined the faculty of Acadia College as professor of rhetoric. He became professor of theology at Acadia, studied in Germany, and returned as professor of Hebrew and systematic theology. In 1881, in the wake of efforts to establish a Baptist institute to serve all of Canada—an institution that later became McMaster University—Welton accepted an appointment at the institute. He was replaced at Acadia by Theodore Harding Rand.

Mud Creek notes that in 1879 Dr. Welton was making plans to build the house shown in this picture, and Kirkconnell and Silver confirm that "about 1880, he built a handsome house, named 'Maplewood,' on the corner of the later University Avenue and Park Street, but facing on Main Street." Maplewood was therefore very new when Dr. Welton left to teach at McMaster. To the left of the house is the second College Hall, while in behind is Chipman Hall. The College Hall was built in 1879 and burned in 1920, while Chipman House was built in 1875 and burned in 1914. Maplewood was used for a time as a residence and was demolished by the university in the summer of 1968, to make way for the Huggins Science Hall.

The last days of the old Baptist church, April 1911

In 1910, Ernest Porter was paid ten dollars to remove the weather vane on the 120-foot high steeple of the old Baptist church in Wolfville. He was accustomed to working on the church; his painting of the steeple and tower in 1908 was described in the press as "a daring accomplishment." The church, however, was to come down, which is why the weather vane was removed. The church had been standing for fifty-two years.

In the 1850s, under the leadership of John W. Barss, plans were made for a new meeting house to replace the one built across Main Street in 1820 at the southwest corner of the old cemetery. A lot was purchased on the southeast corner

of Main Street and Highland Avenue, where the church was built at a cost of eight thousand dollars. Ronald S. Longley's history of the church describes it as an inspiring structure, 70 feet long by 44 feet wide, with pews equipped with doors. A gallery extended around three sides, the north gallery eventually becoming "the exclusive preserve of the young ladies of the Seminary." The church was dedicated on January 15, 1860, with Acadia President John Mockett Cramp preaching in the morning, and Professor Artemas Wyman Sawyer in the evening. A new pipe organ was installed in the church in 1878. At the same time, a new baptistery was constructed, meaning that it was no longer necessary for the congregation to go to the Gaspereau River for baptisms.

In 1904 Dr. Ingraham B. Oakes, who had served as principal of Horton Academy and who, by the time of his death in 1948, was Acadia's oldest living graduate, moved a resolution to the church's governing body that the church establish a building fund in order to build a new house of worship. His resolution passed and on March 28, 1911, the building committee was authorized to sell the old church and have it removed by April 30. Before the church was taken down the pipe organ put in place in 1878 was removed and sold to the Kentville Baptist Church for $800.

BAPTIST CHURCH, Wolfville, N.S.   GRAHAM.

The Baptist Church, built 1911-1912

The new Baptist church, replacing the one torn down the previous year, was dedicated in two formal ceremonies on Sunday, October 27, 1912. The minister of the congregation, Rev. Edward D. Webber, had worked hard to make the new church a reality. He led the morning service to dedicate the church, at which time it was reported that the work had cost $69,000. The president of Acadia, Dr. George B. Cutten, gave the sermon. Speaking at the evening service was Simeon Spidle, professor of philosophy and theology at Acadia, later dean of theology. The cornerstone for the church had been laid on August 31, 1911, by Miss Margaret Barss, representing the prominent Baptist family of John W. Barss. The cornerstone contained a sealed box, in which were such documents as the calendars from Acadia College, Acadia Seminary and Horton Academy, as well as a Baptist yearbook and copies of *The Maritime Baptist*. The inscription on the cornerstone reads "Baptist Church organized 1778. This house erected 1911."

The church was designed by C.B. Chappell Ltd. of Charlottetown and Sydney, and was built by Wolfville's C.H. Wright, who at the time was working for the firm of Allen and Sons, of Middleton. *The Acadian* said that it was only just to say that to C.H. Wright and his corps of workers was due the credit for the church: "Mr. Wright's presence on a contract insures honourable treatment and high class work." In its issue of October 25, 1912, the newspaper reported that the church was 106 by 72 feet, with gables, buttresses and the massive tower giving variety and distinctive character. Stone for the structure came from Dorchester, while the brick was imported from New Hampshire. The roof was slate, with copper gutters. *The Acadian* noted that the great window on the north side of the church had a central portion which "shows what Canadians can do in art glass."

Wolfville's first public schools, c.1890s and 1910s

The MacKay School shown in both of these photographs was built in 1893, just east of the first public school in the community. That earlier school can be seen in the winter photograph, to the right of the MacKay School. It was constructed at the beginning of the free school system in Nova Scotia in 1864, and from then until 1893 housed the primary, intermediate and advanced departments.

The Acadian kept a close watch on the town's schools. In its issue of May 9, 1884, the editor, writing of the village's first school, was "struck by the extremely dirty and uncouth appearance of the different rooms. The walls are rough and awfully dirty. The floors were quite thick with dirt, and the whole appearance of the rooms was one of neglect. We don't know just who is to blame, but the matter should be remedied at once. We pity the teachers and scholars who have to spend such a large part of their time in such a place." By the end of October, *The Acadian* reported with some satisfaction that the school had been closed for repairs and that new chimneys had been built, which gave "a perfect draught and do away with yards of pipe, which hitherto, have been a bill of expense, with very little satisfaction. Two chimney posts have been removed from the east and west rooms. The vent holes in the ceiling have been closed up, thereby preventing the escape of a large amount of heat. The stoves have been renewed or repaired, so that now, in the absence of smoke, the teachers can see their pupils in their seats."

By the next year, 1885, the newspaper was reporting on crowded conditions. Temporary seats and desks had been put in place. The advanced department was particularly crowded, since a number of young men from surrounding communities had paid the fees and were attending school in Wolfville. Agitation grew for a new school. In April of 1892, the board of

school commissioners voted to build a new school and, when it was completed the next year, gave it the name of provincial superintendent of education, A.H. MacKay. The new school, shown best in the second photograph, had two floors, modern heating, ventilation and sanitation systems, and was second to none in the province. It was built by contractor Fred W. Woodworth and had as its principal Judah L. Bishop, who had innovative ideas about discipline. In order to keep his students from using bad language he provided them with equipment for the game of cricket, which they could use so long as they gave up swearing. The MacKay School eventually housed all departments from primary to grade eleven. In 1897 Robie W. Ford, from Milton, Queens County, took over as principal. He served until 1921, when the brick Munro School was built, and the old 1864 school removed.

The Munro School, built in 1921 and demolished in 1971, c.1930

These girls are shown leaving the grounds in front of the Munro School, designed by Wolfville architect Leslie R. Fairn and constructed on Acadia Street in 1921. A story in *The Acadian* on June 24, 1921, announced that the contract for building the new school had been awarded to C.H. Wright, for the sum of $34,559, the building to be completed by the end of the year. Excavation for the new structure began on June 21. By December 23 the school board was making plans for the formal opening of the school, to be held between Christmas and New Year's Eve. Harry Farris, who had fought so valiantly during the burning of College Hall the year before, was hired as the new janitor.

The Munro School was named for the provincial superintendent of education, Dr. H.F. Munro, and was home to students from grades five to eleven. Its first principal was B.C. Silver, who occupied the office from 1922 to 1940. Silver was born in Lunenburg, graduated from Lunenburg Academy, and was briefly principal of the school in Blue Rocks, Lunenburg County, in 1915. He graduated from the Normal College, Truro, in 1916 and then was principal at Hantsport before taking the Wolfville position. Noted as a musician, educator and author, he eventually became an inspector of schools. He went on to receive a master's degree from the University of Edinburgh in 1966, and an honorary doctorate from Acadia. In 1940, O. Rex Porter took over the job, serving as principal until 1970.

In 1972 the newspapers carried the story that the Munro School would be torn down to make way for a new school. In the course of its story, *The Advertiser* of Kentville remarks that the Munro School had cost the taxpayers less than fifty thousand dollars, and that "surely it has given good service during the last half century and justifies the superhuman efforts of the faithful few of Wolfville citizens of that day who worked so hard to obtain the affirmative vote necessary for its construction."

The Wolfville post office, c.1920s

The post office in Wolfville was constructed in 1911, from sandstone quarried in Cumberland County. The first postmaster in the new building was E. Sidney Crawley, whose photographs have preserved so much of Wolfville's history. Crawley, son of Edmund A. Crawley, succeeded George V. Rand, who had kept the post office in his drugstore on Main Street.

For years the post office was the centre of community life. The people who ran it knew everyone and were known by everyone: postmaster Carl Angus had thirty-four years of service, seven of them as postmaster, and employee Churchill "Church" Connor served for thirty-six years. Esther Clark Wright called the post office the centre of the town: "It is the forum, the market place, the exchange, the club. It is the place where you see your friends. If you want to know what is going on in Wolfville, you go to the post office." The grounds were looked after by the community garden club, which celebrated the removal from the property of a laundry building—and the last of the apple orchard seen in the photograph—in a ceremony in 1938. Later, the sandstone was covered by grey stone, but the structure was still imposing.

An announcement in February of 1969 spelled doom for the magnificent structure, saying that the federal government had put aside $200,000 to build a new post office. Officially, the reason given was that were flaws in the structure's foundation, but its destruction seemed to be part of a widespread process. Other towns—Liverpool, for example—had had their historic old postal buildings replaced by ugly, squat buildings. Rex Porter, who was retiring as supervising principal of the Wolfville Schools, was one of many unhappy with the situation. While the post office was coming down in March 1971, Porter wrote in *The Advertiser* that the demolition was being watched "with wonder and disbelief." He said that the building was a highly regarded landmark, one of the most imposing post office buildings in the province, "and a Cinderella of architectural beauty compared to the ugly duckling built to replace it." Rex Porter told the staff making the transition from the old building to the new that "you and the people of Wolfville deserve a better building than you are getting. It is regrettable that those who decide such matters did not possess imagination and foresight at least equal to that which conceived and built the structure now being demolished."

THE ACADIA VILLA HOTEL, WOLFVILLE, N.S.

The Acadia Villa Hotel, c.1920s

The Acadia Villa Hotel stood at the top of Linden Avenue, on the northwest corner of Linden and Acadia Street. Rockwell and Company were proprietors of the hotel, opened in 1901 by Frank P. Rockwell, who also operated the summer hotel in the Acadia Ladies' Seminary, and the resort at Evangeline Beach. In the November 1914 issue of *The Athenaeum*, Acadia University's student publication, an advertisement described the Acadia Villa Hotel as a "fine new modern house.[…]thoroughly up-to-date in all its appointments. Hot water throughout. Situated in the centre of the town. Only a step from Post Office, Railway Station and College Buildings." The Acadia Villa had room for thirty guests. Other hotels in the town at the time included the Evangeline Cottage, also on Linden Avenue, owned by J.B. Merrill, and the Royal Hotel ("brilliantly lighted with new Electric Fittings"), owned and managed by T.S. Sanford. Acadia University students sometimes occupied rooms in the hotels once the tourists had gone for the season. In 1919 a large, three-storey addition to the Acadia Villa, designed by architect Leslie Fairn, was built to the left and slightly back of the hotel; today, it is the only part of the complex that remains.

The Acadia Villa Hotel was popular with generations of Acadia students. It was with regret that the *Acadia Bulletin*, the university alumni magazine, reported a disastrous blaze on the morning of November 26, 1940, when the "big, red Acadia Villa Hotel" was destroyed. The bulletin said that hundreds of Acadia students would recall many a happy gathering held within the hospitable walls of the old villa. It is difficult to pick them out, but there are several people relaxing in chairs on the verandah, while someone perches on the railing and reads a newspaper.

Acadia Villa, home of the Prats, c.1890s

At one time, Prospect Street in Wolfville ran across Highland Avenue; on it was this home, which belonged to Wolfville's first station master, Samuel Prat, whose family had a major impact on the life of Wolfville. The home was called Acadia Villa (not to be confused with the Acadia Villa Hotel, or with the Acacia Villa School in Grand Pré).

On September 6, 1895, there was a note in *The Acadian* that Professor G.D. Roberts, late of King's College, Windsor, was spending a few days in Wolfville. A noted Canadian writer, he later became Sir Charles G.D. Roberts. Roberts was the brother of Goodridge Bliss Roberts and the cousin of Bliss Carman, the poet. Goodridge Bliss had been a frequent visitor to Acadia Villa and was engaged to Samuel Prat's daughter, Minnie Sophia. In 1892, when he was twenty-two and Minnie Sophia twenty-four, Goodridge came down with influenza while visiting at the house and died; Minnie's father Samuel died nine days later, also from influenza. Bliss Carman, interestingly, fell in love with the Wolfville area and his first book of poetry was called *Low Tide at Grand Pré*.

Acadia Villa was a social beehive in Wolfville. A 1987 exhibition of the work of the Prat sisters at the Nova Scotia Archives and Records Management said that "the Prat household in Acadia Villa, Prospect Street, Wolfville (about where Acadia University's Divinity College is now), must have been a lively meeting place when Rupert and his four sisters, with their many cousins, friends and beaux, were young people."

House given to Edmund A. Crawley on Prospect Street, c.1880s

The grandson of Edmund Albern Crawley was named for him and grew up in this house, called Hillside, built in 1864 by Presbyterian minister Robert Sommerville and his wife, Elizabeth. Edmund wrote that the house had been given to his grandfather soon after he and his family returned from the southern United States in recognition of his service to the university as founder and one-time president.

The elder E.A. Crawley's son, E. Sidney Crawley, who took many of the photographs used in this book, lived in the house until the 1920s. In a notice in the April 10, 1924, edition of *The Acadian*, Crawley offers the house, garage, and its orchard for sale, furnished or unfurnished, for possession by June first. The younger Edmund (Sidney's son) remembered that behind the house was a barn with a horse and cow stall, a small carriage house, above which was a hay loft. The privy was just inside the wall of the barn facing the house, protected by a trellis—visible in the photograph—which provided hops used in the making of bread. Edmund said the bread was baked in a brick oven in the ell on the east side of the house; the oven was later demolished, though its foundation remained under the floor. The privy was done away with soon after the town incorporated and the house was connected to the town water supply and sewers. A bathroom was installed in what had been the first E.A. Crawley's study, located on the second floor at the back of the house. Heat for the house, which is still standing, was first provided by four fireplaces, two on each floor; later by a wood box stove and kitchen stove; and later still by a hard coal burner in the front hall.

The saga of the Presbyterian church, 1885 and 1913

The Presbyterian church stood for forty-five years on the street now known as Prospect Street, as seen in the previous photograph. E. Sidney Crawley took this picture in 1885 as the church was being moved to a new foundation on the south side of Main Street, between Locust and Seaview avenues, where the United church stands today. Crawley purchased the land on which the church stood, later selling it to Dr. I.B. Oakes, who built a house that stands today.

The church, which had been moved so carefully down the hill, was destroyed by fire in August 1913, as seen in the photograph by Edson Graham. On the back of this particular postcard is the handwritten inscription: "Take your last look at the old church where you did (did not) worship."

PRESBYTERIAN CHURCH, Wolfville, N.S. Aug. 14, 1913.

The church built to replace the Presbyterian church, c.1920

The destruction of the Presbyterian church by fire in 1913 necessitated "construction of the present edifice, which is of red sand-stone quarried at White Rock. Like the Phoenix, the new architecturally beautiful building arose from the ashes within the year, with C.H. Wright the contractor" (Davison, 1985). The church was designed by Andrew Randall Cobb, who studied at Acadia and in Paris, and who designed a number of the buildings on the Acadia and Dalhousie University campuses. Cobb designed Emmerson Hall in 1913, Horton Hall in 1915, and was responsible for the fine home of the late ornithologist and author Dr. Robie Tufts, which stands on Highland Avenue just south of the Baptist church.

The new church was completed in 1914. By 1925 it had become the United Church of Canada, after union between the Presbyterians, Methodists and Congregationalists. The Methodist church, which appears in other photographs in this history, was located on the corner of Main Street and Gaspereau Avenue, but was torn down in 1925.

The C.R. Burgess home, now Blomidon Inn, c.1900s

This home was built by shipbuilder C.R. Burgess, who purchased the property in 1881 and began building the house the next year. Already wealthy through his activities as a merchant and ship owner at Kingsport, in 1883 he bought the shipbuilding business of Philip R. Crichton and for some years afterwards built and owned more ships than anyone else in Kings County. His fleet of tall-rigged ships had among it some of the largest ships ever built in Nova Scotia. The Burgess home was grand, with over a hundred Victorian brackets nestled up against the eaves. There are marble fireplaces throughout the building, and tall mirrors in the large drawing room. A library contains beautiful fireplaces and mirrors. A grand staircase leads to the second floor. Three bay windows are on the east side, and two on the west side. There are three floors, the third featuring dormer windows and a mansard roof.

After Burgess died in 1905 the house was sold by auction, and was occupied by families until 1949, when it became a hotel known as the Blomidon Lodge, which operated until 1960. In that year it was bought by Acadia University as a residence, and the university bussed its sixty students to the campus for meals and classes. Acadia used it first as a residence for men, then for women, selling it in 1968. In 1980 it was bought by Peter and Gail Hastings, who restored the house and opened the Blomidon Inn the next year. Since 1988, it has been run by Jim and Donna Laceby as an inn with twenty-eight guest rooms.

Thornleigh, home of John W. Barss, built in 1850, rebuilt in 1888

One summer afternoon in 1850, a strange procession wound its way through Wolfville. As the story was told to Walter D. Barss in 1916, it went from the T.A.S. DeWolf House east to the driveway leading up to a big, new house beside what is today the Blomidon Inn. People in the village had watched the house being built for John W. Barss, son of the legendary Liverpool privateer Joseph Barss Jr. John's mother was Olivia DeWolf Barss, daughter of Judge Elisha DeWolf, the son of the Planter Nathan DeWolf. Barss had lived in the DeWolf house when he first came to Wolfville. It had taken two years for builder John Woodworth to build the house. The procession was for what history calls the blessing of Thornleigh. Leading it was the Reverend Theodore Seth Harding, pastor of the Baptist church for fifty-nine years. Among those following were John W. Barss, his wife Lydia Kirtland Fitch and five of his children— Andrew, Margaret, Minnie, Alfred and Willie. As the daughter Margaret told the story to Walter Barss, neither Lydia nor the children had been allowed to see the house while it was under construction. Sadly, the house burned in 1886 and had to be rebuilt. The new dwelling, shown in this picture, was also named Thornleigh. John W. Barss died on May 22, 1902, and Thornleigh was offered for sale. Today it is owned by King and Ruth Butler.

A.W.H. Eaton's *History of Kings County* called Barss one of the most successful men of business Kings County ever had. He was a shipbuilder and banker. He was born in Liverpool in 1812, but when his famous father was captured and imprisoned in New England after a privateering raid—then released on the condition that he no longer go to sea—the family moved to the Benjamin Peck farm, east of Kentville. Not being near the ocean broke the father's heart. He died at the age of forty-nine and was buried in Kentville. John W. went into business in

Halifax from 1836 to 1850, was highly successful, then moved to Wolfville. He brought his family to the town looking for a healthier place to live. In that year, 1850, there was a crisis in the finances of Acadia College, and Barss was one of those who gave a significant sum of money to help it out. He then got more directly involved. As Longley's history of Acadia views it, "in 1861 John W. Barss became treasurer of the College and at once the finances began to show improvement." *Mud Creek* notes that he also provided half of the money to erect the Baptist church and parsonage, and was both a deacon of the church and superintendent of the Sunday school. It was Barss, *The Acadian* commented in 1937, whose influence led to the establishment of the first Wolfville bank, the People's Bank of Halifax, and who donated to the community the property that is now Willowbank Cemetery.

Brightbank, home of William Henry Chase, c.1900s

Millionaire William Henry Chase built this magnificent home west of the centre of Wolfville in 1893. He and his wife, Fannie C. (Webster), are shown in this picture with an unidentified woman partly hidden by a shrub. Chase, a businessman and apple exporter, was sometimes called the Apple King. He began working at his father's general store in Port Williams at the age of fifteen, and by the age of eighteen was making a profit with potatoes he shipped to the West Indies. That was in 1867; he later moved to Wolfville, building this home in 1896. He became a civic-minded citizen, serving on Wolfville's Town Council, as president of the Board of Trade, and on the board of the Eastern Kings Memorial Hospital, which he helped to found. When W.H. Chase died, the house passed to his daughter, Lalia. Born in Port Williams, she graduated from Acadia in 1918 and from Dalhousie Medical School in 1924. Lalia and her brother William were at medical school together. Fannie Chase died in 1924, William Henry in 1933, William in 1978, Lalia in 1979.

The late industrialist and financier Roy Jodrey, whose own home was west of Brightbank, was a teenager when Chase was in his sixties. Jodrey is quoted by Harry Bruce as saying that "W.H. Chase was a big man and he thought big. He was once the biggest supplier of barrelled apples in the world." Bruce also quotes an apple grower saying that Chase was the Bank of Canada in the valley: "He owned everything and everybody," had mortgages on many of the farms, and was "probably one of the biggest financial wheels in the country."

In 1940 Brightbank was sold to Clifford W. Fairn, then to George Brister, and then, in 1945, to Eric W. Balcom. Aaron Fishman owned it between 1947 and 1965. It was Eric Balcom who created an inn of Brightbank, naming it The Rivaron (later the Revaron). With an exterior remarkably unchanged from when it was built, Brightbank is now a registered historic property called Victoria's Historic Inn and run by the Cryan family.

The Roy Jodrey home at the west end of Wolfville, c.1940s

This beautiful white home is one of Wolfville's best-known houses. Between 1917 and 1936 it belonged to Roy A. Jodrey, the Kings County boy who made a fortune through hard work and entrepreneurship. Earlier it had been owned by W. Marshall Black, once mayor of Wolfville. Jodrey sold it to move to the former home of an important shipbuilder in Hantsport.

Roy Jodrey was born on Christmas Eve, 1888, in White Rock, and was driven all of his life to work hard and make money. He and his friend, the builder Charles H. Wright, brought electricity to homes all over the Annapolis valley, and his Minas Basin Pulp and Power Company was the most senior of all of his businesses. Harry Bruce calls the house in this picture "the most handsome of the handsome properties in Wolfville." It was, Bruce says, the house in which Jodrey's three children grew up, and it was Jodrey's domestic anchor "in all the time he helped build power companies and pulpwood companies, during the careful erection of his fortune, the collapse of that fortune, and the awful struggle to get a foundation in for the raising of an even bigger one."

In the 1920s the house was the operational headquarters for the Gaspereau Valley electric utility Jodrey had founded. Electric light bills were paid at the house and the books were kept at the house by Jodrey's wife, Belle Coldwell Jodrey. The children brought up in the house were Florence, John and Jean. In 1917, Roy Jodrey, already well off at the age of twenty-seven, bought the house for ten thousand dollars. The Jodreys lived well, entertaining two hundred people in their first year in the house. They had two cars, according to Bruce, as well as a big playroom in the attic, a glass sun porch where they ate, a vegetable garden, a silver cat named Bobby, and an English setter.

In 1942 Eric Balcom established the house as the Paramount Hotel, a superior inn that played host to notables from prime ministers Louis St. Laurent, John Diefenbaker and Lester Pearson to Governor General Roland Michener. It had a ballroom which was even used by Wolfville High School's graduating classes for their senior proms in years when the school had no gymnasium. Later it became Landmark East, a school providing children with enhanced learning opportunities. A footnote to the house's history is understood to be true by all who lived in Wolfville at the time: In 1965, while still the Paramount Hotel, it was the first location in Canada to fly the new Canadian maple leaf flag. The minute debate began over the design for the flag, one was made locally and flown over the hotel—though some remember the flag as having blue borders.

SUNNY-BRAE, Wolfville, N.S GRAHAM DU

Lloyd E. Shaw and Sunny Brae, c.1930s

This imposing house, which still sits at the top of Victoria Avenue, was built in 1905 on land owned by Eardley Randall and his sister, Elizabeth Cogswell. The house, called Sunny Brae, was owned by Alice Borden until 1919, at which time it was rented by Lloyd E. Shaw. The picture presents a peaceful Wolfville scene in which three young women and a man play croquet, while an older man and two women sit on chairs behind a hammock.

Shaw was born in 1878, spent his early years in Hantsport, and followed his father into the brickyard business. In 1914 he decided to open up a new brickyard in Avonport. At the same time he moved his family to Wolfville, thinking of the education of his children. Each morning, he would take the six-thirty train from Wolfville to Avonport, east of Wolfville, and return on the evening train. The new brickyard got an unfortunate boost with the great Halifax Explosion of 1917, when large quantities of brick were suddenly required. The Shaw family also found it needed a larger house. Shaw wrote that within a year they were able to buy Sunny Brae.

Shaw became involved in the life of Wolfville. He became president of the Board of Trade, insisting that George Nowlan be the secretary. One of their actions was to send Roy Jodrey and Charles H. Wright to investigate the possibility of securing power for Wolfville from the Gaspereau River (see Chapter four). Shaw won election to the Town Council, led the battle to build a new school in Wolfville, served on the Acadia University Board of Governors, and expanded the brickyard to be a major industrial force. He also expanded his business operations to Halifax and moved there in 1936, buying a home on the Northwest Arm. The family included his children Jean, Leon, Ronald, Greta and Lloyd. Lloyd had a son, Robbie, and a daughter, Alexa, who went on to become leader of the New Democratic Party at both the provincial and federal levels.

The Godfrey house, Main Street, c.1920s

This fine home was located just to the east of the Baptist church. It was built in the 1830s by Louis Payzant Godfrey, who bought the land from Elijah Fowler at the same time as the Baptist church bought land from Fowler for its church. In a small building between this house and the church, Godfrey had his boot and shoe operation. The building was later occupied by a small business called Tweedell's Jewellery Shop, and still later by a jewellery store owned by J.W. Williams, who moved to Wolfville from Prince Edward Island in 1911.

Originally from Windsor, Godfrey moved to Wolfville around 1833. One of his student employees was Charles Tupper, a student at Horton Academy who went on to be prime minister. Godfrey and his wife, Rachel, had a son, John Fowler Godfrey, in 1846. Though he studied medicine, he had a career in education, teaching in Barrington, where he married Annie Trefy. He became principal of Windsor Academy in 1877, then taught in Hebron, Parrsboro, and Digby, before becoming principal of the Wolfville schools, a position he held from 1894 until 1897. It was John Fowler Godfrey who had the bay windows added to the house. He died in 1913.

In 1930 the Irving Oil Company bought the property and erected a gas and service station. The house was moved to Linden Avenue, just south of Herbin's Jewellery. A story in *The Acadian* on July 9, 1936, reported that Williams' jewellery store was being torn down to make more room for the Wolfville Service Station, with Williams moving to the McKenna-Eaton Block on Main Street. The newspaper said the building was perhaps the oldest and most historic of Wolfville's business places: "thus, one by one, disappear the ancient landmarks that connect the past with modern times."

Peck home, Highland Avenue, c.1940s

This was the home of Wolfville's Peck family, including architect Ron Peck and his wife Jean. Ron Peck's father, Henry, was manager of the Wolfville Fruit Company's apple business, a Wolfville town councillor, and was involved with the chamber of commerce, the Boy Scouts, and the school board. His wife was Ethel (Connor). Henry was born in New Brunswick, son of G.M. Peck, who moved to Wolfville with his family in 1901. Henry and his father were involved in the nursery business, experimenting with ways of propagating apple trees. Henry Peck died in June, 1927.

Ron Peck was part of a long line of architects who made Wolfville their home. He was born in 1915, taught at Acadia, served in World War Two, then worked with Leslie R. Fairn. By 1947 he was practising on his own. As an architect he made the restoration of historic buildings a specialty. He worked with Parks Canada from 1972 to 1979 on the conservation of historic sites, serving as head restoration architect for the Atlantic region. He also found time to serve for many years on the Acadia University Board of Governors and as master of the Masonic Lodge. One of the buildings he designed was the Acadia Dairy building on Front Street. All that remains today of the building is the big chimney used as a centrepiece for the Robie Tufts Park, opened in July 1989, where people can watch the chimney swifts swirling down at dusk. A son, Warren, now works for Parks Canada as asset manager for mainland Nova Scotia. Another son, Drew, is a graduate architect working at Acadia University as manager of construction and planning.

The house on Highland Avenue has been in the family almost continuously since the turn of the century. It was built by John C. Woodworth in 1883. In 1890 it was purchased by E.N. Archibald, a clergyman, who had it until 1901, when it was bought by G.M. and Nancy Peck. It was turned over to Fred Peck in 1922, then to Clarence Brown, and then in 1934 to Henry Peck. Ownership of the house went to Ron Peck in 1937, though it wasn't until later that he moved into it. Ron Peck died in 2000, Jean in 2001.

The Earnscliffe Avenue home of Dr. Eugene Eaton, c.1920s

This home on Earnscliffe Avenue belonged to Dr. Eugene Eaton, who with his brother Leslie practised dentistry in Wolfville for many years. Both Leslie and Eugene had been dentists in India, and on returning home Eugene lived in this house with his family, which consisted of his wife Elsie and children Marion, Karl and John. In this picture Eugene's son John may be the figure at the top of the turret on the front of the house. John and Karl also became dentists, graduating from Acadia and then from Harvard. Like their father and uncle, they spent part of their careers practising in India. When they returned, John set up dental offices in Wolfville, and Karl in Kentville. John married an Englishwoman, Joan Templeman. Their daughter Sally is married to dentist Wayne Hills.

The house sits on land that was the site of a garden operation run by William Charles Archibald, begun in 1881. There were two Archibald family homes in the area; the second burned and the land became the site of the Eastern Kings Memorial Hospital. William was also the owner of the Wolfville Knitting Factory and for a time managed the Wolfville Fruit Land Improvement Company. The editor of *The Acadian* paid a visit to Earnscliffe Gardens in July 1893, and reported that there were some four thousand plum trees alone on the grounds, two thousand of which were filled with fruit. Together with apple and other fruit trees, Earnscliffe Gardens and its associated Wolfville Fruit Land Improvement Company were said to have the largest number of fruit trees under one management in the Dominion of Canada. The newspaper said that Archibald had systematically solved most of the problems connected with fruit culture: "The most economical methods are employed in preparing the ground, fertilizing, planting and cultivating these orchards." The operation had already attracted wider attention. A year before, *The Nova Scotian and Weekly Chronicle* commented that anyone interested in fruit growing should not fail to visit Earnscliffe Gardens, where an orchard of plums, peaches and other fruits could be seen, W.C. Archibald being a gentleman of original and independent views and an enthusiast in fruit culture. "He is carrying on extensive experiments in line with his ideas, and is meeting with substantial success."

The Evangeline Inn, the old Royal Hotel, c.1920s

Used as a postcard in the 1920s, this photograph shows the Evangeline Inn at its location on the corner of Main and Elm streets, the site today of a little park. At this time, the inn was owned and managed by T.S. Sanford, whose brochure describes it as situated on Main Street, one block from the railroad station, overlooking the Minas Basin. The largest and most modern inn in the Annapolis valley, it had fifty rooms, according to the brochure, remodelled and refurnished, including private baths and hot and cold water. With its large, spacious dining room, its "unexcelled cuisine makes it the most attractive resort hotel in the Evangeline land." It featured private tennis courts and was advertised as being within easy reach of a beautiful nine-hole golf course.

The Evangeline Inn was originally built by the Rev. John Chase for use as a school and quickly became the Grand Pré Seminary for girls. When the seminary closed, the building became the Acadia Hotel, and by 1893 had become the Royal Hotel. *The Acadian* noted on June 16, 1894, that J.W. Beckwith was "moving this week to the Royal Hotel, which he has leased and thoroughly renovated." The inn was badly damaged by a fire in 1896, but two years later the *Halifax Herald* was able to report that it was rebuilt: "The house is new and furnished with all of the modern conveniences of electric light, bells, hot and cold bath." The hotel was sold in 1912 to Trueman Sanford, who changed the name from the Royal Hotel to the Evangeline Inn in 1927. In 1928 it cost four dollars for a room, six for a room with an adjoining bathroom, or twenty-five and thirty-five dollars per week. The inn advertised that it paid special attention to college banquets.

The announcement was made in September 1945 that Acadia University was leasing the inn for a period of three years, to serve as a men's residence. Trueman Sanford had died in March and it was his son Max's decision to help the university, which was facing a housing shortage as men returned from war service. Many townspeople were upset that the town's largest hotel was being taken out of circulation. Dining room service was discontinued immediately and those who lived in the hotel had to seek space elsewhere, while the Rotary Club, under chairman Dr. M.R. Elliott, backed a move by the Paramount Hotel to increase its space. Fifteen years later, on August 30, 1960, the news appeared in the *Chronicle-Herald*, Halifax, that one of Wolfville's landmarks, the old Evangeline Inn, was to be torn down and replaced with a service station.

The Orpheum Theatre, c.1920s

Originally built as a hotel, the building was converted to a theatre in 1911. The Opera House, established by W. Marshall Black, could seat over five hundred people, had steam heat, electric lights, a telephone and could be used either for live theatre or moving pictures. It was purchased in 1923 by Nat Evans and the name changed to the Orpheum.

High school students, under the direction of the principal, B.C. Silver, put on Christmas pageants at the Orpheum, many of the students having their first theatrical experiences under Silver's direction. The theatre went all out for the Christmas season. *The Acadian* noted proudly that at Christmas 1923, the front stage was "banked with red carnations and evergreens and ornamented with Japanese panels hung over the entrance to the stage, while at the front of the house the balcony was festooned with green and red streamers and Christmas wreaths of carnations giving a most pleasing effect."

The Orpheum closed in April 1947, replaced by the Acadia Theatre, the first movie house in Canada with radiant heating. In 1953 Al Whittle became manager of the Acadia Theatre, beginning a long term during which he became a friend to both young people from town and Acadia students. He worked on the Acadia campus, helped with the Winter Carnival, and got involved in town organizations. Among the young people he employed to work as ushers in the theatre was the author of this book. This photograph shows a sign in an upper window for the office of George C. Nowlan, barrister and later federal cabinet minister. The shop on the ground floor, which opened on February 16, 1924, belonged to F.C. Bishop, who sold men's wear and advertised a "nifty" assortment of "nobby" clothes. Today, Just Us Coffee Roasters operates a café in the lobby and shares are being sold to provide funds to reopen the theatre.

The Eastern Kings Memorial Hospital, c.1940s

On August 6, 1920, *The Acadian* reported that it had the pleasure of inspecting the Westwood Hospital, set up the year before by Dr. C.E. Avery DeWitt. It informed its reading public that the operating room had been enlarged and additional lighting provided, and that it was now regarded by surgeons as being decidedly well arranged and adapted to operations of any description. "Since our people do not appear willing to provide a public institution of this kind we are very glad that the proprietor of the Westwood Hospital has the courage and enterprise to undertake the work and wish him abundant success in what is certainly a most worthy undertaking." Dr. DeWitt, whose father, Dr. George E. DeWitt, came to Wolfville in the 1890s, bought a large house on Westwood Avenue for use as a private hospital, which he ran until 1929. The idea had not been exactly alien to Avery—when his sister Carrie came down with tuberculosis, his father George had opened a private sanatorium on the land above Wolfville. Both DeWitts served as town medical officer.

As the 1920s ended, fundraising was underway for a public hospital, under a board chaired by William Henry Chase, the wealthy apple exporter and businessman. With funding in place from the town, university and individuals, construction began on Earnscliffe Avenue, at the heart of what had been the fruit orchards of Earnscliffe Gardens. The cornerstone was laid by W.H. Chase on October 22, 1929, exactly one week before the stock market crashed. Nevertheless, construction proceeded. Brian Cuthbertson says it "went forward with such speed that on the day the Eastern Kings Memorial Hospital opened, 26 May 1930, doctors performed their first operation." The building was designed by Leslie R. Fairn and built by Charles H. Wright, at a cost of $117,800. Its first three doctors were Perry Cochrane, Malcolm Elliott and William Eager.

In 1972 the Nova Scotia Health Council called for the EKM Hospital to be phased out by 1980. Massive protests from the people of the town temporarily prevented the closure, but what passed for progress was relentless. In November 1995, Health Minister Ron Stewart, who as a student had been president of the Acadia University student representative council, announced that the hospital would become a community health centre. It is today the Eastern Kings Memorial Community Health Centre.

Chapter 3

Acadia University

⤳

The formation of the university now regarded as one of the finest in Canada is a fascinating story, with its own published histories, notably those of Albert Coldwell, who wrote a prize-winning essay published in 1881 as part of the half-century celebrations of Horton Academy and Acadia College; Ronald S. Longley, who in 1939 wrote the history of Acadia University from 1838 to 1938; and Watson Kirkconnell, who continued that history from 1938 to 1963. The university's story is told too in the pages of the various histories of the Baptists in Nova Scotia; in *The Athenaeum*, the student magazine and newspaper which began publication in 1874; in *The Acadia Bulletin*, published by the university's alumni association; and in *The Acadian*, the town newspaper, started in 1883. What comes through in the early history of Acadia is that, while it was founded by Baptists, it was intended from the beginning to be an institution tolerant of other faiths. As will be seen, this was an important issue.

First came Horton Academy. In 1828 it was proposed, in an emotional meeting of the Baptist church association in Wolfville, that an institution of higher learning be founded for the education of Baptist youth. Those who spoke were in tears when they described the difficulties stemming from not having a better education, and it galvanized those at the meeting to push forward with the plan. The Nova Scotia Baptist Educational Society was formed with a board of directors. As Coldwell wrote in 1881, Wolfville was chosen as a site because of its natural beauty and its central position. The society bought sixty-five acres of land and in 1829 opened Horton Academy, with the intention of developing it into a college. The academy's first principal was a man named Asahel Chapin from Amherst College, in Massachusetts. The next year he left the position, and Rev. John Pryor was appointed in his place.

"The first building used," Coldwell writes, "was an old, low, one-storey dwelling-house, situated exactly where the main street now runs, and nearly in front of the late college building." (The first College Hall had burned.) Deacon William Pick's reminiscences about Wolfville in the 1830s, published in *The Acadian* in 1930, speak of "a yellow building on Main street to the west of the present entrance to the university grounds, which was the first home of Horton Academy." P.S. Hamilton wrote in 1888 that he remembered "close upon the street and about midway of the width of the academy—now college—lot, was 'the old yaller house.' Here was originally the 'Horton academy,' eventually developed into Acadia College. When I first knew it, it was a somewhat nasty tenement house."

Things got better. By 1831, after an expenditure of one thousand dollars, the Academy Hall had been built on the hill. By 1835 the Academy Boarding House had been built, sufficient, quotes Coldwell from a report, "to accommodate the principal and his family, the assistant teacher, steward, and fifty boarders." With Horton Academy up and running, thoughts turned to the next step: making it into a college. Many in the province were of the opinion that there should be one provincial university, located in Halifax, and by 1838 Dalhousie College was opened. Baptists initially agreed, providing they would have positions at the university. Reverend Edmund Albern Crawley, a Baptist pastor of a church in Halifax and a member of the society that had established Horton Academy, was thought to be the logical choice for the Chair of Classics. He applied, but was turned down—not because of his qualifications, which were eminent, but apparently because he was not a member of the Church of Scotland.

It seemed to Baptists that only people of certain faiths would be welcome at Dalhousie. The Education Society that managed Horton Academy met in Wolfville on November 15, 1838, and according to Coldwell, "resolved to commence a collegiate institution in that place, in accordance with their original design." The institution would be called Queen's College. Funds were immediately raised, and by December a public notice was issued that classes at Queen's would begin the next January 20. E.A. Crawley and John Pryor were appointed to the faculty, and Pryor's position at Horton Academy was taken by Edward Blanchard of Truro. In October, Isaac Chipman was also appointed to the teaching staff as associate professor of Natural Philosophy and Mathematics. With twenty students, the college was already the largest in the province. None of those who were admitted had to undergo any religious tests.

The granting of a charter to the new college was not an easy process. The incorporation bill was introduced to the House of Assembly in 1839, where it ran into opposition and was

CANADIAN ILLUSTRATED NEWS. SEPTEMBER 27, 1879.

WOLFEVILLE, N.S.—THE NEW BUILDING OF WOLFEVILLE COLLEGE.

Engraving of second College Hall, 1879

The Canadian Illustrated News for September 27, 1879, published this engraving of the second College Hall, which replaced the one burned in 1877. Chipman Hall, built in 1875, is depicted at the right.

defeated, 23-22. A second attempt was made in 1840, the opposition coming from those who wanted a provincial university in Halifax and saw the new college as an obstacle to that. There were eloquent speeches for and against, but the vote this time was in favour, 27-15. The idea of a single provincial university was defeated. The act of incorporation was sent to England for approval, since the college was to be called Queen's; the authorities in England sent back the information that it would be approved, provided the name were changed. The name chosen in its stead was Acadia.

More political skirmishes were to come over the next several years. Joseph Howe was involved in efforts to cancel the charters of the rural colleges, again in order to set up a single university in Halifax. Each time, these efforts were defeated. In the meantime, in Wolfville, plans were being made to construct a proper building for the new college, since the facilities provided by the Horton Academy building and its boarding house were proving inadequate for the new university. Herein lies the story of how the third professor hired, Isaac Chipman, managed to "build a College without money."

By all accounts, Chipman was an extraordinary man. He was born in Cornwallis in 1817 and at the age of twelve went to Horton Academy, in the first year of its existence. Five years later he was appointed to the academy staff, but he left a year later, not having finished with his education. By 1837 he was a student at Waterville College in Maine, and was offered a position at Acadia College in 1839. He was a hard worker who relaxed by making trips across the Minas Basin to Blomidon, where he collected, among other minerals, amethysts. On June 7, 1852, he set out for Blomidon with seven others, the party including the editor of the *Christian Visitor* journal, four students, and the two men who were in charge of the boat. The day had been fair, but on the way back, the wind came up and the seas became rough. A boy standing on a point of land saw what happened: "The southwest wind blew a gale. The little sail became unsteady. There was confusion as of men quickly moving from place to place in the boat. A few moments of suspense and the boat disappeared." The drama was described in the January 1940 issue of the *Acadia Bulletin*. The boat was near Long Island, where Evangeline Beach is located. When swamped by the waves, the men set about bailing out the water, turning for Long Island. According to the one man who survived, a second wave swamped the boat, and it went down by the stern and turned bottom up. Several of the party clung to the boat and managed to get aboard, but it flipped around again. The four who were left kept returning to the upturned boat only to be washed off again, until finally only one was left. George Benjamin of Gaspereau, one of the two men in charge of the boat, managed to make it to shore.

The drowning of Chipman and the others was an enormous tragedy for the young college, which was struggling financially. The president of the college at the time, John Mockett Cramp, said he could scarcely think, the accident being such a stunning stroke. The young college had lost Chipman, and the entire graduating class of the next year, as well as a member of the board of governors. Isaac Chipman's body was recovered on June 20, and was buried in the Old Burying Ground across from the Baptist Church. That the college was at its lowest point was evident from the fact that its opening was delayed that fall, when the new president, Cramp, was forced to call upon a student and a teacher from the academy to help him teach the classes.

The college slowly rebounded. Crawley, who left in 1846 to return to the pastorate of the Granville Street Church in Halifax, was asked in 1853 to come back to Acadia, which he agreed to do providing the college allowed him to occupy a leadership role. Cramp became principal of the college's Theological Institute, and Crawley the president of the university. It was an odd arrangement, with Crawley and Cramp essentially sharing the work. They hired Artemas Wyman Sawyer to take the position of professor of classics, an appointment that turned out to be historic for the university since he served as its president for almost three decades. Crawley hoped to increase the funds available to Acadia through investing the money the university had raised, but the investments quickly failed and the money was lost. He resigned, taking up a position in the United States as principal of a ladies' college. Cramp resumed the duties of president.

Despite the setbacks, Acadia grew, and, by the accomplishments of its graduates, its reputation grew as well. Students had a fairly regulated existence during the years of Crawley and Cramp. Ronald Longley's history notes that "they arose at six o'clock each morning and a short time later presented themselves to a monitor in one of the class rooms to attend prayers. After breakfast classes began and continued, with an interval of an hour at noon, until four o'clock when they met again for prayers. The evenings were generally devoted to study by light of a candle or lamp. In winter the rooms were heated by the use of small stoves."

What Longley calls "the Age of Sawyer" came next. Artemas Wyman Sawyer was first appointed to the faculty in 1855, took over the presidency of the Literary and Scientific Institute of New London, Connecticut, after leaving Acadia in 1861, and returned to Acadia in 1869 as president. He was to serve for twenty-seven years, retiring in 1896, though continuing after that to teach at Acadia. Five years before he retired, in May of 1891, the name of Acadia College was officially changed to Acadia University.

Albert Coldwell, later on the faculty of Acadia, concluded his essay about Acadia's early years by saying that the site of the college was one of the finest in North America: "The lover of natural scenery will find here landscapes of rare attractiveness. The eye can never tire of the beautiful panorama spread out before it of mountain, river, valley, sea and sky." For Coldwell, the setting lingered in the memory of the Acadia graduate long after he had entered the business of life, leading him to look back yearningly on the pleasant days in Wolfville, when he "allowed his eyes to drink in with deep delight the enchanting scenery that stretches from bold Blomidon to the beautiful valley of the Gaspereau."

The legendary first College Hall, "Built Without Money," c.1860s

Isaac Chipman, who had been hired in 1839 to teach mathematics and science at the new Acadia College, had much to do with the building in this old photograph. Very early on in the life of the new college it became clear that a new main hall would have to be built. The college used the facilities of Horton Academy for its first two years, but it was an arrangement that suited neither the institution's need for prestige nor the requirements for such things as laboratories and a library. An appeal was made for funds but these were hard times, and little money was forthcoming. Isaac Chipman stepped in and proposed that the building be put up not with money but with donated materials. He suggested that supporters of the college up and down the Minas shore donate timber, boards and shingles, and that other materials be solicited in Halifax and Saint John.

Longley's history of Acadia tells the story well: "In announcing his plan Chipman counted on its novelty to make it a success and he was not disappointed. During the winter of 1843 the woods of Wilmot rang with the sound of the woodsman's axe as the trees were felled and prepared. By the spring 22,000 feet of timber had arrived, ready for the frame." It was a project that involved people from all over the Maritimes. In 1881 Albert Coldwell wrote the Vaughan Prize Essay on Acadia's history, in which he says that "the first load of timber was landed at Wolfville by the late Mahew Beckwith, Esq., from his own vessel, and two other loads soon followed. From Liverpool, came a cargo of valuable pine lumber, shingles, laths, sashes, and doors. From the Annapolis Valley, a vessel loaded with shingles, hemlock, spruce and pine boards. St. John sent lime; while from Halifax there came an important contribution of oil, putty, sheet-lead, nails, paint and glass. The inhabitants of Horton rendered valuable aid in preparing the foundation of the building, removing the materials from the wharf to College Hill, and erecting the large frame." At 150 feet by 40 feet, it would have three floors, and four Ionic pillars at the front, carved in Greenwich by brothers Lewis and Edmund Davison. Workers had the building boarded in by winter and ready for use the next year.

Tragedy struck both the builder and the building, however, when, in 1852 Isaac Chipman was asked by a member of the Board of Governors to lead an expedition by sailboat to Blomidon. The boat capsized and only one man, George Benjamin survived. The second tragedy was the burning of College Hall.

The photograph also shows Sawyer Hall, a house to the left of College Hall, before additions were made and the house was turned to face Acadia Street. Watson Kirkconnell and B.C. Silver note that at the time the picture was taken the house was lived in by Edmund Albern Crawley, one of the founders of Acadia.

The first College Hall after the fire of 1877

Some of the students at Acadia lived right in College Hall, where rooms were set aside as lodgings for about thirty students. There was no central heating; students kept warm with stoves in their rooms. "On Sunday afternoon, December 2, 1877," Dr. Ronald S. Longley has written, "the students assembled to hear a lecture by a visiting clergyman. After the lecture they replenished the fires in their rooms and went for a walk. When they returned they found the Hall in flames." The students were able to save the books from the library, but as the *History of the Baptists* put it, "the President's residence, the Academy Hall and Recitation rooms, the College Recitation rooms, the Library, Chapel, Museum, Laboratory and Dormitories...were all swept away." Two students, Walter Barss and Oliver H. Cogswell, were recognized for their bravery; pictures of them were placed in the new university library, "in memory of the valiant services of these two students, who entered the burning College building and saved the books, pictures and laboratory apparatus." Also on the scene was John Bogart, later a medical doctor, who wrote in the *Acadia Bulletin* in June 1933 that he did what he could to salvage the library, on the second floor: "The flames spread so rapidly that the books had to be thrown out of the windows." One of Bogart's teachers was Albert Coldwell, who wrote in his Vaughan essay that "as ruthlessly as the waters engulfed the lamented Professor Chipman twenty-five years before, did the flames consume the fruit of twelve years of his toil given to the erection of this College-building and the collection of the Museum."

On the morning after the fire the entire faculty, the members of the Board of Governors, students and friends of the university gathered to inspect the ruins and to have a group portrait taken. In that picture, published in the *Acadia Bulletin* in 1933, are visible Professors Kennedy, Jones, Sawyer, Crawley, Higgins and Tufts. A few minutes later the photographer, W. Chase of Halifax, took this picture as the members of the Board of Governors look at what is left of College Hall.

The second College Hall, 1890s

The day after the first College Hall burned in 1877 plans were being made to build the second. In fact, the Board of Governors quickly decided that not one, but three new buildings were needed: one to house the College, one for Horton Academy, and one for a ladies' seminary. *The Athenaeum* said that the new College Hall "is to be built where the ashes of the old now lie," and asked that "everyone help in building the temple on our fair hill. While the men heave up the stone pillars let the children carry bricks." As the newspaper reported, appeals for funds went out immediately and in the first weeks after the fire an almost spontaneous movement to provide the necessary money began. Professors of Acadia College, teachers at Horton Academy, students, ministers and laymen all went about soliciting funds, and before long, over half the money needed was raised. Haste was encouraged, in the hope that the College Hall would be ready by the next August and there would be no interruption in study and teaching.

Architectural plans for the building were prepared by F.P. Dumaresq, of Halifax. The new building was 154 feet by 70 feet. The central tower was approximately 110 feet high. Ten classrooms were on the main floor, and an assembly hall, offices, museum and library were on the second floor. "The exterior is exceedingly graceful, as the architects and builders have succeeded in securing a very pleasing effect through a harmonious combination of ancient and modern styles of architecture, without any sacrifice of interior accommodation," wrote Albert Coldwell of the new building.

The new College Hall cost over twenty thousand dollars. It was erected by one of the largest design and construction companies in Nova Scotia, Rhodes, Curry and Company, of Amherst, which undertook the construction of the new ladies' seminary building on the Acadia campus at the same time as it built the second College Hall; eventually it would be responsible for the third College Hall, in 1920. In the town of Wolfville itself, the company built, among other structures, the Skoda Discovery Plant in 1892, the railway station in 1912 and the Bank of Montreal building in 1921. The photograph was in an album of photographs collected in the 1890s and belonging to John S. Crockett.

Flames destroy second College Hall, December 2, 1920

The Halifax Herald of December 2, 1920, plastered a headline across its front page that announced that, earlier that day, College Hall in Wolfville had burned. Early in the morning, the newspaper said, the Wolfville Fire Department, several hundred students and many other volunteers "who had valiantly fought the flames since eleven-thirty at night, gave up their attempts to save any part of the main building." Instead, they turned their efforts to saving the ladies' seminary. In its report the next day, *The Acadian* concluded that it had been fortunate there was no wind, because had conditions been otherwise the whole town might have been wiped out. It was, coincidentally, the same date as the first College Hall fire.

The blaze was first noticed by a student in Rhodes Hall, who sounded the alarm. In a few moments, the newspaper reported, the whole student body and a large number of citizens had joined the firemen in fighting the blaze. However, it was burning from the bottom up and from inside out, and being of wood it proved easy prey. On their arrival, the firemen located the blaze in the centre of the building, but the whole basement was a mass of flames and it soon became obvious that the building was doomed. According to *The Halifax Herald*, the only theory advanced about the origin of the fire was that one of the furnace doors may have blown open, since it appeared that the flames were fed from below and from the centre of the building. A week later, *The Acadian* reported that it was now generally accepted that the fire was a result of defective wiring.

Lost in the fire were the president's office, some of the university classrooms, the administration offices and the museum. "The latter contained the German airplane presented to the University and a valuable collection of birds of Robie Tufts, Canadian naturalist," *The Acadian* noted. Furniture on the lower floor was saved, in addition to most of the university records in the president's office, and the contents of the treasurer's office. There was no loss of life, though a member of the junior class named Brenton tried to save his academic gown and was trapped in the room where the gowns were hung. The janitor at the seminary, Harry Farris, heard him crying for help and rescued him, dragging him through the halls and delivering him to his fellow students. The newspaper noted that Farris "did splendid service" during the fire in quieting the fears of the women at seminary and in working to save the seminary building. "He also summoned Dr. Cohoon [bursar and general superintendent] and assisted him in saving the contents of the College office."

Third College Hall, the present University Hall, c.1926

The Acadian of February 22, 1924, gave a progress report on the new college building, noting that the foundation walls had been completed and the first floor laid before the frost could do any damage—"Already a forest of steel beams and posts are in place. Some of the latter are over 40 feet high, on which will rest the roof trusses." The newspaper said that the work of making the granite blocks for covering the basement walls was going on in the basement. These blocks were made in wooden moulds, and were of crushed granite and cement. "Above the granite base, the outside walls are to be built of brick and hollow tile, faced with white stone, with columns and trimmings of the same material." This stone was called Benedict Stone, an artificial stone made of crushed marble and cement. In May, all of the floors had been laid and the roof trusses put in place.

University Hall was designed by architect Leslie R. Fairn, with construction by Rhodes, Curry and Company. Fairn, at one time the principal of the Young Manual Training Hall, had a long and distinguished career in Wolfville. He received an honorary doctorate from Acadia.

The cornerstone for the new building was laid on Wednesday, May 28, 1924. Dr. George B. Cutten, president of Acadia when fire destroyed the previous hall, performed the ceremony. Among the items in the cornerstone were the contents of the cornerstone from the previous College Hall, as well as such items as copies of the *Acadia Bulletin*, *Maritime Baptist*, *Morning Chronicle*, and *The Halifax Herald*, current postage stamps, the annual report of the town of Wolfville, and the calendars of Acadia, the Acadia Ladies Seminary, and Horton Collegiate and Business Academy. Longley describes the building as having a large auditorium, twelve classrooms, a room for the faculty, and sixteen offices for the professors and administrative staff, at a cost of $425,000. In this picture, the grounds are being landscaped, and the grass is not yet sown.

Chipman Hall

Horton Academy

Prof. Coldwell

Prof. Wortman

Dr. Sawyer
President

Prof. Kierstead

Prof. Jones

Prof. Higgins

JUBILEE
ACADIA COLLEGE
1838.   1888.
SOUVENIR.

Prof. Tufts

Acadia College

Ladies Seminary

Acadia College Jubilee, 1888

On August 28 and 29, 1888, Acadia College celebrated fifty years of existence. Graduates and friends of the college gathered in Wolfville for the jubilee, which began with an alumni reception—the first, as Dr. Ronald Longley notes, in the history of the university—described as the grandest affair that ever took place in the province outside of Halifax. One of those present was E.A. Crawley, one of the founders of Acadia. Though in good health at the jubilee, he died just a few weeks later.

The president of Acadia College at the time was Artemas W. Sawyer. During the ceremonies the president of the alumni, Dr. J.B. Hall, called Sawyer to the platform, "and amid loud cheering the brilliant and popular president ascended the platform, blushing like a maiden." *The Morning Herald*, Halifax, went on to speak of the contribution Sawyer had made to Acadia as a teacher and administrator, and congratulated him on the prosperity of the college during his administration. Deeply touched, Sawyer "awarded large credit" to his faculty. Next, "three ringing cheers were given by an enthusiastic assemblage, with waving of handkerchiefs by the ladies and demonstrations of appreciation."

This souvenir postcard, issued to commemorate the occasion, shows, clockwise, Chipman Hall, Horton Academy, College Hall and the ladies' seminary. Dr. Sawyer and the college professors are also shown.

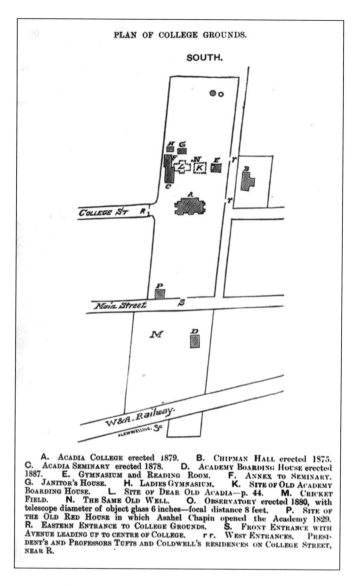

Map of the Acadia College campus during the jubilee, 1888

The map shown here appeared in *Golden Jubilee*, a book published to celebrate the Jubilee of Acadia College. The legend reads as follows: "A—Acadia College, erected 1879. B—Chipman Hall, erected 1875. C—Acadia Seminary, erected 1878. D—Academy Boarding House, erected 1887. E—Gymnasium and Reading Room. F—Annex to Seminary. G—Janitor's House. H—Ladies' Gymnasium. K—Site of Old Academy Boarding House. L—Site of Dear Old Acadia. M—Cricket Field. N—The Same Old Well. O—Observatory erected 1880, with telescope diameter of object glass 6 inches—focal distance 8 feet. P—Site of the Old Red [sic] House in which Asahel Chapin opened the Academy 1829. R—Eastern entrance to College Grounds. S—Front entrance with avenue leading up to centre of College. Rr—west entrances. President's and Professors Tufts and Coldwell's residences on College Street, near R." (Note that there are no letters I, J or Q in the legend.)

The first Horton Academy residence, built 1835, c.1880s

Horton Academy opened for students in March 1829. The Academy Hall was built in 1831, on the site of the current University Hall. The building shown in this picture was erected in 1835 as the Academy Boarding House, and was large enough to accommodate the principal and his family, fifty students, an assistant teacher and a steward. The building located behind and slightly west of College Hall was enlarged to twice its size in 1839. It burned in 1887.

Horton Academy had a long and glorious history, but in October 1958 *The Athenaeum* reported that its work would be suspended indefinitely at the close of the academic year and its resources devoted to university use. University President Watson Kirkconnell said the decision had been taken only after exhaustive study and long deliberation. Horton Academy had been founded as a classical high school to prepare young Nova Scotians for more advanced study. It had passed through several phases: Horton Collegiate Academy, the Acadia Collegiate and Business Academy, and from 1926, Horton Academy. During the latter period it was coeducational, though the Acadia Ladies Seminary was for a time the Female Department of Horton Academy. Kirkconnell said that "the governors' decision to suspend this phase of their work ends a long and notable record in which many thousands of students passed through the Academy's halls and classrooms."

Grand Pré Seminary, c.1870

The idea of allowing women to have a college or university education took hold in Nova Scotia in the mid-1800s. The Rev. John Chase opened a school for women in Wolfville in 1858, and two years later the school was taken over by the Baptist Education Society. Alice Shaw, who had a school in Berwick, became the principal in 1860 of the school known as Grand Pré Seminary. Twenty of her students followed her to the school in Wolfville. Alice Shaw, like the daughters of John Chase (who were the first teachers at Grand Pré Seminary), was a graduate of Mount Holyoke in Massachusetts. She died in January 1921 at the home of her son in Berwick.

A note on the back of this old photograph identifies this as the first of the Grand Pré Seminary buildings. A book published as a memorial to Acadia College and Horton Academy for the half century from 1828 to 1878 says that Grand Pré Seminary was opened in Wolfville by John Chase "in the house now known as the Acadia Hotel." It was located on the site of the present Town Clock, or Founder's Park, across from the Baptist Church. For twelve years, a ladies' seminary continued on these premises, until in 1872 the Committee of Management for Horton Academy "decided to open its classes to young ladies until some better plan for their education should be adopted." As it turned out, this plan was not so provisional, as the Acadia Ladies Seminary developed from it, under the direction of Acadia College, and from 1872 classes were conducted on the Acadia Campus.

The Academy Residence, later Chipman Hall, c.1900

By the time the smoke cleared after the first College Hall had burned in 1877, the only important building left on the campus was Chipman Hall, built in 1875 at a cost of $18,000. It was originally established as a Horton Academy residence and for a time academy students and college students shared the building, but by 1886 it had become exclusively a residence of the college. It was a building in the modern style, four storeys high, with a French roof. It was 80 feet by 40 feet, with an ell measuring 30 by 40. "The first flat contained a dining-hall, 40 feet by 40 feet, and apartments for teachers. The other flats were used for studios and dormitories" (Coldwell).

Chipman resident John Bion Bogart entered Horton Academy the year after this residence was constructed. He wrote about his experiences for the *Acadia Bulletin* in 1933, saying that as the students were "not permitted to mingle with the Seminary girls, except at occasional receptions, and then only under the constant scrutiny of the teachers, and as there were no social functions in the village, there was nothing to distract us from our studies except such outdoor sports as then prevailed." Those sports were football (a predecessor to rugby), baseball and cricket. After fire destroyed College Hall in 1877 a number of temporary buildings were put up, one of them later used as a gymnasium. Bogart pondered the lack of interaction between the sexes, describing the way the women of the seminary always walked two and two and were both preceded and followed by monitors. Except for the rare receptions at seminary, he writes, "our sole intercourse was restricted to gazing upon one another at a respectful distance."

The destruction of Chipman Hall c.1914

On May 26, 1914, at one-thirty in the morning, fire alarms went off on the Acadia campus and in the town of Wolfville. The old Acadia gymnasium, situated close to Chipman Hall, was on fire, the flames being fanned by a strong wind. As the *Acadia Bulletin* told the story, the fire seemed to create a southwest wind that sent the sparks towards both Chipman Hall and the town. Chipman Hall caught fire in one of the gutters "and very readily the flames were communicated to the inside and appeared on the top of the roof." Gale force winds made it difficult to fight the flames, but worse still, burning cinders were falling on the main college building. Meanwhile, streams of water were being directed on Rhodes Hall, to prevent it from burning. "Fires broke out down on the Main Street taking the attention of some of the firemen, but the main College building was in gravest danger; three times it caught fire and these fires were with difficulty extinguished." The wind changed once again, leaving the College Hall in less danger. Danger of further fires subsided around four in the morning, "leaving the Gymnasium and Chipman Hall but a pile of smoking ashes, but the College building and the rest of the town safe."

A.W. Rogers, one of the editors of the student literary magazine, *The Athenaeum*, wrote that he had stood by the grave of old Chip Hall, which he described as a pitiful ruin of bricks and mortar, unfit evermore for human habitation. He thought of the generations of students it had sheltered, and concluded he would rather it had been Carnegie Science Hall that burned, rather than "that homely home of Acadia's traditions, known as 'Old Chip Hall.'" The photograph of Chipman Hall on fire was taken by Hugh Crawley, son of photographer and barrister E. Sidney Crawley.

The historic Acadia Ladies Seminary, c.1889

Three months after College Hall was consumed by flames in December 1877, advertisements were placed for tenders not just for a new College Hall, but also for a ladies' seminary to accommodate seventy-five women. Work began on June 10, 1878, and an official service to lay cornerstones for both College Hall and the Acadia Ladies Seminary was held on July 9. A Yarmouth woman, Mrs. J.W. Lovett, had contributed the largest single amount to the construction of the seminary, so she was asked to perform the cornerstone ceremony. The firm of Rhodes, Curry and Company, Amherst, handled the construction, and in September of 1879 both buildings were ready for use by Acadia.

An architectural gem, the ladies' seminary is now a National Historic Site. Albert Coldwell describes it as 90 feet by 40, with an ell measuring 30 feet by 40; it was four storeys high, "thoroughly modern in its construction and equipment, being heated throughout by hot-water radiators, and having bath-rooms with hot and cold water on the flats occupied by the boarders. The furniture of this building was made to order, as was also the table and bedroom ware and every piece of this ware has the name 'Acadia Seminary' stamped upon it by the makers[…]In the healthfulness and attractiveness of its site, in the architectural beauty of its exterior, and the comfort and elegance of its interior, this building is without a rival of its kind in the Lower Provinces, perhaps in the Dominion."

In 1892 the building was renovated and enlarged, in a manner to fit in with the original structure. The Acadia Seminary Calendar for 1901-1902 says that the building contained an assembly hall for morning prayers and public entertainments, large and pleasant classrooms, a laboratory, studio, gymnasium, reception room, library, hospital, "a large and cheerful" dining room, eighteen music rooms and several bathrooms. The outside was not neglected. The grounds were landscaped and in the rear of the building were two lawn tennis courts, in addition to croquet and ball grounds.

Officials were ever mindful of the possibility of fire—in 1893 the chimney on the north end of the seminary caught fire and made a spectacular scene for a short time, but no damage was done—and worked continually to ensure the safety of the women who lived in the seminary. *The Athenaeum* noted in February 1915 that "during Christmas vacation, all of the doors of exit from the Seminary were changed, so as to swing outward. Two specially constructed fire escapes have been added to the east and west wings. Fire extinguishers have been distributed in all the corridors. These precautions added to the presence of a standpipe and hose in each corridor and to the fact that there are no fewer than eight exits from the building, reduce danger from fire and panic to a very low minimum. This is as it should be and will be appreciated by the patrons of the school." This 1889 photograph shows a girl on the lawn and a boy by the tree and is a good portrayal of the front of the building.

Acadia Ladies Seminary, first graduate, Lois Bigelow, 1880

Lois Bigelow, shown in this photograph by the W. Notman Company, was the first graduate of the Acadia Ladies Seminary. She was also the only graduate in 1880. She was the daughter of J.W. and Sarah (Payzant) Bigelow, J.W. being the secretary of the Acadia College building committee and the one who oversaw the construction of the seminary building. Lois Bigelow graduated from the Literary Course.

Lois left seminary in June. On October 12 she married D. Graham Whidden, who had been born in Antigonish and who had travelled all over North and South America. The pair settled down, had ten children and became one of Wolfville's prominent families. Graham was a member of Wolfville Town Council,

elected in 1922, and then the town's stipendiary magistrate, and was active in many town organizations. He was also a writer, a contributor to *The Acadian*, and the author of a history of Antigonish and of many other historical and genealogical articles.

While Lois Bigelow was the first graduate of seminary, in 1880, the first female graduate of Acadia College was Clara Belle Marshall, born in Mount Hanley, Annapolis County, who received her degree in 1884 and later was matron of Whitman House, or "Tully." The second, Alice Maud Fitch, who graduated the next year, was the first woman to serve on the editorial staff of *The Athenaeum*, the student literary magazine, and the first woman to receive a Master of Arts degree from Acadia. Alice Fitch taught for many years at seminary, was principal of Moulton Ladies' College in Toronto, and was also the first woman to sit on the university senate, in 1893. Grace McLeod Rogers and Margaret Marshall Saunders, both of whom were born in Queens County, were the first women to receive honorary degrees from Acadia, in 1911. Rogers also sat on the Acadia University board of governors. Both were writers: Saunders is well known for the classic animal story *Beautiful Joe*; Rogers was the niece of the celebrated South Brookfield writer, naturalist, lawyer and minister R.R. McLeod, and the mother of Acadia graduate Norman McLeod Rogers, Minister of National Defence in Mackenzie King's wartime cabinet.

Roommates at Acadia Ladies Seminary, 1902

The three seminary roommates in their home away from home in 1902 are, from left to right, with their married names in brackets: Ruby Darrach (MacNeill), from Kensington, Prince Edward Island; Mabel Elliott (Morse), from Clarence, Nova Scotia; and Bertha L. Schurman, from Summerside, P.E.I. The photograph, in the Esther Clark Wright Archives, was given to the archives by Ruby MacNeill, daughter of Ruby Darrach MacNeill.

Today the seminary, built in 1878/1879, is the oldest building on the Acadia campus, a National Historic Site, and is still used for classes and as a dormitory. When this picture was taken it was over a hundred years younger than it is today. In 1935, Helen Beals, then Acadia's assistant librarian, reported in the *Acadia Bulletin* that "the Sem" was no longer to be Acadia's neglected dowager, that her "ill-assorted" towers had been removed and her music hall shorn of its "unsightly projection." She said that with its new coat of paint (reddish with white trim), seminary was in harmony with nearby brick buildings. New floors had been laid, partitions removed, walls and woodwork refinished, and furniture enamelled.

As the picture shows, life in Sem was pleasant. Beals described the rooms as usually two bedrooms connected by a study. Rooms were furnished with a few necessary pieces, and the women were expected to bring extra comforts with them. Heating was by a hot water system. "Electric lights," Beals writes, "were not introduced for many years, but in the meantime the girls managed very well with oil lamps." In 1892 the "East Wing" portion of the building that faces Blomidon was built, making rooms for one hundred students and most of the thirteen teachers. As an institution, Acadia Ladies Seminary closed in 1926 and was merged with Acadia University and Horton Academy.

The tennis courts behind seminary, c.1907

Lucretia Florence Nicholson had this picture of her friends on the tennis courts behind seminary in her photograph album, which was put together from pictures taken while she was a senior at Acadia Seminary in 1907. Lucretia was from Charlottetown, Prince Edward Island. For women at Sem, recreational activities included tennis, popular in Wolfville (there were two courts behind Sem, as well as courts for croquet and basketball), walking, holding suppers, painting, singing in the glee club, playing music, and putting on entertainments. While the catalogue said the purpose of the seminary was to "mould character and implant lofty aims and ideals," with religious culture recognized as the basis of true womanhood, the women managed to have a good time.

In 1935 Helen Beals wrote in her history of seminary that "receptions were held in the large room opposite the front door monthly, and seemed to have been popular, though the only entertainment afforded was the promenade, with conversation, up and down the long corridor." She said that callers—carefully vouched-for young gentlemen, brothers or cousins, "of whom there are said to have been a surprising number"—were permitted occasionally. Apart from that, recreation consisted of the daily walk to the village, within strictly defined limits. Calisthenics were permitted. More strenuous gymnastics were frowned upon, Beals said, yet athletic material was not wanting. "At a hilarious midnight 'feast' it is said that one of the girls turned a nicely placed somersault from her chair on one side of the table to a vacant one on the other." The girls had the use of their own gymnasium, between seminary and Tully, and were allowed an afternoon at the skating rink.

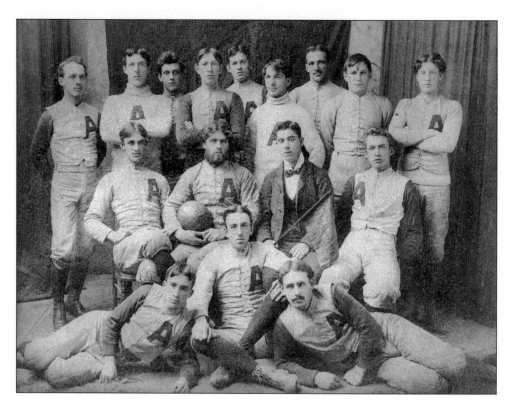

The 1895 Acadia College Rugby Team

Until 1876, Acadia's premier team sport was cricket, a game understood by few North Americans today but immensely popular in many parts of the world. Few pictures exist of it being played at Acadia. In 1876, according to Ronald S. Longley's history of Acadia, R.G. Haley came to Acadia after spending his first year at McGill, bringing with him association football, a modified version of which became rugby. He taught it to his fellow students, and the game caught on quickly. A game of association football was played between Acadia and King's College in 1879, and in 1883 the first rugby game was played between Acadia and Dalhousie, ending in a scoreless tie. This photograph was taken in the new studio of Lewis Rice, whose main studio was in Windsor, but whose Wolfville studio was set up in 1893. He apparently did so because he was grateful for the support given Windsor by Wolfville merchants during Windsor's great fire.

In the photograph are, top row: Clifford A. Tufts, William L. Hall, and Charles W. Rose; next row: Fred O. Foster, F. Tupper, Edgar Nelson Rhodes, Harry A. Purdy, E.B. Jonah, and N. McLeod; third row: Wilford E. Dimock, George B. Cutten, Charles H. Freeman, and Frederick M. Fenwick; front row: Edwin Howard Moffat, G.M. Parson, and William Reginald Morse. Amherst-born Cutten, with the beard, would become the president of Acadia in 1909 and later spend many successful years as president of Colgate University. Edgar Rhodes was to be a premier of Nova Scotia and later a federal finance minister. His father, Nelson, had been a member of the university board of governors; the family had donated the funds in his memory for Rhodes Hall. William Hall went on to be an attorney-general of Nova Scotia. His daughter married Robert L. Stanfield, Nova Scotia premier and leader of the federal Progressive Conservative Party. Charles Rose was the first university chaplain.

William Oliver, superintendent of Acadia grounds and buildings, c.1901

Acadia University President George B. Cutten wrote that William Oliver helped him greatly when he came to Wolfville as president of the university in 1910, and that no man ever had greater love for Acadia than Oliver. *The Athenaeum* in 1915 said William Oliver was a friend and counsellor, and that he was remembered "as a unique personality, an indefatigable worker, a genial and trusted friend."

Oliver was born in Halifax County and began working for Acadia in the mid-1890s, looking after the seminary building, shortly afterwards taking over as superintendent of all of Acadia's buildings and grounds. Oliver served under five presidents and had overseen the construction of every building on the campus except the seminary. Whenever he visited Wolfville, after leaving to become president of Colgate, Cutten's first call was always to the university president, his second was to Oliver; after that he went to see professors and friends: "Mr. Oliver's greeting was always friendly and genuine, and no call I enjoyed more, for we were friends." Oliver and his family lived on campus, in a house near the seminary.

Oliver died in 1934, and his son Clifford took over his role at Acadia. Clifford and his wife, Dorothy Moore, were the parents of the Reverend William Oliver, who served for many years as pastor of the Cornwallis Street Baptist Church in Halifax, and who received honorary degrees from both Acadia and the University of King's College. He and his second wife, Helena White, were the parents of Donald Oliver, who received a scholarship to the Dalhousie University Law School, became a Canadian senator and received an honorary doctorate from Dalhousie University in 2003. The photograph was taken by W.W. Robson, who began working for the Lewis Rice Studio in Windsor and Wolfville, and who eventually opened his own studio on the north side of Main Street.

The Edward W. Young Manual Training Hall, c.1900s

In 1891 the Board of Governors of Acadia began to raise funds both for a manual training teacher and for a building in which to conduct manual training classes. The next year Charles E. Young of Falmouth donated this building in memory of his son, Edward, who had been a student at Horton Academy. Both it and the academy were located close to where the gymnasium and football field are today, across Main Street from University Hall. Two years after it opened it was deemed a success. The hall represented the first teaching of applied science at Acadia. One principal was the noted Wolfville architect Leslie R. Fairn, who can be seen with his students assembled in front of the school. Fairn studied at Horton Academy and was already designing houses in Wolfville by 1902, when he took on the position of principal. He resigned after a few years and moved to Aylesford, where he served as an architect and undertook such projects as the design and construction of the present University Hall. He moved back to Wolfville permanently in 1929.

By 1913, Edward Young Hall had been superseded as a manual training school by Rhodes Hall. The Board of Governors of Acadia decided to move the old hall to the northwest corner of the academy building. As the *Acadia Bulletin* reported in December 1913, moving the hall would enable it to serve as a dining room, kitchen, hospital and matron's and servants' quarters: "This will give additional room in the Academy Home for twelve new students, which is much needed, as several students have to board outside the Home. The building is now being fitted up, and it is expected that it will be ready for occupancy at the beginning of the second term, January 1." Moving the hall ultimately proved fatal, however. On the morning of February 3, 1915, the Horton Academy building caught on fire, as did the Edward W. Young Manual Training Hall, which toppled to the ground twenty-five minutes after the academy building collapsed.

Horton Academy residence, c.1907

Taken in 1907, this unusual photograph of the Horton Academy residence was in a scrapbook belonging to Lucretia Florence Nicholson. It is interesting to compare it with the photograph of the same building during Acadia College's Jubilee, 1888, shown earlier in this chapter. This picture shows the addition to the building, on the right side in the picture.

The academy residence was built in 1887, again by the Amherst firm of Rhodes, Curry and Company, which built so many of the buildings on campus. It was three storeys, had a basement, was heated by hot water heat, and had electric lights. There was room in the residence for almost ninety students. It was located across the main road from the college proper, not far from the site of the present gymnasium.

GRAHAM
PHOTO

Fire destroys Horton Academy residence, February 3, 1915

At ten minutes past nine on February 3, 1915, fire alarm bells sounded in Wolfville. The academy residence was on fire. Before long, as *The Athenaeum* described it, all collegiate and college activity had stopped and hundreds had gathered by the burning building. One of those was photographer Edson Graham, who took this picture as fire destroyed the building.

A cold northeasterly wind fanned the flames, it was reported, as dozens of students and firemen tried to save the building, furniture and student belongings. It soon became obvious that fire had penetrated all parts of the structure. "As a consequence, with the exception of a few trunks and miscellaneous articles from some of the students' rooms and the dining-room and kitchen [visible in the photographs], everything was consumed." The building fell to the ground in three-quarters of an hour, and shortly afterward the attached Manual Training Hall also was destroyed. The two buildings were worth more than thirty thousand dollars, but were insured for a little over twenty. An investigation held later concluded that the fire began in the chimney and spread to the attic, burning unnoticed for some time, as the students had left for classes at 8:15 A.M. It was not until the fire had burned through the ceiling that the alarm was sounded.

The Athenaeum noted that there had been eighty-two students, monitors and teachers living in the residence, and that temporary accommodation had been provided for them in Willett Hall, in the college residence on Main Street, and in different homes around town: "Although the students and teachers underwent such bitter experiences and lost practically all their books, Academy classes were resumed the following morning." Plans were quickly made to rebuild, but in a different location. The decision was made to leave the old site free in order to increase the space available for the athletic field. A new stone residence would be built, to be designed by architect Andrew R. Cobb, a graduate of Acadia.

Artemas Wyman Sawyer, president of Acadia for twenty-seven years, c.1880s

Artemas Wyman Sawyer was born in Vermont in 1827. In 1855 he moved to Wolfville to become professor of ancient languages. He left in 1861 to become a pastor and then principal of the Literary and Scientific Institute of New London, Connecticut, and in 1869 was appointed president of Acadia College. A.W.H. Eaton's *History of Kings County* describes him as a man of dignity and culture, who successfully filled the responsible office he so long held. Sawyer, whose large white house can be seen in photographs in this chapter and in chapter one, died in 1907.

Dr. Ronald S. Longley devoted a chapter to "The Age of Sawyer" in his book on the history of Acadia. Sawyer began his work at Acadia at a time when the teaching of classics was making room for science. Oxford and Cambridge had only started offering science courses the year of Sawyer's appointment as president. Under Sawyer's guidance, legendary professors of science like George T. Kennedy and Albert Coldwell, and history professor John Freeman Tufts (seen in the 1888 souvenir postcard reproduced earlier), were given appointments. Tufts' scholarship at Harvard had been of such a high standard, Longley writes, that thereafter graduates of Acadia were admitted to Harvard without a preliminary examination. Sawyer also appointed Theodore Harding Rand as professor of English and history, and Elias Miles Keirstead as professor of English literature and logic, a post he held from 1882 to 1905.

Longley points out that another innovation of Sawyer's presidency was the admission of female students to classes at Acadia. Women at the Acadia Ladies Seminary had asked permission to attend classes at the college, permission that was granted with some misgivings, although in 1884 the first woman graduate was awarded a degree. In 1896, after serving almost three decades as Acadia's president, Sawyer resigned that position but continued teaching at the university and became honorary president of the seminary.

The Acadia girls' hockey team, 1914

The women in this photograph are, left to right, Deb Crowell, Class of 1915; Rae Wilson, 1915; Charlotte Layton, 1916; Dorothy Burdett, 1917; Elizabeth Starratt, 1917; Grace Blenkhorn, 1915; May Raymond, 1914; Margaret Palmer, 1914; and Lillian Chase, 1916. The photograph was in the album kept as a student by Bessie Lockhart, whose picture appears later in this chapter.

In 1983-1984, Acadia University mounted an exhibition to celebrate the centenary of its first woman graduate, Clara Belle Marshall. The catalogue notes say that the subject of women in sport had been controversial, and that when the seminary opened in 1879 women's sports were limited to catch, tag and croquet; "However, by the 1890s women were playing tennis and basketball and in another decade had their own hockey team." While sports were voluntary, exercise was not: the women put on bloomers every day between four and six in the afternoon and engaged in drills that involved swaying, stretching, statue-like poses, wands, scarves, fans and head and toe exercises. "These drills were universally hated by most of the girls but town and gown loved watching the yearly spectacle in which women publicly displayed their feminine deportment." The drills were eliminated when the War Memorial Gymnasium opened in 1921 and gym classes were instituted.

The sophomore Easter hat parade, 1915

Each year the sophomore class staged a hat parade where the members marched as a body downtown, but the custom stopped in 1912. According to *The Athenaeum* in April of 1915, the Class of 1917 had revived the parade; it had been held on Sunday, April 10. "About thirty members of the class took part in it," the newspaper said. "Lack of space and vocabulary prevent a detailed description of the different hats, but it is sufficient to say that the creations were of such wonderful designs that the Class was followed in its march by nearly a thousand spectators." It said the hats were exhibited in Calkin's drug store on Monday and Tuesday, "and were the objects of delighted approval from all who were so fortunate as to see them."

In this photograph the sophomore class is seen marching in front of the Wolfville Baptist Church, which had been built just four years earlier.

Big winter slide at Acadia, 1915

Physical education instructor Lyman W. Archibald was always looking for ways to keep students active, and especially to get the women outdoors. In 1913 he had the idea of erecting a giant slide for coasting, which began near the back of the Carnegie Science Hall and ended at Main Street, a run which took the students nearly a quarter of a mile. The *Acadia Bulletin* wrote in 1913 that the students "enjoy this form of exercise very much." This photograph, taken by Edson Graham in 1915, shows a similar slide, which began in the university orchard, went past Whitman House and ended at the seminary. A man is steering a toboggan while five laughing co-eds hold on behind.

Students harvesting the Acadia farm crop, 1918

The students in this picture are bringing in the harvest from the Acadia farm, south of Willett Hall. As *The Athenaeum* told the story in its January 1919 issue, the war had created a scarcity of labour, so on Thursday, November 7, the students volunteered to help with the work of harvesting the fall crop. The university, in turn, announced that all of those who wished to assist would be excused from classes. More than fifty students went to work, labouring until five o'clock. "By this time almost the entire crop of turnips, about eight hundred bushels, had been pulled, topped, and hauled to the vegetable cellar. The remainder of the task was completed by the students the following morning." Just after the students had gone out for the afternoon work, there was word that Germany had signed the Armistice. The news turned out to be false, but despite the excitement the fellows continued their work vigorously and faithfully.

The farm had been established at the back of the campus "to provide milk and produce for the dining table and healthy exercise and needed money for students" (Moody, 1988). Acadia and agriculture were closely associated in the early days. A school of horticulture, promoted by the Nova Scotia Fruit Growers Association, was established at Acadia in 1894. Things did not always go smoothly at the farm, however. In 1911 Dr. George E. DeWitt, for many years Wolfville's medical officer (and mayor between 1903 and 1905), reported to Town Council that there had been an epidemic of typhoid in March and April 1910 among the women at Acadia seminary. He said the milk supply was suspected of being the cause of infection, as a well contaminated by sewage had been used to cleanse the milk cans and water the cows. He said the milk supply from that source had immediately been stopped, and no further cases had occurred.

DeWitt was a forward-thinking physician; when his own daughter, Carrie, came down with tuberculosis, he studied treatment for this killer disease and in 1899 set up a centre in Wolfville where patients—including Carrie—could get plenty of rest, fresh air and medication. At the time it was one of only three such centres in Canada and was the forerunner of the provincial sanatorium set up in Kentville in 1904.

Four Acadia women destined for great things, c.1916

Four Acadia women from the Class of 1916 who made their mark in Canada and elsewhere stand in front of their residence, Trotter House. On the left is Lillian Chase, born on Church Street in Cornwallis in 1894. She went to Wolfville High School and graduated from Acadia with her BA. She became an eminent medical doctor, a specialist in internal medicine and a Canadian authority on diabetes. Graduating from the University of Toronto in 1922, she was a pioneer in the introduction of insulin and worked with the Banting and Best Clinic in Toronto, and after serving in the Medical Corps during the war was involved in the Women's College Hospital in Toronto. Next to her is Esther Clark Wright, Lillian's roommate, author of *Blomidon Rose*. She was born in Fredericton, the only New Brunswicker in the Class of 1916. She married a member of the faculty of Stanford University, Conrad Payling Wright, studied at the University of Toronto and at Oxford, and earned her PhD from Radcliffe-Harvard in 1931. She lectured at Acadia between 1943 and 1947, retiring to Wolfville and carrying on a career as a prolific writer. She received an honorary doctorate from Acadia in 1975 and was made a Companion of the Order of Canada in 1990, just a few weeks before she died.

On the other side of the tree, in the black dress, is Bessie Lockhart, from whose photograph album in the Esther Clark Wright Archives, Acadia University, this photograph is taken. Bessie was born at Castle Frederick in Falmouth in 1890 and went to Windsor Academy before coming to Acadia, where she graduated with a BA. After graduation she worked with the Canadian Baptist Mission in India. She stayed there until 1934, then returned for service between 1955 and 1959, and again in 1963 and 1964. On the right, holding the tennis racket, is Hettie Morse Chute, born in Nebraska in 1888. She attended school in Waterville, Nova Scotia, and graduated with her BA. She earned her MA from the University of Toronto in 1918, taught in Toronto and at Colchester County Academy in Truro, then was an assistant in biology at Acadia. She received her PhD from Cornell University and went on to be a professor at Rutgers.

Trotter House, later a women's residence, c.1920s

After Artemas Wyman Sawyer gave up the presidency of Acadia, the board of governors went on a search for a new leader, leaving the university in the hands of faculty committees until it came up with the right person. They found the ideal candidate two blocks away, the pastor of the Baptist church in Wolfville. He was Thomas Trotter, born in England, ordained in Shelburne, later a graduate of the University of Toronto, then a minister in Ontario and professor at McMaster University in Hamilton. In September 1895, Trotter came to the Wolfville Baptist Church and was offered the presidency of the university two years later. Longley calls Trotter "clear, forceful and inspiring," crediting him with energetic fund raising that cleared the university of debt. In 1906 ill health caused Trotter to resign and accept a pastorate in Ohio. His son Bernard, who wrote a book of poetry about war and peace, was killed in France in 1917 at the age of twenty-seven.

Trotter lived in this house, located just east of seminary. According to Kirkconnell and Silver, the house was built around 1873 by George W. Borden. From 1907 to 1909 it was the residence of Acadia President W.B. Hutchinson, and from then on, because of its proximity to seminary, was used as the college women's residence. In 1912 the *Acadia Bulletin* described it as accommodating twenty young women, under the care of a matron, with preference given to the women of the freshman class. In 1914 it was used to house ten- to fourteen-year-old girls—students at a junior department of seminary—after which it became, once again, a residence for the college women. It had the nickname "the Crow's Nest." On July 29, 1997, *The Advertiser*, Kentville, carried photographs of a backhoe knocking down its walls, as the university had it demolished. Built near the location of Manning Memorial Chapel, the building was moved to Horton Avenue in the 1960s to allow for construction of the chapel, and most recently had housed an international student centre.

Tully, the women's residence, after construction in 1915

For generations of women who attended Acadia, Tully was home. Fires in 1914 and 1915 had destroyed both the Horton Academy residence and Chipman Hall, so Acadia set about building new residences to take their place. One was Willett Hall, for men, which cost $35,000, and the other was Tully, which cost $40,000. Both were completed in 1915.

Esther Clark Wright was one of those who lived in Tully. In *Blomidon Rose*, she tells the story of how the new residence got its name: It was named Tully by the boys in the first winter of its existence. The year before, a boy had gone to a dance and met what he considered to be an unattractive girl (Wright describes the boy as unattractive himself, an ungainly stripling with a pimple on his nose). The girl's name was Tully, so the boys began using "tullies" as units of measurement in evaluating women, the highest value possible being one thousand tullies. When the girls moved into their new residence in the fall, the boys, giving the residents high scores, named it "Tully Tavern." The girls loved the name, Esther Clark Wright said, and even developed a song about it. A wooden boardwalk, later a cinder path, from the new building over the red mud, was named the Tully Tavern Scenic Railway. Wings were added in 1919 and 1926. In 1927 the building was given the official name Whitman Hall, but unofficially remained Tully.

McConnell Hall, the university dining hall, c.1927

In 1926 the university built what it first called the University Dining Hall, and later McConnell Hall. This photograph shows the interior of the dining room, with room for ten students per table. In its last years, before being turned over to a catering service, the dining hall was run by dietitian Elizabeth Eaton Stuart, who continued the practice of using students as waiters. The head student waiter in the year the picture was taken was a young man named Tommy Kirk, a friend of Harry Starr's.

In 1936 the *Acadia Bulletin* published a brochure that included pictures similar to this one, with the caption "Acadia students dine together at small round tables in the beautiful University Dining Hall, a spacious room, well lighted and perfectly ventilated, with a seating capacity of 600." The brochure said the dining hall was modern in every respect. The "spotless" kitchen was equipped with a large electric oven, steam jackets of various sizes, a mixing, cutting and grinding machine, "the bakeshop with a coal oven, brick-floored, and a large bread-mixer." There were heated tables to keep the dishes hot, electric bread cutters and toasters. Throughout, the brochure said, one was impressed with the air of quiet efficiency and spotless cleanliness.

Acadia University's bookmobile service, c.1930

These two bookmobiles were run by Acadia University in the early 1930s to provide outreach library service to various points in the Maritimes. In the photograph, T.A.(Tommy) Kirk is at left, and Hubert (Hugh) Miller at right. The bookmobiles are parked by the rear of University Hall, just before leaving on their run.

The service began in 1930 with two bookmobiles, each holding 2,400 volumes. Tommy Kirk took his bookmobile around Nova Scotia, dropping off books at appointed stations and picking them up on the next call. Hugh Miller took his to New Brunswick and Prince Edward Island. Mary Kinley Ingraham wrote about the service in the *Wolfville Acadian* of August 25, 1938, saying that "it was a good system but a costly one. In August, 1931, the bookmobile service ceased, not because the people were uninterested or unresponsive, but because of the financial strain on the university."

The Superline station and the president's house, c.1940s

This excellent photograph was taken from the steeple of the Baptist church and shows in the foreground the Superline service station, located in front of the university rink, with the house used by the presidents of Acadia University next to it. That house had been built by one of Wolfville's most important businessmen, John L. Brown, in 1852. Presidents who occupied the house included George Cutten, F.W. Patterson, Watson Kirkconnell, James Beveridge and James Perkin. Notice the Ionic pillars at the front of the house, which match the portico of the first Acadia College Hall (Kirkconnell and Silver). The building now serves as the home of the university alumni.

West of the house can be seen the War Memorial Gymnasium, with the athletic field in front and the tennis courts beside the field's grandstand. The original gym burned in the same fire that took Chipman House in 1914. Delayed by the war, construction began in 1919. The decision was made to use the facility to honour the sixty Acadia students who had died in the war. Ronald Longley's history of the university notes that the building would cost $125,000. Plans were drawn by F.P. Dumaresq of Halifax, who graduated from Acadia in 1899, and the contract to build the gym was awarded to Charles H. Wright. It was completed in 1921. Built of local quartzite from White Rock, it contained a running track nine feet above the gymnasium floor. There was also a swimming pool, locker rooms, a wrestling and exercise room, and Memorial Hall, devoted to the memory of the students who died.

Acadia from the air, c.1938

Until 1946 there was very little growth of the university south of the old laundry, the Great Depression putting an end to building at Acadia for almost seventeen years. The drought ended when the need for residence space became overpowering. War Memorial Residence opened in 1946, and since it had to be left with its walls unplastered for a time, it received the nickname "Barracks." With post-war registration booming, the university took over the Evangeline Inn for a number of years, where it housed eighty-two students. Professor Daniel M. Welton's elegant old home, Maplewood, built around 1880 (see Chapter two), was used by the university for a girls' residence. A number of cottages were built on university property for married war veterans and the university even put students in buildings at Camp Aldershot and in Canning, running a bus service between there and Wolfville. Army huts from Aldershot were set up on campus for a variety of purposes.

In the area occupied by the orchard in this picture, Acadia built residences as soon as the money became available. Chipman House, south of Willett House, went up in 1960, its cornerstone laid by 1903 graduate Dr. Leverett deV. Chipman. Dennis House was next, helped by funds from the newspaper-publishing Dennis family of Halifax. It opened in 1961. Eaton House, named for the Eaton families of Kings County, opened in 1964.

Chapter 4

Shops, Businesses, Agriculture, and Industry

Wolfville, Its People and Their Work

Business and commercial life grew up in Wolfville first around the creek. The early records are sketchy, depending on old account books, diaries and the reminiscences of people who took the time to write them down. A.W.H. Eaton wrote that the Planters brought many of the basic tools they needed and that they were able to provide for themselves in large measure. What they didn't have could be purchased at Edward DeWolf's well-stocked shop, said to have been at Horton Landing between 1773 and 1796. The Planters set up blacksmiths' forges, for mending carts and shoeing horses and oxen, and carpenters' shops for building furniture and making household utensils. They built grist mills, saw mills, carding mills, brickyards and tanneries and opened small general stores in both the Horton and Cornwallis town plots, stores which in time had rivals in many nearby communities.

The DeWolfs had been granted much of the land that came to be Wolfville, with Elisha DeWolf having a shop and post office. By the 1830s, businesses were well rooted in Wolfville. Horton Academy had been established in the village, one of its students being Charles Tupper, whose great-grandfather was one of the original Cornwallis Planters. Tupper went on to be premier of Nova Scotia, one of the Fathers of Confederation and prime minister of Canada. In 1837, on the grounds of the academy, he planted an elm tree that lasted for 166 years before succumbing to Dutch elm disease. On April 29, 2003, the old tree was cut down. The historic plaque that had been placed on the tree during the Dominion Diamond Jubilee in 1927 is now in the Esther Clark Wright Archives, Acadia University. While Tupper was at Horton, he worked in the shoe-making shop of Louis Payzant Godfrey, located to the left of the current Baptist church.

Peter S. Hamilton was a classmate of Sir Charles Tupper. He started at Horton Academy in February of 1838 and later remembered every building in Wolfville. Fifty years after he was at Horton Academy he described the town in the *Morning Herald*, Halifax. Starting at Johnson's Pond west of the centre of the village, Elisha DeWolf's shop would be on the left. Moving eastward and continuing on the left, there was Irishman Luke Franklin's shoemaking shop on the eastern boundary of the grounds of Horton Academy; the inn of Jonathan Graham, whose lands on both sides of the road were divided among his sons and eventually became Acadia University; the shop owned by Thomas Andrew Strange DeWolf, Elisha's son, whose house was later the home of the town's museum; a carpenter's shop well past Mud Bridge; and finally, near the edge of town, a "grimy looking old house, used as a grog shop."

Hamilton then cast his mind's eye on the right side of the road, starting back at Johnson's Pond. He mentions the location of Horton Academy, goes past the Baptist Church, and comes to a two-storey house belonging to Elijah Fowler bearing a sign for the Temperance Inn. There was a home and shop owned by Stephen DeWolf, and on the west end of Mud Bridge, a house and carpenter's shop, plus a blacksmith's shop owned by Israel DeWolfe. The next building was occupied at the time by Margaret Best, who ran a seminary for women; today it is the Randall House Museum. Dr. Edward S. Brown had what Hamilton called a drug shop and surgery, and then there was a carriage maker's shop "belonging to the brothers Armstrong." Finally, there was Scott's general store, on the corner of the road to Lower Horton and Gaspereau, now Maple Avenue.

The famous Ambrose Church maps include one of Wolfville, begun in 1864, an original of which hangs in Randall House. A sample of the businesses that appear on the map gives a sense of what the business face of Wolfville looked like in the 1860s. The drugstore run by George Valentine Rand was located in the block between Highland and Linden Avenues, established in 1853. Rand owned much of the land between Main Street and Acadia Street, having bought it from Elijah Fowler Jr. He sold off the lots on both sides of Linden Avenue. The store built by John L. Brown was situated on land he purchased in 1849 at the southwest corner of Highland and Main; that historic store was torn down in 1966. Also identified was the shop of one of Wolfville's earliest photographers, J.B. Davison.

The Church map also shows Thomas Andrew Strange DeWolf's shop, still in business a quarter of a century after it opened in1838, and Joseph Weston's tailor shop, which was on the north side of Main, in the block between Elm Avenue and Central Avenue. When Joseph died, his wife continued the place as a candy shop. Henry B. Witter is listed as a flour merchant. At this time his store was located, according to Church, on the south side of Main Street, in front of today's University Hall and near the site of the first Horton Academy building. J. Loran Franklin is listed as a ship and country smith. Franklin moved to Canard from Windsor when he was sixteen in order to learn the blacksmith trade, went from there to Kingsport to do iron work on ships, then came to Wolfville in 1869 to work on vessels being built by David J. Harris on the east side of Mud Creek. Not planning to stay in Wolfville, he found he liked the place so much that he opened a business of his own next to D.A. Munro's carriage factory, which he operated for many years. He eventually bought the F. and H. Brown hardware business which had been opened in the shoe factory building near the street leading to the Wolfville wharf. Franklin later erected a large building facing Locust Avenue, where he and Charles E. Starr ran a hardware business known as Starr, Son and Franklin. That building is still there, part of the historic Wolfville streetscape. Franklin died in 1926, his obituary in *The Acadian* providing a good summary of his life.

On June 27, 1898, three decades after the Ambrose Church maps were begun, *The Halifax Herald* carried a story called "Men and Firms of Wolfville—Who are the Representatives of Business Progress and Prosperity in This Seat of Learning, of Horticulture and Paying Trade." Apart from the awkward title, the report was a good glimpse at what Wolfville's business area was like just before the turn of the twentieth century. Featured in the story were the dry goods and millinery business run by J.D. Chambers, later Wolfville's mayor; J.F. Herbin's, the jewellery business started by John Frederic Herbin in 1895 and still in operation today; the People's Shoe Store, started by a man from Liverpool named N.M. Sinclair; and W.W. Robson's studio, Robson being the photographer who had taken over the Lewis Rice operation out of Windsor and Wolfville, and who would eventually turn that over to Edson Graham, Wolfville's most famous photographer.

Featured too was the store of former mayor T.L. Harvey at the corner of Main and Gaspereau, called one of the finest grocery establishments in the county. In 1915 a spectacular fire would destroy that store, along with a number of other buildings. The article also included information about the Royal Hotel, later the Evangeline Inn, located where a little park featuring a town clock has today been created; L.W. Sleep's hardware and stove store, then one of the oldest firms in town, established forty years before and situated on Main near Locust Avenue; Starr, Son and Franklin, also a hardware store and seller of the "favourite Columbia bicycles"; Hotel Central, run by J.W. Selfridge, on Main Street, fitted with electric lights and hot and cold baths and connected to a livery stable owned by W.J. Balcom; and F.J. Porter's, one of the largest groceries in Wolfville. There was also the Acadia Seminary Hotel, run by F.P. Rockwell,

Turn of the century advertisements

These advertisements appeared in the November 1899 issue of the Acadia University student publication, *The Athenaeum.*

who had the brilliant idea of renting the Acadia Ladies Seminary during the summer and turning it into a tourist establishment. The newspaper states it was undoubtedly the largest summer hotel in Nova Scotia, having accommodation for one hundred and fifty guests.

There was mention of the R.E. Harris business, which sold china and glassware, plus souvenirs and groceries, Harris also being an apple and potato exporter, as well as the agent for the steamer Beaver; A.J. Woodman's, the only furniture store in Wolfville, Woodman previously being an undertaker; the Wolfville Coal and Lumber Company, run by C.M. Vaughan and F.W. Woodman, selling both fuel and building materials; the Wolfville Clothing Company, the "only ladies' tailoring establishment in Kings County;" O.D. Harris's, a dry goods store on Main Street, three storeys high, each floor containing things for the buying public; C.H. Borden's, selling boots and shoes; and William Regan's, a leading manufacturer of harness for horses.

All of these merchants are a part of the story of Wolfville. They represent a particular point in time, yet they also represent a continuum. A few years earlier or a few later, the stores might or might not exist, or might be owned by someone else, but there would likely be links from one era to another. For example, James Patriquin had started a harness shop in 1863. His son Charles took it over, finally passing it on to William Regan, who had first come to work in the business in 1880. The Lewis W. Sleep hardware store had been started by Lewis's father, Simeon R. Sleep, among the first to advertise in the town newspaper in 1883. The store was run by others in the Sleep family after Lewis. Likewise, John Frederic Herbin started Herbin's Jewellery in 1885; it passed to his son, Frederic, who took it over at age twenty-two after his father's death in 1923. Frederic died in 1951, to be followed in the business by his son John, whose son Peter is a member of the firm today.

While this commercial activity was going on, Wolfville was growing in a civic sense. Until the 1890s Wolfville had been a village, but a movement grew to have it incorporated as a town. In January of 1893 notices were posted around Wolfville that there would be a vote on incorporation on January 22 at the James Morse store. It was a simple ballot: one would either vote "for" or "against." There was a bit of a snag, however, since an appeal had been launched over the proposed town's boundaries, and Sheriff Stephen Belcher issued a notice that the poll would be postponed until the appeal had been heard.

By the end of February the appeal had been decided, the poll taken, and the decision made to incorporate. *The Acadian* editorialized that the success of incorporation depended on who was chosen for council, saying it trusted that the people would look into the matter fully and elect such officers to manage the town's affairs as would bring credit upon the town. When the election was held, Dr. E.P. Bowles was chosen mayor by acclamation. The newspaper congratulated him, remembering that he had been a resident of Wolfville for a number of years and was well acquainted with the requirements of the town. His councillors were C.H. Borden, George Thompson, Everett W. Sawyer, George W. Borden, A. DeW. Barss and C.R.H. Starr. Defeated were such well-known names as J.B. Davison, S.P. Benjamin, R.E. Wickwire, F.J. Porter, J.L. Franklin, A.E. Coldwell and O.D. Harris. Almost all of the names on the list made their mark on Wolfville's history, whether on Town Council or not.

Mayor Bowles was sworn in on Saturday, March 25, 1893 by Justices J.B. Davison and J.W. Caldwell. George Thompson was chosen deputy mayor, and a town clerk—Walter Brown—was appointed at a salary of $300 per year. Committees established included Finance and Tenders; Streets, Public Properties and Waterworks; the Poor; Laws and Legislation; and Bylaws.

One of the issues that occupied this first council was the question of names, not only of the streets in the town, but of the town itself. According to a letter writer to *The Acadian* in March of 1893, the name Wolfville was not easily pronounced or understood; suggested

Looking down Highland Avenue, c.1900s

Highland Avenue had different names over the years, one of them being School Street, because the village's first school faced it from what became Acadia Street. The photograph is from the Ron Peck collection and is courtesy of Warren Peck.

replacements were Acadia, Acadie, L'Acadia, Evangeline, Minas, or, incomprehensibly, Basil. A meeting of citizens was called to consider the name and the newspaper urged people to attend: "If the people wake up some morning and find they are not living in Wolfville, they will have no person to blame but themselves, and if they find they have lost an opportunity to start their town on a new career, they will not find much sympathy from those who favour the change." A Haligonian wrote to say that it was wrong to have "ville" tacked on the end of the name of a town, and suggested instead the name Marshfield, given the nearby marshes. From a person who had passed through Wolfville, calling it the "prettiest town in the province," came the suggestion of Wengoosoonake, the Mi'kmaw word for apple. The writer of this newspaper account had tried to imagine a brakeman on the W & A opening a car door and singing out the new name. "Oh my," the letter said, "do not spoil part of the beauty of the town by changing the name." At the meeting, James S. Morse moved that the present name be retained, a vote was called, and it passed unanimously.

The Town Council's attention was turned to the names of the streets. At a meeting in November 1895, Councillor F.J. Porter moved that the town streets be renamed, with those running east and west to be called by numbers (Main Street thereby being given the name Second Street), while those running north and south be called avenues. C.R.H. Starr moved an amendment that the streets running east and west be named, beginning by the waterfront, Front Street, Main Street, College Street, Prospect Street and Pleasant Street. The vote was tied on the amendment, but the mayor, James W. Bigelow in 1895, cast his vote in favour of Starr.

It was then unanimously decided that the streets running north and south would be called avenues. Starting at the east side of town by Scott's Corner, the names adopted were Maple, Oak, Orchard, Cedar, Willow, Locust, Gaspereau, Central, Linden, Elm, Highland, University, Westwood and Cherry.

Among the names consigned to history were Water Street, which became Front Street; McKeen Street, which became Prospect; the Old Post Road to Melanson, which became Maple Avenue; Barss's Lane, which became Oak; Pick Lane, which became Orchard; Franklin Street, which became Cedar; Chapel Street, which became Gaspereau Avenue; Earl Street, which became Central Avenue; Rand Street, which became Linden Avenue; Railway Street, which became Elm Avenue; School Street, which became Highland Avenue; College Avenue, which became University Avenue; Chipman Avenue, which became Westwood Avenue; and Ferry Lane, which became Cherry Lane.

There was never great happiness with the names chosen. As late as February 1921, Anglican rector R.F. Dixon wrote in *The Acadian* that the names of the streets in Wolfville were absolutely meaningless. "Why," he asked, "wasn't the street running from Main to the school house, known by some absurd fancy name which I forget at this moment, named Rand Street? Most of the land through which it passed was given by the late George Rand, in his day and generation a worthy unselfish citizen and member of an historic Nova Scotian family." Dixon argued that the names should perpetuate eminent men or old and respected pioneer families. Two months later, a writer who signed himself "Citizen" wrote to agree with Dixon, saying that a town which shows itself grateful to those who have laboured in its interests invites others to add to the improvement of the town. The writer wanted Earnscliffe to be named Cramp Avenue, Westwood to be Sawyer, University to be Crawley, Highland to be Trotter, Linden to be Rand, Gaspereau to be Cutten, Locust to be Rockefeller, Seaview to be Carnegie, Willow to be Rhodes and Victoria to be Chipman. They were good suggestions, but none were acted upon.

The Skoda Discovery Company Plant, later a flour mill, c.1900

The Canadian Skoda Discovery Company in Wolfville was the Canadian branch of a Maine-based patent medicine producer, organized in January 1892 with Wolfville shipbuilder C.R. Burgess as president and G.W. Borden as business manager. The plant was seventy feet long, forty-five feet wide and four storeys high. The floor space equalled nearly one-third of an acre, almost all of which, according to the Saint John *Messenger and Visitor* (Sept. 1893), was used in putting up the "well-known Skoda remedies." The newspaper explained that the ingredients were mixed in large oaken tanks and there was a bottling room with an automatic bottle filler "having a capacity of 1,800 bottles per hour, which takes the medicine from the tanks and places it in the bottles ready for use." The bottles were then cooked, sealed, washed, wiped, labelled, packed twelve to a box, and readied for shipping.

Sadly, within a few short years it had failed. On November 3, 1897, the *Bridgetown Monitor* reported that a new flour mill was planned for Wolfville, using the Skoda building. Marshland had been acquired just north of the wharf and a gang of workers from Canning was driving piles and laying sills. The building was moved from its location slightly east of the railway station by its new owner, Acadia and Harvard graduate Arthur L. Calhoun, who renamed it Beaver Mills. Tragedy struck Calhoun, however. On January 10, 1899, while he stood on a platform where corn was being unloaded from the schooner *Leonard B.*, a container struck him and knocked him to the wharf below. He was killed instantly.

Later, the Skoda building was bought by R.E. Harris and Sons, who "fitted up" the upper part as a community hall, while using the lower floor for storage. On Wednesday, September 16, 1931, a freight train crew shunting cars at two o'clock in the morning discovered the Skoda building on fire and sounded the alarm, but nothing could be done to save the building or its contents.

Wolfville businesses before the turn of the century, c.1890s

This classic photograph of Wolfville shows some of its businesses from the middle of Main Street, facing west. On the left is T.A. Munro's tailor shop, and next to it is the O.D. Harris dry goods store. O.D. Harris set up shop in Wolfville in 1881, purchasing the Glasgow House, then building the store in this picture in 1884. It was the first store in Wolfville to have plate glass windows. The Halifax Herald described the store, in 1898, as an up-to-date establishment "second to none in the country." The building was three storeys high, sixty by thirty feet in size, and had artistically dressed windows. The first floor carried fancy dry goods such as ladies' dresses, silks, laces and gloves, while upstairs were carpet and clothing rooms.

The T.A. Munro tailor shop, next to the Harris store, was described in 1893 as having a fine assortment of cloth for boys' and men's wear "and is prepared to manufacture the same at short notice." Across the street and just past the corner of Central Avenue was the Burpee Witter store, its distinctive roof evident. The store, built in July 1880, was sold in 1895 to John Calder, who kept it for three years and sold it to G.W. Borden. Borden ran it until 1903, when it was taken over by John Chambers, who later was a mayor of Wolfville. Chambers sold it in 1920 to Charles H. Porter, in whose family it remains.

**The Caldwell and Murray dry goods store, next to the former
J.L. Brown store, c.1879**

In the early days, the southwest corner of Main and Highland was part of a farm owned by Daniel Whipple, whose holdings included the land from Highland to University Avenues. It passed to his son-in-law, Jonathan Graham, who later divided it between his sons, James and George. James sold his land to Acadia, while George sold his to John L. Brown, in 1849. Brown soon built a store on the property, while next to it, J.W. Caldwell later established a store called Caldwell and Murray's.

In the photograph, taken circa 1879, the Caldwell and Murray store is shown at centre, with what had been Brown's store on the left. In the January 21, 1880, edition of *The Star*, published in Wolfville, an advertisement for Caldwell and Murray describes a new boot and shoe store in Wolfville. The two stores became something of a one-stop shopping centre: In 1879, Professor Kennedy (who taught natural science at Acadia College), bought substantial quantities of milk and vegetables from John L. Brown and a woollen shirt, drawers and black straw hat from Caldwell and Murray. The milk was four cents a quart and the straw hat a dollar (Davison, 1985). Kennedy died in Wolfville in 1907, after a career that went on to include the vice-presidency of King's College in Halifax.

The John L. Brown store eventually became Porter Brothers. Born in 1815, Brown had come to Wolfville from Grand Pré in 1847 and became one of Wolfville's most important businessmen. He was the son of Charles and Frances Lothrop Brown and was a direct descendant of the Planters who settled Horton. His brother, Frederick, bought the store, and John Brown moved on to other ventures in town, eventually becoming a member of the provincial parliament. It was he who built the house across the street which at one time served as the home of Acadia University presidents, and which today is the headquarters for the Alumni Association.

Simeon R. Sleep, hardware and stoves, c.1890s

On the left in this post card of Wolfville is the S.R. Sleep hardware and stove store, located at the southwest corner of Locust Avenue and Main Street. Several children watch the photographer, while a horse and wagon head west along Main Street, which is a gravel road with dirt sidewalks. The entrance to Gaspereau Avenue is a little farther up the street, while across the street is the Thomas Andrew Strange DeWolf house. The large, three-storey building to the west of the Sleep store was that of T.L. Harvey. In April 1915, fire destroyed that and a number of other buildings, and for a time, the whole eastern part of Wolfville was in danger of going up in flames. The Sleep store was damaged, but not before all the stock had been removed.

The business was started in the 1850s by Simeon R. Sleep, whose home was in the building on Main Street now occupied by Acton's restaurant. Sleep was a tinsmith and stove dealer. An advertisement in the *Young Acadian* of September 26, 1883, tells readers that "S.R. Sleep has a very fine assortment of Coal and Wood stoves, comprising some twenty different kinds among which may be found the celebrated Soft Coal Base Burner 'DENMARK,' which is no doubt designed to altogether superseed [sic] the hard coal base burners. The prices are very low." By 1898 the store was owned by S.R. Sleep's son, Lewis W. Sleep. A story in the *Halifax Herald* of June 27, 1898, reported that the store was well stocked with general hardware, comprising stoves, ranges, and kitchen furnishings. "A specialty is made of plumbing and furnace work," the newspaper said. The building later housed Cavanagh's, then the Mermaid Theatre Centre. In July 1988, the building—the oldest commercial structure in the town—was torn down.

ACADIA Iron Foundry.

The subscribers respectfully inform the Public that they have opened a Foundry in

WOLFVILLE, N. S.

and are prepared to manufacture

RANGES, STOVES, PLOUGHS, Hollow Ware,

And General Castings

—AT—

WHOLESALE & RETAIL.

—ALSO—

TIN and SHEET IRON-WARE

In connection with the above.

STOVES

Repaired at shortest notice.

ORDERS SOLICITED

BY

SLEEP & McADAM, Proprietors.

Wolfville June 13th 1884

Advertisement for the Acadia Iron Foundry, June 13, 1884

In 1884 Wolfville merchant Simeon R. Sleep opened an iron foundry to produce kitchen ranges, stoves, and ploughs. Before it opened, *The Acadian* of April 11, 1884, told its readers that Sleep had indicated that the foundry project was a settled matter and that it would probably be in operation by June. Sleep's partner was William McAdam, a foundry man who had been working in the business in Halifax. The newspaper said it anticipated great things for the company and hoped it was only the beginning of a manufacturing industry in Wolfville. On Monday, June 9, the Acadia Iron Foundry made its first cast.

The foundry had a pattern and carpenter shop, where mouldings were made for iron castings; an engine room and machine shop; a boiler room; a moulding shop; and a room housing the shipping facilities. By late June, advertisements like the one above were appearing in the local newspaper. The business did not last, however. Five months later, the November 21, 1884 issue of *The Acadian* carried an advertisement from S.R. Sleep drawing attention to the fact that he was selling off a large stock of stoves, the remnants of the stock manufactured by the Acadia Iron Foundry. He also advertised a six horsepower engine, an eight horsepower boiler and a "number four" fan, "almost as good as new."

A piece in *The Acadian* on the same date sarcastically referred to Wolfville as being unusually quiet and "free from the annoyance and discomforts of business." It said a foundry had been started but its existence was short-lived: "it had just got nicely to work when cold water was thrown from all directions upon it, the fires were extinguished and all operations were forthwith terminated." Later, Wolfville took pride in the fact that it was a town without the pollution of industry.

Benjamin's Mill, White Rock, c.1884

S.P. Benjamin was a mill owner and entrepreneur who owned many thousands of acres of land in the Gaspereau valley. Lumber from his mill in White Rock built houses and businesses all over the valley, some of it sold through the S.P. Benjamin store in Wolfville in the 1880s, 1890s and 1900s. Much was shipped out by rail and by schooner; lumber from the mill was hauled by ox cart to Greenwich and Port Williams and sent out from there. In 1910, Eaton's *History of Kings County* called Benjamin "the most considerable lumber merchant in the county for the past twenty or thirty years." His ownership of lumber woods and his large shipments of lumber had given him a conspicuous place in the county's roll of enterprising men.

In the 1870s, Benjamin had two gang mills on the LaHave River at Bridgewater, where they and two mills owned by E.D. Davison and Sons produced more than thirteen million board feet of lumber a year. It was in 1879 that Benjamin relocated to White Rock, using water power to run his mills. By the 1890s he had expanded to a steam-powered mill on the Avon River. Barbara Robertson's important study of sawmills in Nova Scotia says that he innovated with band saws in that mill, and that he used scows and steamers on the Avon to haul his lumber. Benjamin shipped a great deal of lumber from Port Williams harbour, and one year—during which his mill ran night and day—shipped seven million board feet of lumber to South America. The lumber was hauled to Port Williams by horse and ox teams, each making two trips a day. Thirty teams hauled lumber, with seventy-five men running two crews at the mill (O'Leary).

The John Frederic Herbin store, c.1890s

In 1885 Arthur W. Hoare, the manager of the Western Book and News Company, invited a young native of Windsor to begin a different kind of merchandising in his store. The invitation was accepted by John Frederic Herbin, who went on to become a jeweller and one of Wolfville's best-known citizens. For a short time he operated out of a small part of the Western Book and News, but in 1885 bought a building on Main Street and set up shop for himself. Until 1895, the building was also the post office. In 1893 it was noted by *The Acadian* that Herbin had purchased a lot from J.W. Vaughan, west of the Wolfville bakery, in order to move his building to it. This was the lot at the corner of Main Street and Linden Avenue. The building quickly proved too small, so in 1898 a larger one was constructed on the lot. The picture above shows J.F. Herbin outside the first store, before it was moved to its new location. The left side of the building housed the office of the *Acadian Orchardist* newspaper.

Herbin was never content with just one role in life. Besides being a noted poet and writer, he served as mayor of Wolfville. He was something of a geologist as well: *The Acadian* in the fall of 1893 reported that he had gone out on a geological expedition and had brought home a nice collection of stones which he had arranged on exhibition in his shop. He had visited Partridge Island and Five Islands, near Parrsboro, Blomidon, "and a number of other points of interest to geologists." He used the stones in his work. By 1898 the *Halifax Herald* was able to report that Herbin was the only manufacturer of jewellery in Wolfville, and that he carried an excellent stock of jewellery and silverware. As well, "His collection of Bay of Fundy minerals is perhaps the finest in the province, and comprises some splendid specimens of the mineral wealth of these shores."

Herbin's store, built in 1898

The store in this picture still stands at the corner of Main Street and Linden Avenue, and is still a jewellery business, now run by John Frederic Herbin's descendants. Herbin replaced his first store in 1898, and in the new one, he carried a full line of jewellery, silverware and clocks, and in addition had a large practice as an optician. The *Acadian Orchardist* newspaper made the move with him, and was located on the right of the new building. Herbin's establishment was fully equipped with appliances for use in his profession, including such costly instruments as the ophthalmoscope and retinoscope.

By 1917 Herbin had joined his store with the building next to it. That building was apparently originally constructed as a tea room, according to *The Advertiser* of Kentville, and the joining made a common façade along Main Street. While Herbin's remained, the additional store space was occupied by such businesses as the J.C. Mitchell shop and Peter and Gladys Jadis's restaurant. Later still it was a children's and ladies' wear store, and then Norwin Fashions. After J.F. Herbin died in 1923 his son Frederic, only twenty-two, took over the business. Frederic improved the efficiency of the store, installing showcases custom-made in Wolfville, which are still used today (Davison, 1985). Upon his death in 1951 he was succeeded by his son John, also only twenty-two, who joined the firm in 1950. John's son Peter trained as a watchmaker in Toronto and Switzerland and became a member of the firm in 1975.

Rupert Prat, Wolfville merchant, c.1890s

Rupert Prat was the son of first stationmaster Samuel Prat and the brother of Annie Louisa, Charlotte Elizabeth, Minnie Sophia and May Rosina Prat. He was born in 1863. For a number of years Prat, who married Lillian Harris, was a merchant in Wolfville. In October 1883, while a young man of twenty, he was advertising choice family groceries, in addition to china, glass and earthenware recently imported from Boston, Montreal, Saint John and Halifax. He had cornmeal, oatmeal, choice molasses, white wine and cider vinegar, soaps, tea, Graham flour, cracked wheat, buckwheat meal, pickled herring, dry codfish, and pollock.
Also advertised were pork, ham, rolled bacon, and the finest stock of biscuits and confectionery, tobacco, pipes, cigars and smoker's sundries in Wolfville. If more were wanted, Prat also sold lamps, dinner sets, tea sets, chamber sets, vases, and toys.

In March of 1893, Prat and his partner, E.J. Collins, sold their business to the firm of Harris and Harvey, who announced that they were prepared to do a first-class grocery business. In May a notice advised that Prat and Collins were dissolving their partnership by mutual consent. Shortly afterwards, a story in *The Acadian* said that R. Prat had opened a new grocery store at the corner of Main and School streets, next to Caldwell's. The store, which had been completely remodelled, had been the premises of J.H. Bishop, who ran a flour business. It was so changed in appearance as to be completely unrecognizable: "The whole building has been raised and now presents a very handsome appearance." The store was filled with new goods, and "the large and handsome plate-glass windows which have been put in afford a grand opportunity of showing his goods to advantage, and when lit with the electric lights in the evening attract the attention of all."

Prat shows up often in the public record. Like other young people of his time he enjoyed dancing, and was a member of the Quadrille Club. He and his sisters attended a successful ball in June 1884 in Canning, and four years later he is reported as the organizer of an all-day excursion to Parrsboro on the ferry *Hiawatha*, with a fare of sixty cents and the best of order promised (Davison, 1985). Prat left the grocery business in 1894. An advertisement on July 20, 1894, is signed R. Prat, while that of July 27 is signed Estate R. Prat. By 1909, Annie Prat was writing to her brother on Markham Street, in Toronto. He became involved in the tea business and later in life insurance. He died in Toronto on August 30, 1945.

The Wolfville Fruit Land Improvement Company, c.1890s

Amos L. Hardy took this photograph of apple orchards to the west of Acadia College, showing some of the trees that made up Earnscliffe Gardens and the Wolfville Fruit Land Development Company. Earnscliffe Gardens was run by W.C. Archibald, who until 1894 also managed the Wolfville Fruit Land Improvement Company. The lands were beside and above the university.

The company undertook a fascinating effort at town planning. *The Nova Scotian and Weekly Chronicle* reported on October 8, 1892, that Wolfville was almost one large orchard, that it was enjoying a building boom, and that in the past year a factory, a manual training hall, a seminary building, a store and a dozen houses had been built. The company was financed by a group of Halifax and Wolfville capitalists, its president being Dr. George E. DeWitt, who had recently moved to Wolfville from Halifax (and who would later be mayor of the town, then its medical officer). The company's aim was to make Wolfville "an aristocratic residential town." The newspaper said the quality of the soil, the gentle northern slope and the freedom from injurious freezes rendered the town unsurpassed for fruit culture, and that the disagreeable fogs were shut out by the North Mountain and by Cape Blomidon. Local enterprise had given an excellent water supply, and there were electric light and telephone connections from Halifax to Annapolis.

The Fruit Land Company had purchased a hundred acres of land close beside the university grounds, an area known as the Wolfville Highlands. These lands were being divided up into building and garden lots, water and electric lights. Tenders for four new houses had already closed and new streets were being opened throughout the property. Men were at that moment laying out Chipman Avenue, extending from Main Street to the Ridge Road, and another road, Blomidon Avenue, would contain some of the best building sites in Wolfville. Lot sizes would range from a sixteenth of an acre to the size of a small farm and were being planted by the developers with pears, plums, peaches and dwarf apple trees. "The aim is to make this the centre for high class fruit culture, and to demonstrate that town populations can be supported by agricultural pursuits as well as by manufacturing or mining," *The Nova Scotian* wrote. "The promoters believe that two acres of fruit land properly cultivated will yield sufficient income to support the average family."

Rand's drug store, c.1910s

It would be difficult to find shops more central to the history of Wolfville commerce than Porter's, Herbin's and the Rand Drug Store. The interior of the latter is shown in this photograph. George Valentine Rand bought the land east of Louis Godfrey's house and shoe shop, on Main Street, in 1855. He was the descendant of an original Planter family, his great-grandparents being Thomas and Mary (Marchant) Rand, who had come to Cornwallis from Nantucket to take up a land grant after 1760. George, born in 1829, was a brother of Theodore Harding Rand, a noted educator and writer serving at different times as the Nova Scotia and New Brunswick superintendent of education, chair of education and history at Acadia University, principal of the Baptist College at Woodstock, Ontario, and professor and vice-chancellor at McMaster University.

George Valentine Rand's role in life was somewhat different. He used the land bought in 1855 to build a drug store, one which continued under the Rand name until well into the twentieth century. He lived on what was to become Linden Avenue, the land for which he gave to the town. His home, described by *Wolfville Acadian* editor Bowman O. Davidson as facing Main Street but standing well back, was located behind Herbin's jewellery store. Rand's drug store and post office were located where the Rand Building—today the Brownell Block—is today. In 1897, Rand's was described in the press as "thoroughly equipped," containing, in addition to all of the leading remedies and requisites, an abundant supply of Christmas goods. The photograph shows a good collection of medicines on the wall, shaving brushes in the glass case, and an assortment of rubber sponges. George died in 1908 and his son, Aubrey Valentine Rand, carried on the business. In 1929, the drugstore business was sold to Dalton R. MacKinnon. For a photograph of George Rand and family in front of their house, see Chapter six.

William James Regan, harness maker, c.1890s

This was the shop of William Regan, harness maker for many years in Wolfville. An article in *The Halifax Herald* in 1898 described the shop as an old established house in Wolfville, noting that William Regan manufactured harnesses of superior style and quality. He also carried a complete stock of rugs and all horse furnishings, and was prepared to do repairs. The shop contained a life-sized model of a horse, the tail end of which is visible at the right in the photograph. The store was centrally located on Main Street, east of the post office. While William ran the harness shop, his wife, Bella, and the sixteen Regan children ran Babbling Brook Dairy, on the corner of Gaspereau and Willow avenues. Regan had dykelands, as well as land above Willowbank Cemetery, and Bella's fifteen cows provided butter, milk and buttermilk to many in Wolfville. They also sold eggs.

The Acadian of April 2, 1920, reported that William Regan had sold his harness business to a Mr. Parker, of Canning. Regan had been trying to dispose of the business for some time, owing to the condition of his health. On January 15, 1924, the newspaper reported that William Regan died, at the age of sixty-six. He had come to Wolfville in 1880 to work in Patriquin's harness shop and had eventually purchased it. "As a citizen he took a lively interest in local institutions, was an active member of the old fire company, and for three terms filled a place on the Town Council where he gave efficient and faithful service."

Making barrels and shipping apples from Port Williams, c.1890s

The Acadian wondered in February of 1885 what railway station could beat Port Williams when it came to shipping apples. It said there were over eleven thousand barrels of apples shipped from Port Williams between August and December of 1884, and that week in February nearly a thousand more went out by the morning train, heading for markets in England. By contrast, during the same period, Horton Landing had shipped 100 barrels, Avonport 60, Grand Pré 841, Wolfville 3,726, Coldbrook 1, 767, Cambridge 4,330, Berwick 10,161 and Aylesford 4,330. The newspaper noted it didn't have the figures for Kentville, Waterville, Morden Road, and Kingston, which would probably have brought the total figure to over fifty thousand barrels.

This photograph has been identified as the cooperage of Silas L. Gates, 1895. Gates manufactured ten thousand barrels yearly, according to the Port Williams Women's Institute history of Port Williams. In 1908 a modern cooperage was erected with an output of two hundred thousand barrels a year. Gates also sent molasses barrels to the West Indies.

The McKenna Block, c.1900s

The building on the far right of this picture was known as the McKenna Block, later the Eaton Block. It was built by Wolfville dentist Dr. A.J. McKenna, whose office was next door in the Herbin building. A Halifax newspaper reported in January 1899 that the new McKenna block was approaching completion, and when finished would be a conspicuous addition to the town. The building was to be heated throughout by hot water (heat provided by a hand-stoked coal furnace). The first floor on the west side of the building would have the Union Bank agency, fitted with a brick vault at the rear. On the east with the large plate glass windows would be a "first class grocery store" operated by H.W. Davison.

Upstairs, on the second floor, were to be the dental parlours of Dr. McKenna, as well as several offices, one of which would be used by Wolfville barrister J.W. Wallace. The rear of the second floor would be occupied by B.O. Davison and the *Wolfville Acadian*. The third floor was to be the Masonic Hall, St. George's Lodge. The *Morning Chronicle* said it would be one of the most attractive lodge rooms outside of Halifax. In December 1920 the building was purchased by Leslie and Eugene Eaton, and the the dental offices were then occupied by Eaton Brothers, Dentists. The building had many different stores in it over the years. At mid-century Eugene's son John was practising dentistry in the dental offices in the building, its other tenants being J.W. Williams, the jeweller; Otto Porter's grocery store; the Baptist Home Mission Board; the janitor's quarters; and on the third floor, the Free Masons Lodge. Many people in Wolfville called the building the Waldorf, a name taken from the Waldorf Café, which was opened in the building in September 1920 by W.W. Allsop, who had returned from war service. In 1972 Leslie Eaton's daughter, Barbara, sold the building to Horton Developments, which had it torn down.

ACADIA SEMINARY HOTEL,
WOLFVILLE, N.S.

The Acadia Seminary Hotel, 1906

Wolfville mayor George Thompson reported to his council in January of 1898 that during the previous summer some 2,500 tourists had visited Wolfville. He was pleased by this, and said in his Annual Report that "the opening of the handsome and beautifully situated Ladies' Seminary for their accommodation was a new feature in providing for the comfort and enjoyment of these welcome visitors." The seminary had been rented by Frank P. Rockwell during the months of July and August in order to provide tourist accommodations. It was proving popular. Mayor Thompson said that a number of tourists had expressed themselves greatly pleased by Mr. Rockwell's accommodations and table.

The *Halifax Herald*, in June the same year, described the Acadia Seminary Hotel as "undoubtedly the largest summer hotel in Nova Scotia," having accommodations for 150 guests. "This is the second season for this hotel. The experiment of using the spacious rooms of Acadia Seminary for the summer home of tourists was first tried last season, and, proving most successful, is to be repeated again this summer." It said the surroundings were delightful, and all of the comforts of a first class hotel could be found. In this photograph, taken from a post card, horses and wagons line up outside the Seminary Hotel in 1906.

A busy town in the 1910s

Cars and wagons line the street on this sunny day in Wolfville. Drivers have not yet made the switch to the right side of the road, which they did in 1920. The store on the right still belonged to J.D. Chambers; he and his wife, Mary Frances Woodman, were the parents of the late Bob Chambers, one of Canada's best newspaper cartoonists. J.D. Chambers would turn the store over to Charles H. Porter in 1919. On the left is the J.E. Hales dry goods emporium; both Hales and Chambers were mayor during these years.

By early the next decade Wolfville would have two imposing bank buildings. The Bank of Montreal, on the corner opposite Chambers' store, was managed by George W. Munro, while the Royal Bank, a little farther east, was managed by R. Creighton. The Royal was new in 1919, described in the Halifax press as having a large and sunny interior with attractive furnishings, and a large number of safety deposit vaults. The Bank of Montreal was built in 1921. Other financial matters were taken care of by the brokerage firm of Woodman and Foshay, in the McKenna Block, and by Robie W. Tufts, who had earlier worked with the Bank of Montreal and sold insurance and investment securities. Later Tufts would become a renowned ornithologist. There were five grocery stores in operation: R.E. Harris and Sons, T.L. Harvey, S.W. Barteaux, W.F. Bleakney, and Porter Brothers.

More than forty other businesses were operating in Wolfville in these years. They included jewellery shops run by J.W. Williams and John F. Herbin; lawyers John W. Wallace and E. Sidney Crawley; electrical supplies sold by J.P. Mitchell; plumbing by E.J. Delaney; hardware sold by Lewis Sleep and A.W. Bleakney; carriages, automobiles and farm machinery sold by W.A. Reid and F.J. Porter; a garage run by D.A. Munro; and hotels and inns kept by Frank P. Rockwell (the Acadia Villa Hotel), T.S. Sanford (the Royal Hotel), C.M. Gormley (Acadia

Lodge) and Mrs. T.W. Stackhouse (the Stop and Rest Inn). Besides Chambers and Hales, clothing and footwear were also sold by F.K. Bishop and C.D. Jefferson, while A.E. Regan had a merchant tailor business. W.S. Dexter sold millinery, as did Bessie Saxton. There were two drug stores, A.V. Rand's and Hugh Calkin's; Edson Graham, who took this photograph, had his photo studio; Flo M. Harris sold books and stationery, while C.D. Kopple sold gramophones. Charles H. Wright and Ernest Eagles were builders. Food establishments included Edward C. and Arthur Young's bakery; Arthur's brother Cecil's confectionery and ice-cream establishment; and Hugh Watson's confectionery and ice cream. The Acadia Dairy was in operation as well. Western Union had its telegraph office, and the Maritime Telegraph and Telephone Company was underway.

N.S. HORTICULTURAL EXHIBIT. Wolfville, 1911.

Nova Scotia Horticultural Exhibition, Wolfville, 1911

These apples are displayed on tables at the Nova Scotia Horticultural Exhibition, held at the Evangeline Rink in Wolfville October 10, 11 and 12, 1911. Special trains brought people to Wolfville for the event, which was opened by the Lieutenant Governor of Nova Scotia and the Secretary of Agriculture. Member of Parliament A. DeWitt Foster also spoke. In addition to the work of several hundred exhibitors, the exhibition featured a horse parade on the first day, and the same twenty-five cent ticket would admit people to the parade, the exhibition and an automobile show. The parade and the automobile show were held on the Acadia campus.

By all accounts, things were festive. *The Acadian* reported that music was furnished for the opening by the College Band, and that on opening day special trains brought people who gave the town a lively air. The show opened on a Tuesday morning, the newspaper said, in Evangeline Rink, which "proved to be a most satisfactory and commodious building for such a purpose." It went on to say that the exhibit of apples was easily the finest ever shown in Nova Scotia: "The past season has been a most favourable one in every way for the production of fine apples, and the display as arranged on the tables was indeed a picture. There was also a good exhibit of pears, and a few plums. In vegetables, too, many good specimens were shown." The work of local women was displayed on the second floor "and received a great deal of attention."

Porter Brothers store, corner of Highland and Main, c.1921

This store was built by John L. Brown. In the 1880s it was bought from C.E. Bishop by F.J. and G.A. Porter, and in the 1883 *Acadian* was advertising family groceries—tea, sugar, soap, biscuits, raisins, molasses, oil, oatmeal, "and everything to be found in a first-class grocery store." They also had candy, china, glass and crockery ware, lamps, brooms, clothespins, tobacco and smoking sundries. As with many other stores, they often took goods in exchange for their wares, looking for eggs, butter, oats and all kinds of farmers' produce. In the same issue of *The Acadian*, however, there was a notice that the Porter Brothers partnership had dissolved, and that Grant A. Porter was continuing the business. F.J. Porter went on to open another store, sell automobiles, serve as a town councillor and act as a justice of the peace.

The photograph above shows the store forty years later with a delivery car outside, with "Porter Bros." written on the side. A horse and wagon are out front, and also to be seen are a hitching post, and a Ben's Bread sign. A story in *The Advertiser*, in June 1966, deplored the passing of this Wolfville landmark, as it was to be torn down the next month by Acadia University. Grant Porter and his brother Percy had done business there for nearly fifty years and they also operated an electrical appliance business in the adjoining building. It was in the narrow passageway between the store and the building next to it that, in 1879, an infamous Wolfville murder occurred; the story is told in Chapter six.

Hydro power development serving Wolfville, 1921

From Abraham Gesner's invention of kerosene to Roy Jodrey and Charles H. Wright's development of hydroelectric power along the Gaspereau River system, Kings County has contributed greatly to efforts to bring light to the people of Nova Scotia. *Mud Creek* notes that D.A. Munro had the first electric light in 1881 at his ice rink, powered by his wood working plant. A street light was installed in 1888 at the corner of College Avenue and School Street, and lights were installed in some homes by 1891. The Acadia Electric Light Company built a power station in 1893, which was operated by D.R. Munro; it burned both coal and fuel oil. The effort of bringing hydroelectric power to the town of Wolfville and other communities in the area began in 1901 with the assembly of land and river rights for power development, but it was not until 1907 that work began in earnest. Thomas Kneeland began building an electrical power plant and pulp mill, but the work was never completed.

Ten years later, Lloyd E. Shaw and George C. Nowlan were president and secretary of the Wolfville Board of Trade. It was this organization that asked Roy Jodrey and Charles Wright to investigate the use of the Gaspereau to bring power to the town. According to Harry Bruce's biography of R.A. Jodrey, Shaw wrote many years later that "Jodrey and Wright never came back to report. They found more than we had anticipated. [They] found a waterfall, formed a company, built a dam, installed a powerhouse, shot transmission lines out across the Valley; they did what richer men had been failing to do right back to 1901." Their plant was running by 1920.

Things were not always smooth: a dry summer and fall immediately created problems for the power supply. In October 1920, when Wolfville received word that because of a lack of water in the Gaspereau power was no longer available, the old steam equipment had to be fired up and used to generate power. By the 1970s, when talk began of amalgamating all power companies in the province, the plant had become Nova Scotia Light and Power and had, according to the *Advertiser*, an average output of 100,000,000 kilowatt hours per year. The Gaspereau and Black River draining area was said to be the hardest-working power area in the province. Earlier, operators had manned each of the plants, but that had changed; everything was controlled by the plant at Hell's Gate. Almost nine thousand customers were being served. The photograph shows the White Rock plant in April 1921, not long after it was built.

The Wolfville Fruit Company, c.1940s

On April 15, 1921, a front page story in *The Acadian* announced that the Wolfville Fruit Company was planning on opening a cooperative store in Wolfville, and was erecting a new brick building connected to its warehouses in order to carry this out. By November of that year the newspaper reported that the new building, while not yet complete, would be an ornament to the town. The lower floor would contain two stores, that on the west being occupied by the company. It opened for business on Wednesday, November 23, with a staff that included Stanley A. Robinson as manager; Frank C. Welch, of Advocate Harbour, as chief salesman; and Alex Peters as deliveryman. The newspaper said the building was commodious and equipped with all the latest appliances.

Frank Welch became manager and served in that position for thirty-six years, retiring in 1958. He also raised pigs and was a fruit-grower, planting orchards on his farm in town, which was the former Charles William Fitch property. He was a strong supporter of the Conservative party, serving as president of the Nova Scotia Conservative Association for many years, the result being that in 1962 he was appointed a Canadian senator. In 1965 Welch decided to get out of the apple business in order to develop his property in Wolfville, and before long a subdivision had been created.

The Wolfville Fruit Company was one of dozens of fruit cooperatives that formed in the valley in the early 1900s, as people bought shares in the business. It was set up in 1914 by a group of apple growers from the area as a fruit warehouse, expanding later into the selling of groceries. The photograph shows the front of the store, when it sold such items as meats, fish and vegetables. However, the arrival of chain grocery stores forced many smaller stores out of business, and in the 1950s, in order to survive, the Wolfville Fruit Company sold off its grocery business.

The Palms, exterior, c. 1945

For generations of Acadia students and Wolfville youth, The Palms, on Main Street in the centre of town, was the place to hang out. When the afternoon bell rang to end the school day, junior and senior high students from the Munro School on Acadia Street would make the five-minute walk down Linden Avenue to The Palms and settle in with their friends. Horton Academy and Acadia students would make the slightly longer trek once classes were over. Inside were Cecil and Marjorie Young, who presided over the serving of food, ice-cream sundaes, milkshakes, the feeding of coins into the jukebox, and the playing of pinball machines.

Cecil Young's family moved from Bridgewater to Wolfville in the early 1900s. Cecil graduated from Acadia after the end of World War One and married his first wife, May. With help from his mother, Hannah, they opened The Palms on Tuesday, May 18, 1920. By 1921, *The Acadian* was reporting that Young was making changes to the building, including the addition of another storey, to provide a large roof garden: "The Palms is undoubtedly one of the very best establishments of its kind, and something that Wolfville people may justly be proud of." After his first wife died, Cecil married Marjorie Sheenan, and the family, which already had one child, Marion, grew with the addition of Carolyn, David and Edward, or "Butch." Cecil continued the business—with a short interruption when J.M. Newcombe had the shop in the mid-1920s—until 1972. Hannah Young is credited with inventing grapenut ice cream, before long a Maritime favourite, after she had run out of regular ingredients for her home-made ice cream. Cecil died in 1972, and Marjorie in 1985.

Butch Young writes of The Palms: "Folks would gather for a sundae or soda after the movie, or a hockey game, or come and dance to the latest hits played on the jukebox, nickelodeon as it was originally called." A regular weekly feature during the 1940s was Twilight

Hour, when from nine to eleven there would be dancing to the music on the jukebox. The Palms was in a building that used to be the home of Bishop Palmeter, whose store was next door. Information in the town's house inventory indicates that it was built in the 1870s. Both M. Allen Gibson, in *The Chronicle-Herald*, and Eileen Bishop, in *The Advertiser*, suggest that the name of the restaurant came from potted palm trees on the premises, but it is possible that the name also derived from the fact that the building had been Bishop Palmeter's. The two Palmeter buildings are today joined, but previously the one to the left housed the offices of *The Acadian*. The photograph shows the inside during Twilight Hour in 1945. The boy doing the jive with the girl in the plaid skirt is David Young.

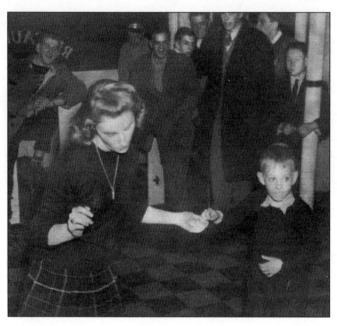

Wolfville's ice-cream parlour and restaurant, c.1940s

A.V. Rand's bookstore, c.1940s

Pictured is Rand's Bookstore, in the Rand block on the south side of Main Street, between Linden and Highland avenues. The shop belonged to Val Rand, son of Aubrey Valentine and Mary Barnaby Rand. Val was part of a line of Wolfville merchants that stretched back to his grandfather, George V. Rand, who kept the drugstore and post office on Main Street, until his death in 1908. The drug store and post office building was moved to Linden Avenue in the late 1890s, and the new Rand building was erected to take its place. In 1924, when the old building was occupied by plumber H.E. Fraser, a fire destroyed the upper part of the structure, the flames having made considerable progress before the fire department arrived.

Aubrey began working with his father in the drug store in the 1890s and took it over on George's death in 1908, advertising in *The Athenaeum* that in addition to his drug service he sold the best line of Canadian and American chocolates, and also the celebrated Pirate hockey sticks. He sold the business in 1929 to Dalton R. MacKinnon, whose store is next to the bookstore. Aubrey Rand died in 1933 at the age of sixty-four. The drugstore burned on New Year's Eve, 1937; the brick building shown here was built in 1938 to replace it.

Val Rand opened the bookstore after his father retired from the drugstore. Eileen Bishop reminisces about visiting the bookstore in the early 1940s and enjoying a drink at the soda fountain. She writes that people would pick up their Sunday reading and just pass the time of day with people from Greenwich, Gaspereau or Grand Pré. Edgar DeWolfe would be there, she notes, keeping a close check on the time, as he was always at the station to see the trains come in.

The store at the corner of Main and Gaspereau, c.1940s

This spot at the corner of Main Street and the little extension of Gaspereau Avenue that went down to the wharf had long been a prime location in the town of Wolfville, particularly for those who lived in the east end of town. The elm trees in front of T.A.S. DeWolf's famous house can be seen across the road, while a two-horse sleigh is parked in front. The Acadia Stores and Robert L. Hancock's meat store sit side by side. In 1944, the Acadia Stores took over the grocery business run for so long by the late Rupert E. Harris. Harris himself, with T.L. Harvey, had assumed the grocery business on that spot in 1893, but Harvey later sold his share of the business to Harris. Eventually, beginning in 1964, the spot was occupied by R.C. Van Wart's Hardware.

Before Harris, the store on the corner belonged to Rupert Prat. The Acadia Stores in the photograph was the first of the chain stores in the Annapolis Valley. Glen Hancock was given a job at the store after school and on open nights—Tuesdays and Saturdays—by manager Elmer Kinnie, and made two dollars a day. "It was hard work but it was fun," he writes. "I liked everyone I worked with, and one of the clerks eventually became my wife." The R.L. Hancock store in the photograph was run by Glen Hancock's uncle Bob. Orders for meat would be shouted through a hatch between the two stores and the meat would appear. Hancock says his uncle made sausages on the premises and had barrels of dried hake, salt pork, corned beef, pickles, and sauerkraut.

Wolfville's main street fifty years after its 1893 incorporation

Wolfville architect Ron Peck climbed to the Baptist church steeple to take this photograph of Wolfville in the 1940s. Years later, in 1993, David Burton made a model of the town's business district as a part of celebrations marking the centennial of the town's incorporation, a model which identified the shops and their locations both in 1893 and in 1993.

In 1893, the building at the bottom left was occupied by the merchant James S. Morse. Afterwards, it was for many years Arthur M. Young's bakery. The shops next to it occupy land that was James Morse's home and gardens; these shops burned in 1963 and were rebuilt. Farther up the street, left of the Acadia Theatre, was the building occupied in 1893 by the tailor Joseph Weston and later Katie Weston's candy shop. Still later it was owned by Leslie Fairn, the right side housing the Sally Starr Gift Shop. The theatre site was occupied in 1893 by the Union House, or Hall. The Orpheum was later built there, eventually becoming the Acadia Theatre. To its east, in 1893, was a meat shop, next was the Temperance Hall, and next to it was Bishop Palmeter's, later The Palms Restaurant. Next to that is the distinctive roofline of Burpee Witter's dry goods store, today Porter's clothing store.

Across the street, at the bottom right, is the sign for the Irving service station, which in 1893 was the location of both the home and shoe business of Lewis Payzant Godfrey. The first visible building is the brick Rand building, built to replace the one that burned on New Year's Eve, 1937. Next to it was the Eaton building, originally the McKenna Block, built by dentist A.J. McKenna in 1898. The roofline of Herbin's Jewellers is visible next. These spaces were occupied in 1893 by George Valentine Rand's drugstore and post office, and by the original Herbin's jewellery store.

Cleveland's Store in winter, c.1940s

Cleveland's was a popular grocery store across from the post office. Earlier it had been the Caldwell-Yerxa store, the Yerxa stores also being located in towns such as Kentville, Annapolis and Digby. Eileen Bishop said of Cleveland's in 1943: "Greta and Bessie Coldwell at Cleveland's Grocery were good-will ambassadors who joked and laughed while Greta weighed sugar on the Toledo scale."

The second picture shows the interior of Cleveland's. Eileen Bishop identified the shop workers as Edith Cook Tanner, left, and Joyce Cavanagh. Cleveland's closed in 1965.

Wolfville Holland Bakery, c.1940s

In 1936, the VanZoost family set up the Wolfville Holland Bakery which grew to be a major Nova Scotian company, marketing its products under the Dutch Maid brand and eventually employing sixty people. It sold bread, cakes, pastries and other bakery goods in the Annapolis Valley, central Nova Scotia and the Halifax/Dartmouth area. A photograph in the Halifax press showed the officers of the company at their first sales meeting, held at the Nova Scotian Hotel: Harry VanZoost was the president; Dean Trimper, office manager; George Seamone, production manager; Curtis Burgess, sales supervisor; and Vince Furlong, Halifax branch manager. Wolfville Holland Bakery was in operation for twenty-eight years. It closed in 1964, the victim of what Harry VanZoost was reported as calling "the stiffest bakery competition in Canada."

The VanZoost family arrived in Wolfville from Holland in 1907. The bakery was established by Hendrick and Feikje VanZoost and bought from them by their son Harry and his wife Naomi in 1941. Harry VanZoost served as town councillor from 1944 to 1951 and was president of the Board of Trade. He was the president of the town's amateur athletic association and also a charter member of the Wolfville Historical Society. These two photographs, from the Randall House Museum, show the bakery itself, on Front Street (above). and part of the fleet of twenty trucks used by the bakery, parked on Wolfville's Main Street in front of the A.J. Woodman store (next page). The bakery was a new cement structure, constructed in 1941.

Part of the fleet of twenty trucks used by Holland Bakery

Chapter 5

Transportation

Where today Wolfville harbour is a scenic little park, at one time it was the centre of commerce and travel. The view from the park across the dykes to the edge of the Cornwallis River shows, on the Beckwith dyke, near the river, remnants of the foundation of one of Wolfville's lighthouses, and Starr's Point in the distance. To the right, across the channel entrance, was the Cornwallis River wharf, where the ferry *Prince Albert* used to dock. The road to the wharf led from just below Randall House out across the dyke. An earlier lighthouse sat at the river edge of the Wickwire dyke. At several wharves along the waterfront schooners brought in goods needed by the town and carried produce out. Bowman Davidson remembered spending many noon hours watching the ships docking, unloading and loading their cargoes, and then sailing. He said that at one time he counted sixteen vessels at their moorings.

Ship in Wolfville Harbour, 1925

The year before the *Kipawo* would begin service, Wolfville's harbour was quiet. When rains, tides and winds damaged the Wickwire dykes, causing the main wharf to disintegrate, ships had to berth beside the DAR tracks, where this vessel is docked. Graham Patriquin, son of Charles A. Patriquin, said that for the *Kipawo*, as for other vessels, the situation made docking in Mud Creek a chancy business. This wharf is gone now, but bits of its pilings can still be seen. The photograph is from the Esther Clark Wright Archives, Acadia University.

At the same time, ferries travelled back and forth, delivering the village's people to Parrsboro, Kingsport, Pereau and Horton Landing. One of the ferry operators was James Ratchford, who, beginning in the late 1700s, had a small schooner that made a trip twice a week between Parrsboro, Windsor, Horton and Wolfville. The Ratchford family carried on business at Partridge Island, near Parrsboro, building a wharf on the bar near the mainland and calling their ferry *The Packet*. The ferry carried people, horses, carriages, cattle and sheep. There was even a ferry crossing the Cornwallis River from Wolfville, a ferry that was abandoned when the bridge to Port Williams was built in the late 1700s. The sea took people farther, too. By 1784 the Planters had access to their old homes in the United States through boats, or "packets," that ran regularly between Halifax and New York, and with the coming of steam power, almost a century later, there were steamers making runs between Minas Basin ports.

Ferry service on the Minas Basin became of enormous importance, with a sequence of ferries on duty. The last of these was the "dear old Kipawo," (as Esther Clark Wright put it, in *Blomidon Rose*), named by the captain for the calls he made in Kingsport, Parrsboro and Wolfville. The ship was pulled off the run for use during World War Two and never restored to that service. Retired Baptist minister and writer M. Allen Gibson writes that two of *Kipawo*'s business affairs were looked after by the Dominion Atlantic Railway's assistant station agent, Horace Jackson. In a little book called *Train Time*, Gibson says that shortly after the vessel appeared in the distance off Longspell Point, Jackson would be seen walking along the track from the station, with the metal box representing the portable business office of the MV *Kipawo* swinging in his hand: "With Captain Trefy at the helm, Kip made a pretty sight meandering up the creek from the Cornwallis River, her bow wave rippling the half submerged grasses at the water's edge. Snug at wharfside, passengers and freight were quickly discharged and loaded. Cars were swung aboard in a massive sling clamped to their wheels, an operation which must have caused more than one owner to hold his breath until it was safely completed." According to Gibson, the lines were then cast off, the bow line first, with the stern line holding until the bow had swung around to face the opening into the creek, "And Kip was on her way once more, racing with the tide for Parrsboro. Horace Jackson locked the shed on the wharf and, metal box under his arm, made his way back to the station."

The water also led to a shipbuilding industry. Bowman O. Davidson's reminiscences state that in the early days many vessels were built at shipyards on both sides of the creek: "In the seventies two vessels, the *Sophie Cook* and the *Terra Nova* were built on the west side at the same time." A report in the *Morning Chronicle* on January 23, 1875, reported that "the pleasant village of Wolfville" had a new industry—the shipbuilding firm of W.A. Cox. Cox had on the stocks a six-hundred-ton vessel "of very superior model, and first-class materials and workmanship, well advanced toward completion, and to be launched as soon as navigation opens in the spring." Preparations were underway for a coasting schooner to be launched in May and for a barque of eight hundred tons to be launched in October of the next year. Cox built a steam mill to provide materials for the ships, manufacturing lumber from logs cut in Gaspereau. *The Morning Chronicle* wondered why a large shipyard had not been established there before: "The situation is very advantageous, having easy water communication with St. John, N.B., and with all the great reservoirs of the well known Bay Shore ship-timbers, rail communication with Halifax, and also with the Western parts of the county, producing the Norway pine, now coming to such good repute for deck plank, topsides, clamps etc., and which is reckoned by many ship people as little, if any, inferior to the Southern pitch pine for many purposes in shipbuilding. The yard is situated that, by means of a railway siding, all materials are delivered immediately in the yard, which, with the water facilities, affords very great advantages in carrying on building operations."

Townspeople looked to the water for other things, as well. A shad fishing industry thrived until the early 1900s; some shad was taken by fishing boats, some caught by nets strung between poles. An editorial in *The Acadian* in July 1924 asked older residents to recall a time when Wolfville was quite a fishing centre at certain seasons of the year. For several weeks each summer a dozen or more boats and their crews would set sail with the tides late in the day, their nets packed away, then "drift" for shad over the night. They would return to Wolfville the following morning "well laden with their harvest of shining fish." The newspaper said that the shad would sell at the door for eight cents each, or three for a quarter, and it blamed the disappearance of the fish on the method of catching shad on weirs, from which thousands would be taken while the half-grown would be left to die. According to the *Natural History of Kings County*, catches of shad plummeted between 1900 and 1910 primarily because shad would not use fish ladders and so could not get past the new hydro-electric dams blocking their spawning rivers in the United States. A further culprit was pollution from cities along major American rivers, like the Delaware, as well as sewage discharged into rivers.

Finally, the water was also used for recreation. Swimming off the wharf was popular with Wolfville youth, and townspeople like D.R. Munro built yachts which they used for sailing around the Basin (see Chapter seven). Partridge Island, a bold bluff overlooking Parrsboro, afforded shelter to vessels navigating the Bay of Fundy. People used the water to sail away on picnics, often to Partridge Island: an unusual story about one such expedition is told in Chapter six.

The turning away from the Minas Basin was a natural progression, partly the result of the

Horse and buggy at Willowbank Farm, c.1895

Richard Sidney Starr sits behind Royal Knight, preparing to set off from Willowbank Farm, located just across the Cornwallis River from Wolfville. Starr married May Rosina, one of the illustrious Prat sisters, in 1904. Photograph courtesy the Esther Clark Wright Archives, Acadia University.

development of travel over land. The Acadians had roads that sometimes followed old Mi'kmaw trails. Eaton notes that in 1720, Port Royal and Minas residents worked to create a road between the two settlements, but the effort was stopped by the governor, who was concerned about the reasons for the road's construction. He was afraid that the Acadians would leave for Annapolis without permission, taking their possessions with them. By the time of the expulsion, passable roads existed from Minas to Annapolis Royal, and eastward to what is now Windsor, where the road connected with a road to Halifax. There were also roads to the north side of the Cornwallis River, and from Cornwallis to Kentville. The scenic road in the Gaspereau Valley running from the village of Gaspereau to Melanson follows a French road, as does the one running across the Ridge. The post road used by the Planters, from the Grand Pré area, followed what is now Maple Avenue, on the eastern side of Wolfville, then continued on the current Main Street as it went to the west. Acadian houses were built along this road.

Travel on the roads was by foot, horse, horse and cart, or ox and cart. A.W.H. Eaton noted that a stagecoach service was set up between Halifax and Windsor in 1816, but that it was not until 1829 that the line extended through to Annapolis: "In 1855 the Royal Western Stage Coach is advertised in the Almanac to leave Halifax for Windsor and Kentville, every morning at seven o'clock." The coach was advertised to connect with steamers from Boston and St. John, and those leaving from Windsor. Eaton quotes Dr. Henry Chipman, who described stagecoach travel to an audience in Lower Horton by saying that either four and six horses were used, hitched up at the starting points in Kentville and Windsor: "Pleasant it was in fine summer weather to sit beside the driver on the top of the coach and bowl away, up hill and down. When the roads were breaking up in the spring, however, it was not so pleasant." He could remember driving through Lower Horton when the wheels were sinking down to the hubs and the passengers were obliged to help pry them out with fence poles.

More comfortable travel came with the arrival of the railway. The Windsor and Annapolis Railway was incorporated in 1865, with rails laid from Windsor to Horton Landing by 1869 and through to Annapolis by 1872. The route made necessary the building of a bridge across the Gaspereau near Horton Landing. In 1893/1894 the Dominion Atlantic Railway (DAR) was formed from the Windsor and Annapolis Railway and the Western Counties Railway, making a single line from Halifax to Yarmouth. The first train went the distance on October 1, 1894. Soon the *Flying Bluenose*, a fast passenger train complete with sleeping car accommodation, was making the run; advertisements in 1897 state that as soon as the train arrived in Yarmouth, the steamship *Prince Edward* would sail for Boston. It was becoming very easy to travel from the Valley to Boston, further cementing the close ties between New England and Nova Scotia. The train also connected with the Royal Mail Steamship *Prince Rupert*, which travelled between Digby and Saint John.

It would be difficult to overestimate the importance of the railway to the town of Wolfville. People used it to travel between Halifax and Wolfville, merchants had their goods delivered by it, students used it to come to Acadia University, the mail was delivered by the trains and taken to the post office, apples and lumber were sent out, tourists arrived by it, and in general it contributed greatly to the growth and prosperity of the town.

It became something of an event when trains arrived each day. Many people are able to remember Edgar DeWolfe, for whom trains were a hobby, meeting each one. For M. Allen Gibson, the daily drama at the train station "mounted to a climax with the arrival of Charlie Delahunt and the mail. His horse-drawn wagon clattered up to the west end of the platform nearest the spot where the railway postal car would halt. Charlie unloaded the bags of mail and then, as ceremoniously as an acolyte, emptied the platform mail box carefully scrutinizing each address ostensibly to make sure that the item was indeed westward bound." Charlie also picked up and delivered student luggage. A train even arrived in Wolfville at midnight, enabling people from the Montreal train to catch the one to the Valley, and permitting Valley people with business in the city to return the same day. In the other direction, the early Halifax train from Yarmouth would go through Wolfville after three in the morning.

Important visitors to Wolfville would arrive by train. William Lyon Mackenzie King, Canada's prime minister, came to town on Friday, September 18, 1925. *The Acadian* reported that Mackenzie King had travelled in Canadian National Railways' private car number 100. Known from coast to coast as "Old Hundred," the car was built for Sir Charles Tupper and had been the travelling home of every prime minister since that time. The newspaper, always fretting about the town, complained that few people knew in advance about the prime minister's visit and that the school children had not been paraded down to the station to see him. It was also embarrassed about what King might have seen: "The tide was low when his train approached Wolfville last Friday morning and conditions at the town dump and along the waterfront presented their normal appearance. When he stepped from the platform of his car he glanced admiringly at the surrounding scenery and remarked to citizens who greeted him 'You certainly have a beautiful town.'"

Blomidon Rose catches the flavour of disembarking from the Digby ferry and taking the *Flying Bluenose* to Wolfville, an express journey with very few stops: "How grand we felt as we raced up the Valley, passing through all the little stations without stopping, and waving condescendingly to friends who had to wait for the regular train which was probably loading apples and fresh cabbages for the Halifax market. With what glee we rushed up to the residence to deposit our bags, and tore down to the station again to meet less fortunate colleagues and commiserate with them on the slowness of their journey and the tardiness of their arrival." The *Flying Bluenose* is no more, and train service today is reduced to an occasional short freight run.

Finally came the automobile. Just as roads, stagecoaches and trains were destructive to Wolfville's relationship with the ocean, so too was the arrival of the automobile destructive to the train. The first car in Wolfville, according to *Mud Creek*, was said to have been owned by D.R. Munro, who ran the town's electrical plant.

Students arrive by train, c.1930

For years, a large number of university students arrived at Acadia by train. This photograph was found in an album kept by Louis Henry Simmons, who graduated from Acadia in 1930.

The arrival of automobiles also ended the era of the horse. Horses had always been notoriously skittish when used for transportation in town, and the local newspaper of the time is full of stories about mayhem on the streets. On May 15, 1885, *The Acadian* described an accident in front of Witter's store on Main Street. Three young ladies, it is reported, started to cross the street while a team loaded with barrels went in one direction. They didn't notice a horse and light wagon coming down the other side of the street. "One of them got across safely, but the next one struck the horse about at the shoulder and fell under the wagon, both wheels passing over her. She was helped into a house near by and it was found that beyond bruises and a severe nervous shock, she had escaped injury."

There is always concern when a new technology is introduced. It was true with automobiles. When W. Marshall Black was a town councillor (before he became mayor), he appeared in Kentville to argue that municipal council should pass uniform regulations governing the speed of automobiles. In 1902, a letter condemning the automobile appeared in *The Acadian Orchardist*: "It is all very fine and interesting for Mr. Black and his family, the Messrs. Munro and their families, Mr. A.M. Young and his relatives, and others to go roaming around the county," but what about the people, the hundreds of women and children, who want to "go pleasuring or shopping" in the towns? Hundreds of families are absolutely prohibited from enjoying any of these ordinary privileges, argues "Farmer," because they are in terror of their lives. Kentville, Wolfville and other towns lost a third or more of their county trade because of these "Hell Waggons," he continues, adding that it isn't a question of speed, but a question of the safety of the general public: it is a crime and a burning disgrace that four or five private men of means, with expensive automobiles, are "allowed to go stalking abroad throughout our fair County at all times of day and night and our wives and children compelled to remain at home because of the fear for their lives."

Regulations were devised to try and control the automobile. *Mud Creek* observed that in 1908, Kings County motor vehicles were not allowed to use the roads on Thursdays, Saturdays and Sundays. However, by 1911, Wolfville had seven Fords. The car was in town to stay.

Early Valley car sets off, 1922

Leila Marriott of Starr's Point drives off in this dark green 1919 Overland, purchased by Leila and her husband Jack in Wolfville. The Overland was sold by W.A. Reid, a Wolfville dealership, which advertised the Overland as the new Canadian car. It was built at the Willys-Overland factory in Toronto. The family loved the car, keeping it for many years. Jack, Leila and their children, Joan and Annette, lived in the historic Planters' Barracks.

Wolfville, the world's smallest registered harbour, c.1920s

Wolfville was often described as the smallest registered harbour in the world. Ships that used it had to sneak into a small channel when the tide was just right, then leave at just the right time. The port was indeed busy—Wolfville had developed a considerable business in shipping local products, chiefly potatoes. Ox carts would be lined up waiting their turn to have their loads weighed and dumped on the wharf. Sometimes as many as sixteen vessels would be inside and outside the port, their bowsprits in the early days sticking across the road and interfering with traffic. In this photograph, taken by Edson Graham, two horses with their carts stand by a four-masted schooner.

In August 1883, *The Acadian* wrote that two men were in Wolfville making a survey of the harbour area for the Dominion Government. There were three possibilities for government work: building a breakwater, dredging the creek, or building a wharf. At that time, the newspaper thought a breakwater would be the most useful, but it had been agitating for a wharf as well. On October 26, 1883, *The Acadian* said better wharf facilities were needed to get Wolfville beyond "her present Sleepy Hollow" condition, and that it seemed as if there were a strong possibility that might happen.

The newspaper saw great things if there were better wharf facilities. It notes that one of the most prominent firms in the region had signified its desire to put on steamers to connect the town with Boston, Saint John and ports around the bay: "Do the people realize the advantages that would accrue to Wolfville by making such a possibility a reality? Do they realize the impetus it would give to our agricultural efforts? Instead of being forced to depend solely upon the potato lottery, cheap connections with these ports would stimulate the production of butter, eggs, mutton, small fruits and vegetables for which there is an unlimited demand in American markets."

The *Hiawatha* sails on an excursion to Parrsboro, c.1880s

The ferry to Parrsboro pulls away from the wharf in this excellent photograph from the 1880s. The *Hiawatha* was one of the many ferries that over the years connected the communities on the Minas Basin. As far back as 1764, two Acadians were given permission to continue the ferry boat they had been running "from Partridge Island to Cape Blowme Down, Horton, Fort Edward and different Settlements on each side of the Basin of Minas" (Davison, 1985). The photograph shows at least two dozen people on the vessel, a large group on the wharf seeing the vessel off.

The *Hiawatha* did not always call at Wolfville, sometimes coming to town just for excursions. In April 1884, *The Acadian* reported that the steamer *Hiawatha* had commenced regular trips between Windsor, Hantsport, Kingsport, and Parrsboro. However, the newspaper said "Wolfville is left out altogether the same as last season, the owners being afraid to let their boat come into the creek. We do hope this state of affairs will not be put up with much longer by Wolfville people. It is one of the difficult things to understand why our Dominion representative failed to get the necessary grant so that the new pier might be got underway this summer and perhaps completed." By 1886, the newspapers were reporting a "splendid wharf now in place."

The ferry *Evangeline*, the CVR, and the Kingsport Wharf, c.1890s

In 1893, the ferry *Evangeline* began service on the Minas Basin run, continuing until 1904. These photographs show the vessel docked at the Kingsport wharf. Meeting the ferry at the wharf is a train of the Cornwallis Valley Railway, complete with passenger car. The Cornwallis Valley Railway was incorporated in 1887, and began running regular trains between Kingsport and Kentville on December 22, 1890. By 1892 the railway was owned by the Windsor and Annapolis Railway, which a year later was known as the Dominion Atlantic Railway.

The Cornwallis Valley Railway ended its operations in 1993. In the 1930s, one of the main functions of the line was shipping apples. The train was mixed in that it had the capacity to carry passengers as well, as can be seen in the photograph. It also had another function. As Ivan Smith writes, the train also served as a school bus: "Students from the Kingsport-Canning-Sheffield area who wanted a high school education travelled on the morning train to Kentville to attend classes at the Kentville Academy; at the end of the school day the afternoon train took them home. The railway and school schedules were coordinated to enable students to attend a full day of classes." At its peak, as many as twenty-two high school students regularly took this train to school, using books of tickets, good for three months, costing $3.30 (Ness).

The wharf shown above where the train is meeting the ferry was the end of this section of the CVR run. Eventually the line could not withstand competition from cars and trucks, officially closing at midnight, December 31, 1961 (Ness).

Entrance to the little harbour at Wolfville, c.1900s

In this photograph, the old Skoda building (discussed in Chapter four), which after its creation as a patent medicine plant saw service as a flour mill, sits near the main wharf. The tide is out.

Wendy Elliott, granddaughter of Wolfville doctor Malcolm R. Elliott and daughter of Robbins Elliott, wrote about the "world's smallest harbour" in 1980. She describes the reminiscences of W.D. Withrow, who came to Wolfville in 1920 as a lawyer, when the port of Wolfville was still thriving. Elliott reports in *The Advertiser* that Withrow had spoken about how in the early days the ships would lie in the harbour with their bowsprits over the road in the general area of the duck pond (now Willow Park), but by the time he arrived the main wharf area was behind the Wolfville Fruit Company, where the Wolfville Waterfront Park is today. Withrow worked to create a park where the old ships had docked, but after the land was turned over to the town by Ottawa, it was sold to the Nova Scotia Power Corporation for their offices.

There were, according to Glen Hancock, several wharves, one of them called "the government wharf," which was used by the *Kipawo*. The wharves were all busy with the commerce of the sea: "Often there were two or more three-masted schooners riding high or resting in the mud, and outside the harbour, on the mudflats of the waterless river bed, another two or three vessels would wait, propped by poles to keep them from tilting over, until the next high water when they could continue on to Wolfville or Port Williams, a couple of miles upriver."

It was the arrival of the railway in 1869 that ended the use of the interior part of Mud Creek for shipping and signalled the end of shipbuilding in the area. The tracks cut off the inner part of the harbour, which was then filled in and developed as a skating pond in the winter, and a duck pond in the summer.

Four-masted schooner Kennebunk docking in Wolfville, c.1920

While four boys and a dog watch from the shore, the schooner *Kennebunk*, out of Calais, Maine, is brought to the Wolfville wharf by two tugs. When it docked in September 1920, *Kennebunk* had a load of over a thousand tons of fertilizer from Boston, for R.E. Harris and Sons.

Wolfville's main connection with the water today is through an attractive little park, complete with interpretive panels, which marks the place where ocean-going ships came and went. The life of the town has turned landward, where once it focused very much on its waterfront. People swam in the waters off the wharf, the newspaper editorialized about the condition of the wharf and the approaches to it, and much of the community's travel and commerce made use of the Minas Basin. A succession of more than thirty ferries connected the Horton and Cornwallis townships, beginning in the days before a bridge was built across the Cornwallis River at Port Williams. The ferries took Wolfville people to Kingsport or Parrsboro. The last and best remembered was the *Kipawo*. Wolfville, being a registered port, even had its own customs officials.

When Isaac Chipman galvanized people from all over Nova Scotia to provide materials for the construction of a replacement for the first College Hall, much of the material made its way to Wolfville by schooner. When the town of Wolfville struggled to keep its muddy roads passable, it brought in schooner loads of gravel. In 1913, when the Emmerson Library at Acadia was under construction, the builder, James Reid of Yarmouth, brought in several schooner loads of stone. Apples and potatoes from nearby went out from Wolfville; coal and retail goods came in.

C.R. Burgess of Wolfville and his sailing ships, c.1890s

C. Rufus Burgess built and owned more ships in Kings County than anyone else. He was born into an original Planter family in 1826, the son of Benjamin and Hanna Cumming Burgess. He married Georgina Dewar, from Prince Edward Island, and the couple had eleven children, five of whom died in infancy. Burgess was a successful businessman and the home in Wolfville reflected that: he built the house now known as the Blomidon Inn. After buying the shipbuilding interests of Philip R. Crichton, he used Kingsport as a base to build a number of vessels, including the *Kammira*, 1,885 tons, launched in 1882; the *Karoo*, 1,900 tons, 1883; the *Earl Burgess*, named for an uncle, 1,800 tons, 1887; the *Queen*, 1,894 tons, 1887; the *Kings County*, 2,071 tons, 1890; the *Canada*, 2,217 tons, 1891; the *Golden Rod*, 1892; the *Skoda*, named for the new medicine factory in Wolfville, 1893; and the *Harvest Queen*, 1894.

Excitement mounted as the day drew near for the launching of the *Kings County* in June 1890. It was 275 feet long and over 45 feet wide. An account in the *Windsor Tribune* said a group of prominent people had gone from Windsor by the tug *Chester* for the big event: "As Kingsport neared it became evident that a large contingent of the inhabitants of Kings County were taking a day off." There were three thousand people on hand: "The long pier was crowded with holiday makers of both sexes, while the shores were black with people. Young men with their best girls in their best clothes, proud young husbands patiently carrying the latest addition to the family, old and young, rich and poor, went to swell the crowd of three thousand people, all seemingly happy and bent on making the most of the lovely June day," the *Windsor Tribune* said. "The great ship lay on the ways with a score or more shipwrights under her huge keel tapping like an army of woodpeckers, splitting out the blocks and knocking away shores and spurs. It was only when close that one could realize the size of this latest addition to the fleet of Nova Scotia shipping. As the time approached when she was expected to start, the interest became more intense, and when slowly at first, but with increasing speed the great ship without a hitch or quiver, glided down the ways to the water, the pent up excitement found vent in cheers from thousands of throats."

The *Kings County* was built by Ebenezer Cox. It arrived at Swansea on July 27, 1893, and on its way across the Atlantic it collided with an iceberg, damaging the vessel considerably. In 1909 the *Kings County* made a visit to Halifax, its first in nineteen years, then on to Hantsport for overhauling. The ship went aground in Cuba in 1911, was pulled off, then lost its mizzen-mast off Brazil. Shortly afterwards, it broke its back near Montevideo and was sold for scrap (Wright, 1957). The photograph above is unidentified but is thought to be one of the Burgess ships coming off the slips at Kingsport, possibly the *Kings County* itself.

The tides at Wolfville Harbour, with the Prince Albert in dock, c.1925

Between 1904 and 1926, ferry services between Wolfville and Minas Basin ports were handled by the *Prince Albert*, shown at a Wolfville wharf in these 1925 photographs by Edson Graham. The wharf in question was the Cornwallis River Wharf, located across the Wickwire dyke. To get to it passengers had to enter the dyke, then drive over the road that ran along the dyke wall, all the way out to the main river's edge. The wharf was built out into the river near the channel that ran into the town itself, and was destroyed when storms washed out the Wickwire dykes in the early 1930s. Graham Patriquin explained in *The Advertiser* that persistent rains, record high tides and violent winds had combined to break the Wickwire dykes and isolate the government wharf: "It slowly broke up and disappeared under the assault of winter's pack ice and the unceasing ebb and flow of the tides."

Patriquin, reminiscing about his boyhood in Wolfville, said the *Prince Albert* "was an ancient coal-burning slowpoke whose cargo-handling operations were scarcely more titillating than those of the two masted schooners that fairly cluttered the wharves of Mud Creek's tidal road-bed." The *Prince Albert*, which had originally been called the *Messenger*, was replaced in 1926 by the just-launched *Kipawo*. The second photograph, also taken by Edson Graham, shows the wharf with the tide out.

Sailing ships in port, c.1930s

These two ships were docked close to the railway tracks in this picture, taken in the 1930s. With the Cornwallis River wharf in no condition to be used due to the washing out of the Wickwire dyke, even the *Kipawo* ferry connecting Wolfville, Kingsport and Parrsboro had to berth at this dock beside the Dominion Atlantic Railway tracks. Restrictions of time and tide made docking a chancy business. At this time *The Acadian* argued that the town of Wolfville should take over the Wickwire dyke, acquiring the rights from the owners at a reasonable price and reconstructing and operating the whole property. The newspaper saw the dyke as "a valuable property of over six hundred acres lying at the town's door" and said its present condition greatly impaired the beauty of the town, as well as endangering a number of its citizens.

The *Kipawo*, the Wolfville-Kingsport-Parrsboro ferry, c.1920s

When the new steel ferry was launched in Saint John on December 25, 1925, its captain named the boat the *Kipawo*, because it would be going into service the next year on the Wolfville—Kingsport—Parrsboro run. Edward Trefry commanded the *Kipawo* throughout its service, which lasted until the war. For Captain Trefry, running the Kipawo across the Bay of Fundy and stopping at the three towns was a dicey business, success and even the time of arrival and departure depending on the weather and the tides. The ferry was 113 feet long, displaced 200 gross tons and had the ability to carry between eight and ten cars. For passengers, there was a large saloon aft of the main deck, in addition to a dining saloon, cooking galley and pantry. Its first voyage to Wolfville was made on May 1, 1926.

The photograph above shows the *Kipawo* loading a car on its deck with a sling invented by Captain Trefry. Its busiest year was in 1929, when the *Kipawo* carried 6,136 passengers. In 1930, it carried 1,250 cars (Gibson, 1973). Year after year, the *Kipawo* was a part of the romance and lore of life in Wolfville. Townspeople and students alike wrote about and took pictures of the vessel. It was owned by the Dominion Atlantic Railway, which waxed enthusiastic about Wolfville, the railroad's publicists calling it "one of the most desirable residential towns in the Maritime Provinces." Of the *Kipawo*, the DAR said, "the boat sails across the Basin of Minas, on the course taken by the transports which carried the Acadians into exile; past Blomidon, the traditional home of Glooscap, the supernatural Micmac hero; by Amethyst Cove, the fabled five islands and the haunted shores of Noel; reaching the mouth of the river at Parrsboro on the incoming of the flood—for the vessel's schedule is regulated by the mighty Fundy tides."

M. V. S.
KIPAWO
STEEL FERRY BETWEEN PARRSBORO, KINGSPORT AND WOLFVILLE

Visitors journeying through the "Land of Evangeline" would do well to take the steamer "KIPAWO" from Wolfville or Kingsport to Parrsboro and return. Accommodation is provided for automobiles as well as passengers.

The Steamer's course on the Basin of Minas is both fascinating and interesting. This portion of Nova Scotia's picturesque shores strongly resemble Norway. The trip from Wolfville or Kingsport, around the base of Blomidon and across to Parrsboro, is one which the traveller cannot afford to miss. Seen from the neighborhood of Wolfville or Grand Pré, the outline of Blomidon is sharp and peculiar. The upper half of its front is sheer and perpendicular, while the lower half is a slope. From the deck of the steamer is now seen the explanation of this strange form. Beyond Amethyst Cove opens out the picturesque Cape Split. When the steamer is half way across the channel interest begins to centre upon the Cumberland Shore. Parrsboro is the centre of a splendid fishing and hunting region, and in all directions lie picturesque scenes. Five Islands is an attractive Summer resort and should be visited. The scenery is excellent.

Advertisement for the *Kipawo* in a government publication, c. 1930s.

The *Kipawo*, nosing into Wolfville Harbour, c.1933

Esther Clark Wright was one of many who loved the *Kipawo*. "Dear old *Kipawo*," she wrote, in *Blomidon Rose*. "How we have missed you these many years, since you, too, went away on war time duties." Wright said the sail out of Wolfville was a two-hour voyage, a delight for road-weary motorists. "It was exciting, too, to see Blomidon from a different angle and look at it full in the face, then, as the boat crossed Minas Strait, to look down the far side of Blomidon. It was new viewing to look down the Advocate shore, past the darkly looming heights behind Spencer's Island, past Champlain's Cap d'Or, to Cape Chignecto, and to see, coming nearer and nearer, the gap in the Cumberland Hills where the river at Parrsboro and the lakes beyond would find passage for their waters. Finally the *Kipawo* would twist through the sand bars to the wharf, which the retreating tide had by this time left high above the ship's deck."

Some people thought the *Kipawo*'s schedule was incomprehensible, but in reality it was governed by the tides. The schedule was dependent on the time of high tide in Wolfville, so it had to leave Parrsboro at a different time each day, "some forty-five minutes later than on the previous day" (Wright). *Kings County Vignettes* says that the *Kipawo*'s whistle told the time of the tides for those living around the Minas Basin, and often meant time for a swim, or time to hurry off and catch the ferry.

The *Kipawo* had been launched in Saint John and made its maiden voyage in 1926. When Canada went to war it was taken off the run and used as a naval auxiliary vessel, then after the war in service in Newfoundland. By 1978, the ship had broken its moorings and was beached, but Acadia professor Jack Sheriff's dream was to bring *Kipawo* back to Wolfville as a site for summer theatre. After years of work, it was repaired and towed back, but only made it as far as Parrsboro, where it now serves as the stage for the Ship's Company Theatre.

Railway service in Wolfville c.1880s

The *Morning Chronicle*, Halifax, praised the new railway station in Wolfville in its issue of Saturday, August 1, 1898. "It is a very creditable building," the newspaper said, "and one of the best on the line." Unfortunately, it burned in October 1911. The Windsor and Annapolis Railway's tracks ran from Annapolis to Horton Landing by 1869, as the bridge over Mud Creek was completed the year before. The first Dominion Atlantic Railway (DAR) train from Annapolis to Halifax made its run early in 1872, while the first train from Halifax all the way to Yarmouth made its journey on October 1, 1894. The DAR had just been formed from the W&A and Western Counties railways. In December 1899, *The Acadian* reported that the DAR had 220 miles of railroad in operation, and had carried 207,249 passengers the previous year, as well as 156,743 tons of freight. The railway line had taken in $579,054 and had paid out $400,472, making it a reasonably profitable enterprise.

The photograph at right shows Samuel Prat, first stationmaster in Wolfville. He had come with his widowed mother from England to Nova Scotia in 1846, and in 1857 married Elizabeth Dupont Morse, who was a sister of the founder of the Morse Tea Company and a cousin to Samuel Morse, inventor of the telegraph. Their children included several whose names are a part of the history of the area: May Rosina, Minnie Sophia, Charlotte Elizabeth, Rupert and Annie Louisa. Samuel Prat's home was located on Highland Avenue.

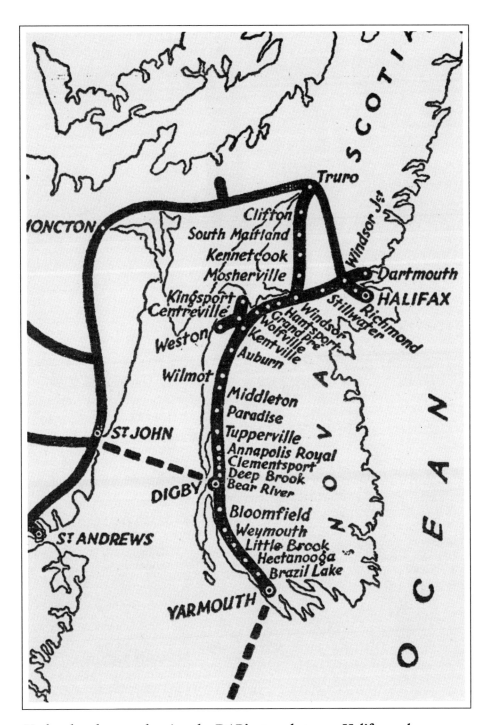

Undated early map showing the DAR's stops between Halifax and Yarmouth, published under the authority of George E. Graham, DAR general manager.

Railway bridge at Horton Landing, c.1870s and 1890s

This early photograph shows the bridge at Hortonville, over the Gaspereau River, under construction in 1871. Six men can be discerned working with a machine, driving piles into the mud to support the bridgeworks. The rail line from Halifax to Windsor opened in 1858 over tracks owned by the Intercolonial Railway. The Windsor and Annapolis Railway opened the line from Annapolis to Horton Landing by 1869, and the missing link—between Horton Landing and Windsor—was completed in 1872 by the W&A.

Wolfville was the headquarters for the railway at first, and engines built in England landed at the town. Disagreements with landowners forced the move of the headquarters to Kentville. By 1894 the Windsor and Annapolis Railway joined with the Western Counties Railway to form the Dominion Atlantic Railway. It was to run trains along this route until Friday, August 26, 1994—thirty-six days short of a hundred years of service.

The photograph above, taken by A.L. Hardy, shows the same railway bridge in the late 1890s. The body of water it is crossing is the mouth of the Gaspereau River, which runs through the Gaspereau Valley and was used for generating electricity. The place from which the Acadians were sent into exile is not far from this bridge. Lloyd E. Shaw, who used the bridge to get to the Acacia Villa School, wrote in his autobiography that he spent two winters at the school, "walking morning and night two miles over the Railway, feeling our way across the Railway Bridge, over icy sleepers at least two feet apart. This was supposed to be a school for wealthy families; Ned Rhodes was a pupil; in later years he became Premier of Nova Scotia and was called to the Bennett Cabinet as Minister of Finance."

The Famous *Flying Bluenose* between Kentville and Wolfville, c.1910

In July 1893, *The Acadian* praised the management of the Windsor and Annapolis Railway for having the foresight to place the *Flying Bluenose* on the run from Halifax to Annapolis (it wasn't until a year later that a single train went all the way to Yarmouth). Two new trains had been put on the run, with new Baldwin engines, at a cost of $100,000. Each train bore the name of the *Flying Bluenose*, and the newspaper said that they had been "a source of great pleasure and satisfaction to all travelers—residents and tourists alike." One train had a new baggage car, a combination smoker and first-class car, palace coaches *Precious* and *Pomona*, and a parlour buffet car called the *Haligonian*.

When the train made its first run in July 1893, "the *Bluenose* started sharp at 9:30 and made a splendid run to Annapolis, stopping only at Windsor Junction, Windsor, Wolfville, Kentville and Middleton, covering the 180 miles in four hours and fifteen minutes. Conductor Herbert was in charge, with James Daino as conductor of the parlour car. The return train [the second train], leaving Annapolis at 1:15, was made up of the engine *Evangeline*, baggage, combination smoker and first class, palace coaches *Jocoas* and *Fleur d'Lys*, and the parlour car *Mayflower*, under Conductor Corbett, with M.B. Bayer in charge of the parlour car." That same year, Rhodes, Curry and Company of Amherst was engaged in building a first-class car for the railway.

Two years later, on July 5, 1895, *The Acadian* noted with approval that "the *Flying Bluenose* expresses made their first trip for the season on Wednesday. They present a fine appearance and will be gladly welcomed by the travelling public. The Dominion Atlantic Railway is making every preparation for the season's travel." The Windsor and Annapolis Railway had become part of the Dominion Atlantic Railway two years before.

The *Flying Bluenose* was fast and made a limited number of stops—only eight between Yarmouth and Halifax.

The Port Williams railway station, c.1890s

At the foot of the hill on the road leading across the dykes to Port Williams, below Greenwich, the Dominion Atlantic Railway placed its Port Williams station. This excellent photograph, taken in the 1890s, shows a locomotive, horses and wagons, and the station itself. The DAR line went from Halifax to Yarmouth and was a vital transportation link through the Annapolis valley, creating a safe and relatively fast means of travel in a time when the roads and stage-coaches were unreliable.

In August 1893, *The Acadian* said that the Western and Annapolis Railway—just before it became the Dominion Atlantic Railway—was seeking tenders for construction of a railway station and freight shed at Port Williams. The first station was on the south side of the railway, but this larger building was constructed in 1893 on the north side (Port Williams Women's Institute).

New railway station in Wolfville, c.1910s

The railway station built in 1898 burned in 1911. By August 23, 1912, work on the new brick railway station in Wolfville was progressing rapidly. *The Acadian* reported that the outside of the edifice was almost completed, and that it presented a fine appearance. The platforms were being laid and would give ample room for handling traffic, "which was formerly considerably cramped in this regard." The newspaper hoped the work would be completed within a few weeks.

The station was built by the firm of Rhodes, Curry and Company, the same company that built the second and third university halls. Known as "the building boom," this was a busy time for construction in Wolfville: the post office had been built the previous year and the Baptist church in the same year, both of them substantial buildings made of brick and stone. The centre of the station building was two-and-a-half storeys high, while the east and west sections were one-and-a-half storeys high. The upper part of the station was an apartment, occupied from 1913 by Chester G.C. Coombs, who was the station agent until 1947. Coombs moved his family to a new home on Earnscliffe Avenue on June 7, 1921. After Coombs lived there, assistant station agent Horace Jackson occupied the apartment.

M. Allen Gibson, whose series on the churches of Nova Scotia captured their history in the pages of the *Chronicle Herald*, grew up in Wolfville. He said of the station that it might not be much by modern architectural standards, but to a boy it was attractive and imposing. Dr. Gibson describes the station as having two waiting rooms, separated by the office. The one nearer the baggage room was for men, while the one on the station's west end was for women. Also using the women's room were college faculty members and clergymen, the assumption being that such individuals preferred to wait for the train in an environment free of tobacco smoke. East along the station platform, as seen in the photograph, was the brick freight shed, with a loading platform that ran along the tracks.

One of the last steam engines at the Wolfville station, August 18, 1956

It was an historic occasion, but it merited only a short notice on the front page of the *Wolfville Acadian* of August 23, 1956. Under the headline "Last Run of Steam Train," the newspaper reported that "the 'Iron Horse' made its last run as a passenger train between Halifax and Yarmouth Saturday, marking the end of an era in Nova Scotia railroad history." The newspaper went on to say that "it was true that no flags were flown at half mast to mark the historic occasion. The almost half-century old steam locomotive, with many of the passenger coaches just as old, had to go to make way for present day progress." The new diesel-operated Dayliner went into service, providing faster and better service to the railway travelling public.

An editorial in the same issue advised that the old must give way to the new, but there was something missing when the "banshee wail of the diesel siren was heard in place of the old familiar whistle of the steam locomotive as the trains passed over the crossings when entering and leaving Wolfville Station." It said that as the train made its last journey through the valley there were many who waved it a sentimental goodbye from stations and points along the line. However, it said sentiment had no place in these days of progress. A lack of sentiment in turn doomed the Dayliner itself, which, despite protests, made its final run thirty-three years later. Information on the photograph identifies this as the last steam passenger train to run through the Annapolis valley, pulled by Dominion Atlantic Railways locomotive 1038, August 18, 1956. If so, either the first few cars may have been freight cars, or the last steam train through carried freight.

Penny-farthing bicycle in front of Prat's Store, c.1880s

E. Sidney Crawley was just learning photography when he took this picture of a man riding a penny-farthing bicycle in front of Rupert Prat's store, at the northwest corner of Main Street and Gaspereau Avenue. In the background can be seen the elm trees that surrounded the old DeWolf House. Crawley was at the time a barrister and property agent but, according to information in *The Acadian*, was already becoming something of an expert in photography by April 1884.

The penny-farthing bicycle was developed in the 1870s and lasted as a mode of transport until the 1890s, when the sort of bicycle in use today came into fashion. Hundreds of companies made penny-farthings, in a variety of sizes. The bicycle is characterized—as seen in the picture—by a large front wheel, as the height of the bicycle was sometimes over five feet. It usually had solid rubber tires, where previous bicycles had steel rims and were rough to ride. Unfortunately, bicycles and horses had an uneasy coexistence, and since Wolfville depended on horses, bicycles were sometimes a trial. At the time this photograph was taken, *The Acadian* was reporting that a team of horses belonging to a man from Gaspereau had been frightened by two bicycles coming down the sidewalk "and turned short around, breaking the axle, one wheel and injuring one of the horses. Had the load not been a heavy one, more serious damage would have been done." The newspaper editorialized that bicycles should not be allowed on the sidewalk. The owner of the team would probably lose eight to ten dollars on repairs, a sum that the newspaper thought should be paid by the bicyclists.

The bridge at Port Williams, c.1900s

Bridges have allowed the crossing of the Cornwallis River at Port Williams for well over two hundred years. The first bridge was built at least as early as 1780, but it—or a second bridge—was carried out by the tide by the time the nineteenth century had been underway. A repaired bridge lasted until 1823. In 1835 a bridge was built by Joseph Winthrop, from Hants County, which for many years served as a toll bridge. Port Williams' history dates the erection of the bridge as the beginning of Port Williams as a village and the decline of Cornwallis Town Plot as the centre of the community.

The people of Wolfville took a great interest in the Port Williams bridge, since it was a vital link to the communities around the Minas Basin, and without it the only practical way to make the journey was by ferry. Before the erection of the first bridge, a ferry made the run from Cornwallis Town Plot, a short distance east of Port Williams, to a spot in Wolfville on Ferry Lane, later Cherry Lane. There was a bell on the Wolfville side to call the ferryman when he was needed; the ferryman kept a roadside house on the north side of the Cornwallis.

Not long after it began publishing in 1883, *The Acadian* noted that there had been three accidents within two weeks on the Port Williams bridge, one when a pair of cattle attached to a wagon got frightened and ran into a carriage being driven by H.M. Sleep, of Canard. In August 1884, the newspaper warned about two dangerous holes in the bridge, and two weeks later noted that plans were being made to have the bridge rebuilt. "We hope," an editorial said, "the Provincial Engineer will have to drive over that piece of road a few times between now and next spring, but if he does he had better get insured against accidents."

The provincial engineer did get to the bridge, in January 1885, and afterwards he reported to a Wolfville bridge committee that a new bridge would be ready for use without fail by March 1. The big issue was whether or not there would be a drawbridge portion of the bridge, but the provincial engineer said it was out of the question. The extra cost for a swing draw, he said, would be $1800 for ironwork and at least $400 more for a pier. Yet even with the new bridge in place, *The Acadian* could not leave it alone. In June it suggested the government establish a semaphore system at the bridge, with a dispatcher in charge to signal to teams wishing to cross. "After night it is funny to see the teams trying to decide whether to back out or lay down to let each other pass on the bridge. Perhaps the bridge will expand enough when hot weather comes to allow ordinary light carriages to pass."

The 1885 bridge, shown in this photograph, was the first iron bridge across the river; it lasted until 1968.

Paving Wolfville's main street, c.1911

The mud on the streets of Wolfville was a constant theme in the community's early years. That good red earth, so fertile for growing apples and vegetables, was not especially useful as a roadbed. Esther Clark Wright said that when the snow melted in the spring and the water rushed down the hillsides, the ditches and sewers were soon overflowing, and Main Street became a morass: "For days on end, only the most venturesome of inhabitants, accoutred in long rubber boots, would essay the crossing."

In 1910, Mayor T.L. Harvey sent the town's Streets and Property Committee to Halifax, Truro and Saint John to look at the way new streets were being constructed. The committee chairman, J.E. Hales, reported back that the members had given the matter a great deal of thought, and recommended buying a crusher and steam roller in order to lay down what was called Tarvia Macadam. A public meeting authorized council to borrow $10,000 to make the purchases, although it was too late in the year for anything to be done immediately. The next year, under new mayor J.D. Chambers, Wolfville put down Tarvia Modern Pavement. A Waterous ten-ton steamroller and a Number 4 Champion stone crusher were purchased, and a contract was entered with the manufacturers of Tarvia for fifteen thousand gallons at ten cents a gallon. As well, the town rented a Tarvia tank wagon, shown in the photograph. Main Street from Highland Avenue to Locust Avenue was paved. The Streets and Property Committee reported to council that it believed that the citizens, "after seeing what can be done to improve our otherwise almost impassable streets, are not going to be satisfied until Main Street is completed its full length, as well as the avenues leading into Main St., and we believe are ready to favour any plan whereby the work may be carried on and as rapidly as possible, especially as we now have the machinery to do the work."

The road between Wolfville and Kentville, c.1920s.

Long before this car drove along the road between Kentville and Wolfville, travel in Kings County was by stagecoach, horseback, horse and buggy, or by walking. Travel by motor vehicle gained slow acceptance after the early 1890s; the first car in town, according to *Mud Creek*, belonged to D.R. Munro. The Wolfville Garage was open by 1912, and in 1920 motorists in Nova Scotia joined those in the rest of Canada in driving on the right side of the road.

Wolfville paved its main street in 1911, the first town in the Annapolis Valley to do so. The road between Wolfville and Kentville was paved in 1932. A story in the *Wolfville Acadian* on September 17, 1931, said that readers would be happy to know that work of a permanent nature was to be commenced at once on the road between Wolfville and Kentville. George Nowlan, Lloyd Shaw, Dr. J.H. MacDonald and G.A. Boggs, along with their counterparts from Kentville, met the provincial minister of highways, who told them that tenders for construction of a permanent road would be called at once. The work to be done in the fall would include widening the whole road to thirty-three feet, grading, putting in permanent watercourses and sub-surfacing the road, at a cost of fifteen thousand dollars per mile. Paving would be done in the spring.

Stuart Graham and his hydroplane at Wolfville Harbour, 1936

The first long-distance airplane flight in Canada is said to have been made by Lieutenant Stuart Graham, son of Wolfville photographer Edson Graham, after the end of the war. In 1918, as *Mud Creek* tells the story, Stuart, accompanied by his wife and his mechanic, left Halifax, passed over Saint John and eventually wound up in Trois Rivières, Quebec. The first airplane to be seen over Wolfville appeared in June 1920, causing a great deal of excitement. It was on an exhibition flight from Truro to Annapolis. Its pilot was Lieutenant Logan Barnhill, and its mechanic E.C. Atkinson, son of Wolfville resident Mrs. E.G. Atkinson. *The Acadian* said that "the plane returned to Truro on Friday afternoon, again passing over the town enroute."

The photograph above shows Stuart Graham and his hydroplane at the Wolfville wharf in mid-July, 1936. In this picture Graham, then living in Montreal, where he was an instructor of civil aviation, had landed on the Cornwallis River and taxied in to the wharf, where he was to pick up his father. They took off for a tour of the western part of the province but found weather conditions unsuitable for flying, so spent the time at Lake Kejimkujik, which straddles Queens and Annapolis counties and today is the centre of a national park. They arrived back in Wolfville two days later. A good crowd had gathered to see the airplane and its pilot, who is standing on the pontoon to the left of the end of the wharf.

Chapter 6

People, events, and daily life

Preserving Wolfville's History

It is the people, not just the businesses, public offices, banks and institutions, that make a town and its countryside. Many of the people who figure prominently in the history of Wolfville are buried in the Old Burying Ground, now a provincially registered heritage property, across the street from the end of Highland Avenue. The cemetery grounds are passed every day by people heading downtown from Acadia University or from the western approaches to Wolfville. The Baptist church on the south side of the street replaced a church on the same site, that church having replaced the first one beside the old cemetery. The earliest burials occurred in 1763. Watson Kirkconnell called the old cemetery "almost a Westminster Abbey" for Acadia University in its record of venerable college names, and said the community itself was notably represented. His words appear on a plaque inside the cemetery gates, placed there by the town's Rotary Club.

Standing in the Old Burying Ground's cool green interior inspires a sense of awe. The grave of Isaac Chipman, who died so tragically at the age of thirty-five on the outing to Blomidon, is there. Edmund Albern Crawley, a founder of Acadia and for a time its president, has a stone. Many of the DeWolf family are buried there, as is Lewis Johnston, whose home, Annandale, is featured in this book. Walking about and studying the gravestones has the effect of connecting one to the history of Wolfville.

Before photography altered the way people kept their history, people relied on oral traditions to pass down stories from one generation to the next, as well as on the writing of books, keeping of diaries, collecting of letters and documents, and publishing of newspapers. It is astonishing how important a local newspaper is to preserving the history of a particular place. Wolfville was well served by *The Acadian*. That there is no such newspaper now is a loss, and one can only hope that at some point it will be reborn. The news that is really important to people is their local news. While Wolfville news is now carried by *The Advertiser*, Kentville, it s not the same as having a newspaper in the town.

The first issue of the newspaper, then called *The Young Acadian*, appeared in April 1883. Arthur S. Davison (later the family spelled it Davidson) published it almost as a whim. In a 1929 article, John E. Woodworth, editor of the *Berwick Register*, said that Arthur Davison, "being possessed of some printing material, started a small paper, mainly for his own amusement." Woodworth notes that Davison originally intended to call the newspaper the Bumble Bee, but didn't have enough "Bs" to typeset the title. By the end of the summer, it was apparent that there was a market for the newspaper. Arthur's brother, Bowman O. Davidson, became a partner and the name was changed to *The Acadian*. A year after it began, in April

1884, the brothers purchased a large Washington press and began issuing the paper weekly.

The Acadian wasn't the first newspaper in Wolfville, nor the first to have that name. In 1859 Campbell Stephens produced a few issues of a newspaper in Wolfville, but gave it up and moved to Windsor. In 1861 the students at Acadia published a handwritten copy of a paper called The Budget. Five years later, an Englishman named M.J. Theakston moved to Wolfville from Canning and with his brother William started the first Acadian. According to Woodworth, it was a creditable five-column paper that was well edited and well printed. It collapsed in 1869, however, after it reported the trial of some boys charged with stealing apples from an orchard. Shortly after the story of the trial appeared, the Acadian offices were broken into and the plant machinery thrown into Mud Creek.

The town's next newspaper was The Star, later The New Star. There was more publishing activity at the college, too. In November 1874, students began producing The Athenaeum, at first a literary magazine. The editors for the initial issue announced that for their new journal they had chosen the name of the existing literary and debating society, made up of all of the male students at Acadia College (the women later had a separate society, called the Propylaeum Society). The Athenaeum continued as a monthly magazine until 1938, when it dropped its literary aspirations and became a weekly newspaper.

In keeping a folksy, humorous watch over the town, The Acadian was just what the community needed. Entertainment was part of the coverage: an item in June 1883 promised the

Church dinner in an open field at Grand Pré, c.1910s

Not only were picnics immensely popular in the late eighteen hundreds, but the newspapers reported on them as important social events. This Paul Yates photograph shows the members of a church group wearing their best clothes, at a picnic in Grand Pré.

Refined Irish Minstrels, Sellon and Burns, plus Miss Maggie Burrell, the world's greatest skipping rope dancer at Witter's Hall. On the same bill was the "accomplished burlesque prima donna, Harry C. Horton," who was supposed to have possessed the most wonderful soprano voice of the age. A week later *The Acadian* reported that Sellon and Burns did not make a vast fortune during their visit to Wolfville: "They gave a very small program to a still smaller house."

Information about upcoming picnics, an important form of recreation, was also included in the regular news. The newspaper commented in June 1883 that several private picnics had been held during the past couple of weeks, "and so far as heard from turned out very well." The Oddfellows were also trying to get up a picnic, and there was also "the whisper of a mass Temperance picnic" some time in August. In August there was a report that the ferry for the Sunday school picnic to Parrsboro had left Horton Landing the previous morning. It was billed as the social event of the season and picked up people from Kentville, Hantsport, Wolfville, Kingsport and Windsor.

The temperance movement was a major force in Wolfville for decades, *The Acadian* solidly behind it. By August, there was more information about the Temperance picnic: it would be held on the twenty-second, readers were told, at Hutchinson's clearing near Ellershouse, Hants County. After it had been held, the newspaper reported that the day had been all that could have been desired. About 450 persons went from Wolfville and surrounding area by special train, arriving there at ten and being met by another 250 people, who came by horse-drawn wagons from Hants County. The picnickers spent the day playing football and croquet, strolling about, visiting the nearby mills and the beautiful grounds. Walking through the grounds reminded the newspaper's correspondent of the Public Gardens of Halifax: "Mr. Harvie, the genial head gardener, made our reporter welcome as he pointed out some of the beauties of the place." All day, music was played by the 68th Battalion Infantry Band, *The Acadian* noting cheerfully that the band members "certainly deserve credit for the marked improvement they are making in their music."

Of course, even though it was a temperance picnic, there were the fallen. The newspaper said that at six in the evening people started for home, "tired, sunburnt but happy and all sober with perhaps six poor exceptions, one of whom was left some miles from home at a flag station, a reward for his foolishness." The conductors of the train were praised for the gentlemanly and careful way in which they ran their train and looked after the comfort of their passengers.

No item was above or beneath the watchful eyes of *The Acadian*. In August 1883 it reported that in some mysterious way, the valve of the water tank at Grand Pré had come open just as the train started from the tank. The leak was not observed until the whole train had passed, and since the windows were open, a certain dampness pervaded those cars, creating an unpleasant condition. When the train got to Wolfville, the conductor did what he could to assist the "unwilling shower bathers" with wraps.

The activities of the area's young men and women were always grist for *The Acadian*'s mill. In January 1884 the newspaper reported that a number of the ladies had procured the town rink near Mud Creek and had sent out invitations to the young men, stating that they would be at home at the rink. The men promptly responded. That night, there were forty couples skating. "This continued," the newspaper said, "the ladies making all the advances and requesting the young men to skate until nine o'clock arrived, when it became in order to ask them to partake of refreshments. Accordingly the poor young men were escorted up to bountifully spread tables where their wants were ministered unto by their fair guardians in the good taste and style which characterizes our Nova Scotia girls." At ten-thirty, D.A. Munro, the proprietor, rang the bell and all headed home. It was agreed that it was the event of the season.

The pages of *The Acadian* are an exceptional record of the life of Wolfville from 1883 onward. Very few people in the community escaped its notice. In June 1883 Everett Sawyer, the son of Acadia President Artemas Wyman Sawyer, returned to town from Harvard. It was noted that he had graduated with high honours. *The Acadian* also made note of Sawyer's professional appointments, community work, and political activity, even keeping track of his movements once he left Wolfville. And when Everett Sawyer died in Woodstock, Ontario, in 1924, it was also noted by *The Acadian*, which said that one of those conducting the service had been McMaster University's Dr. E.M. Keirstead, formerly at Acadia.

In 1919 another newspaper, *The Evening Mail*, published in Halifax, ran a supplement on the town of Wolfville. Wolfville merchants paid for the supplement by purchasing advertising, and town notables provided the copy. Among those submitting material were Dr. W.L. Archibald, principal of Horton Academy; Dr. George B. Cutten, president of Acadia University; Professor W.A. Coit, on the Acadia faculty; Rev. H.T. DeWolfe, principal of the Acadia Ladies Seminary; Rev. R.F. Dixon, rector of the Church of England in Wolfville; John Frederic Herbin, merchant, writer and former mayor; and Robie W. Tufts, author and federal migratory birds officer. It was organized by H.W. Phinney, Ltd.

The supplement was a valentine to Wolfville, singing its praises. It said that one of Wolfville's chief attractions was the total absence of smoke and dust associated with industries. Wolfville had no factories. "There are no belching smokestacks to pollute the clean fresh air which even in the hottest days of summer is tempered by the cooling breezes from Minas Basin." It said the people of Wolfville were largely drawn from the leisure classes, attracted to the town by the unusual educational facilities, business opportunities, and especially desirable living conditions.

There were other things of which to be proud. The newspaper said that car owners who wanted longevity and good service in a car would rejoice in the good roads in and around Wolfville. The town's main street was paved for over two miles and the side streets were shortly to be transformed the same way. And the "whole Canard region, north and west of the town is a network of smooth and well built roads, intersecting that delightful region, where prosperous homes and farmsteads abound." The streets of Wolfville were paved with Tarvia, so that they could stand the heaviest kind of motor traffic without injury to themselves or the car. One could motor in and about Wolfville so smoothly, the supplement said, that riding rivalled the skimming qualities of a canoe or aeroplane. "And you double the life of your car by using it in and around Wolfville."

There were practically no slum houses, the newspaper went on, the homes being uniformly well kept and comfortable. An improvement league had been recently formed, with an ambitious program for civic welfare. A hospital was planned. As well, there was the best opera house in the Valley—clean, comfortably equipped with modern seating and stage and dressing rooms. "The excellent schools, a variety of churches and fraternal societies, the up-to-date skating rink, banking facilities, and fine public buildings can only find passing reference here." Further, the churches, the railway station, the stores, the residence, the banks and the university buildings combined to raise the average of architectural beauty higher in Wolfville than elsewhere in Nova Scotia.

Finally, the air was fresh and sweet, free from impurities, dry and crisp in winter, and never sultry in summer.

Thomas Andrew Strange DeWolf c.1870s

Thomas Andrew Strange DeWolf was the son of Judge Elisha and Margaret DeWolf. He was born on April 19,1795, and died in Wolfville on September 21, 1878. In 1817, he married his first cousin, Nancy, daughter of James and Mary Ratchford of Parrsboro. James Ratchford was Margaret DeWolf's brother. Nancy was born in 1799 and died in 1883. T.A.S. DeWolf, closest to the camera, is shown in this photograph outside DeWolf House, once the home of the Wolfville Historical Society Museum and now demolished.

Between 1837 and 1848, DeWolf was Kings County's representative in the provincial legislature. He was a member of the government's executive council, the cabinet of the day. He was also president of the Horton branch of the Kings County Agricultural Society, which included among its objectives not only the promotion of agriculture, but cultivation of the "social virtues" and the promotion of the good order and well-being of the community. The Horton branch was part of a province-wide agricultural society that by 1898 had nine branches in Kings County alone. The society frequently recommended general reforms to municipal council, one of them being the establishment of a poor farm for the township of Horton (Eaton, 1910). T.A.S. and Nancy DeWolf had fourteen children.

St. Eulalie, home of Judge Robert Linton Weatherbe, c.1910s

Robert Linton Weatherbe was one of the province's most respected judges and a farmer at heart. In 1885, the newspaper reported that Judge Weatherbe had begun active operations on his Grand Pré farm, employing several expert nurserymen to work in his orchards and making plans to plant yet another orchard. *The Acadian* said that before long, Judge Weatherbe would have one of best fruit farms in the province. It called him one of the progressive farmers of the nineteenth century and said he had a fine herd of Holstein cattle.

The newspaper also said that Judge Weatherbe was planning to erect a large residence on the property in the summer. The stone was being quarried in order to make the foundation. Later, Eaton's *History of Kings County*, published in 1910, describes the house as one of the most conspicuous estates in the county, and Sir Robert as "an enthusiastic orchardist [...] He and Lady Weatherbe [the former Minnie Johnson] usually spent their summers on their King's County Farm." The estate included parts of Melanson, once an Acadian hamlet. By the 1930s the house, called St. Eulalie, was described as a "rambling old edifice." The first issue of *Kings County Vignettes* reported on the destruction of St. Eulalie by fire in 1939, saying that by the time the Wolfville Fire Department arrived the fire had made so much headway that the building was a spectacular mass of flames, attracting a large number of people.

Weatherbe (there were at least two other spellings of the name) was born in Bedecque, Prince Edward Island in 1836. He graduated from Acadia with a Bachelor of Arts in 1858 and a Master of Arts in 1861. He studied law and was admitted to the bar in 1863, edited the *Acadian Recorder*, was appointed a judge of the Supreme Court of Nova Scotia in 1878, and was made chief justice in 1905. He received an honorary doctorate from Acadia in 1883 and in 1905 he received a knighthood from King Edward, retiring from the bench in 1907. On his death in 1915, *The Athenaeum* said that Weatherbe had been one of the ablest judges in Canada, and that "his written decisions were distinguished by logical presentation and keen reasoning."

Swimming off the Wolfville wharf, c.1889

In June 1883, in the first year of its publication, *The Young Acadian* (it dropped the "Young" soon after) reported that a group of boys interested in sports had started a subscription list for funds to build a bathing house on the shipyard wharf. The newspaper said that out of the twenty-three people asked, only three refused, and the respectable sum of four dollars and five cents had been raised. The boys took the money, erected a bathing house, and made a very nice shelter for the bathers, in addition to a good platform to get out to the water. "Bathers can now get in and out of the water with some comfort," it was reported. "Their clothes can be kept clean and safe, and the wind won't have the same chance to blow their frail bodies to atoms as heretofore." The public was welcome to use the new facili-

ty, but the bathers wanted to keep it as clean as possible and to preserve it from damage. It was named "Bathers' Retreat."

The careful observer will notice that the boys left *all* of their clothes in Bathers' Retreat. Glen Hancock, reminiscing about the wharf in his book *My Real Name is Charley*, mentions that he and his friends swam every day in the tidal water near the wharf, but that the creeks were popular because "we could swim there without bathing suits. At other times we swam from the wharves...." He says they would swim in the morning tide, then walk to Gaspereau and swim in the fresh water there, washing off the salt and mud. Graham Patriquin also says the wharf was ideal for swimming on hot days, when people could jump, dive or swim to their heart's content. He also notes that the open dykelands provided good privacy for exciting, illicit adventures, including experimenting with tobacco and "devil-may-care girls from the Acadia Ladies Seminary."

The Palace RR Photograph Car Company, c.1880s

In the 1880s, many photographs were taken by travelling photo studios that were attached to trains. The logo above is for the Palace RR Photographic Car Company, which was in Wolfville to photograph both townspeople and students at Acadia College. The quality of the pictures was excellent: this photograph of the Class of 1883, Acadia Ladies Seminary, is just one example. In the picture are Viona Alward, Leonette M. Crosby, Alice R. Hanson, Harriett P. Harris, Emma V. Johnson, and Mary E. Melville. Unfortunately, the information with the photograph did not identify specific people.

Lewis Rice, who had photographic studios in both Windsor and Wolfville, was one of those who used a railway car as a studio. Problems with obtaining payment for the photographs were indicated by a note that appeared in *The Acadian* on January 9, 1885. J.B. Davison, Justice of the Peace, said that "Prof. J.P. Tuck, of the Palace RR Photograph Car, has placed with me for collection, all accounts due them for pictures taken in Kentville and Wolfville. All persons thus indebted will take due notice and govern themselves accordingly." Davison himself was a photographer at the time; the first issue of *The Athenaeum*, in November of 1874, carried an advertisement for "J.P. Davison, Wolfville, N.S., Photographer." He was a dealer in pictures, watches and jewellery, and an importer and manufacturer of picture frames. As well, he "attends to the collection of Debts, and all business in his line, with despatch."

Acadia Ladies Seminary, Class of 1883, taken in the railway car studio

The beautiful, talented and adventurous Prat sisters, c.1890s

Wolfville stationmaster Samuel Prat and his wife, Elizabeth DuPont Morse, brought up their lively family of four girls and a boy in a large house they called Acadia Villa, on that part of Prospect Street that used to run across Highland Avenue towards the Acadia College grounds. The oldest was Annie Louisa (1861–1960), followed by Rupert (1863–1945), Charlotte Elizabeth (1865–1957), Minnie Sophia, (1868–1901) and May Rosina (1872–1965). The young people developed a wide circle of friends including the poet Bliss Carman, who was a frequent visitor at Acadia Villa, regarding it as a second home and mentioning it several times in his poetry. Minnie was engaged to Goodridge Bliss Roberts, the brother of Sir Charles G.D. Roberts, but lost him when he died at Acadia Villa in February 1892. Charles G.D. Roberts later worked as an editor in New York, moving there in 1897 to live with his cousin Bliss Carman; that same year Minnie also moved to New York, followed by her sister May Rosina. Annie went to Chicago to study at the Art Institute of Chicago, and won a number of prizes.

Minnie apprenticed with the first woman bookbinder in the United States, Evelyn Nordhoff. She is shown practising her art at the Elephant Bindery, Ithaca, New York. This was at the home of the Prat sisters' friend Dorothy Cornell, whose grandfather founded Cornell University. Annie, Minnie and May Rosina opened the Primrose Bindery in New York City in 1899, from where Minnie won a silver medal in Paris in 1900 for her binding. In 1901, while visiting her sister Charlotte Wilcox in Windsor, she died of typhoid fever. May Rosina, who had become an accomplished artist in leather, carried on the bindery for two more years, but returned to Wolfville in 1903. She married Richard Sidney Starr, lived at Willowbank Farm, Starr's Point, and later became curator of the Wolfville Museum when it opened in the DeWolf House in 1941.

Annie frequently helped at the Primrose Bindery in New York and became an accomplished poet, painter and art teacher. She is shown with her picture superimposed on that of the Primrose Bindery (which, incidentally, has a picture of Blomidon and the Minas Basin on the wall over the press). From 1917 to 1920 Annie was dean of women at King's College, Windsor, living at the Windsor home of Charlotte and George Wilcox. It was Annie, who lived to be ninety-nine, who restored the famous wallpaper in DeWolf house while her sister May Rosina was curator there.

Evelyn Starr, world-class violinist, c.1890s

By the age of six Evelyn Starr could play on the piano any piece of music she had heard. At seven she took up the violin. She had, according to Wolfville principal and musician B.C. Silver, perfect pitch, and as a young girl could play difficult piano compositions that were being studied by her older sister. By 1914, *The Athenaeum* was reporting on a concert at Acadia by Evelyn Starr, the "Wolfville violinist who recently returned from Europe." Shortly after her performance at College Hall, *The Acadian* was reporting her success at a performance at the Aeolian Hall in New York.

Evelyn Starr was a student at seminary, graduating in 1908. The *Acadia Bulletin* said in 1918 that she had been pursuing her studies with the best masters of the violin in Germany and Russia, and that she had recently made her first professional appearance in Dresden as violin soloist with a celebrated Berlin orchestra. She played exclusively Russian music at the concert, which was held before an audience that included royalty. A review from a German newspaper quoted in the *Acadia Bulletin* said that Miss Starr played most superbly: "The young artist possesses maturity of technique, and a very sympathetic interpretation, delighting the great audience by the charming freshness and fluency of her playing."

Evelyn Starr was the daughter of Evelina Elizabeth Richardson Starr and C.R.H. Starr, prominent Wolfville apple grower and shipper, developer, president of the Acadia Dairy Company on Front Street and member of the Acadia University board of governors. A descendant of the Planter Samuel Starr, C.R.H. Starr at one time owned Willowbank Farm in Starr's Point, before moving to Wolfville in 1888. He was one of the most important members of the Nova Scotia Fruit Growers Association, serving as secretary for many years. He helped establish the Nova Scotia School of Horticulture at Acadia and was a member of the first Wolfville Town Council after incorporation.

E. Sidney Crawley, early Wolfville photographer, c.1887

On April 24, 1884, the editor of *The Acadian* made note of the fact that "Mr. E.S. Crawley is becoming quite an expert in the art of Photography. We were shown some very fine photos, taken by him of Dr. Barss' flock of 'Brahmas' a few days since." E. Sidney Crawley, born in 1830, was the son of Acadia founder and president Edmund A. Crawley and in his lifetime wore a number of different hats. He studied law in Halifax, was admitted to the bar in 1847, and returned to Wolfville to live in 1878. By January 1880 he was advertising in *The Star* that he was not only an attorney and solicitor, but also an insurance agent with "low rates on new vessels." He became a stipendiary magistrate and the town solicitor, a position he held from 1893 to 1922.

He also was postmaster, and was at the helm when the new post office was built in 1911.

At the time that *The Acadian* made its comment, Crawley was taking a series of magnificent photographs of the town of Wolfville, the Gaspereau Valley, and the Acadia College campus. These photographs represent some of the best visual records of the town's early history. Crawley lived in the house called Hillside, on Prospect Street, which was given to his father in recognition of his service to Acadia College. From that high vantage point, E. Sidney Crawley took a number of compelling photographs of the vista before him. He also documented the area's history, taking photographs, such as a series depicting the 1885 move of the Presbyterian Church from the land next to Hillside down to the Main Street (see Chapter two).

At Crawley house, the tallest to the shortest, c.1894

In 1894, E. Sidney Crawley took this whimsical photograph of relatives and family friends arranged from the tallest to the shortest. The photograph, taken at the rear of the family home on Prospect Street, shows, left to right: Ted Barss, Hal Tobin, Edith Tobin, Nell Crawley, Edmund Crawley, Bernal Sawyer, Fred Crawley, Nahni Power, Phil Sawyer, Ted Power, Edward Sawyer, Sidney Crawley, Helen Sawyer, and Hugh Crawley. Several of the photographer's children, among them Edmund, Fred, Sidney, and Hugh, are in this picture.

It was Edmund, who was born in 1884 and who died in 1977 at the age of ninety-four, who wrote a fascinating letter of recollections, quoted elsewhere, in response to the Watson Kirkconnell and Basil Silver book on Wolfville's historic houses. Edmund, later a civil engineer, met and married an Englishwoman during World War One. Her sister was married to Londoner Jack Marriott, the Crawley connection convincing the pair to move from England to Nova Scotia, where they bought the Planters' Barracks near Port Williams. Jack became Wolfville's customs officer.

George V. Rand and family, on the steps of Rand house, c.1890s

In 1855 George Valentine Rand bought a lot on Main Street and established a drugstore. He quickly became a strong citizen. In 1888 he took on the position of the town's health officer, working to establish a good water system for its citizens. In 1891 he served on a committee to rename the town streets. He served as the town postmaster and was involved in the temperance movement, becoming such a spokesman for it that liquor interests burned his barn. His interest in music led him to work with different church choirs.

In this photograph, George V. Rand is shown second from the right. To his right is his son, Aubrey V. Rand, who worked with him in the drugstore business from 1896 until George's death in 1908, at which time Aubrey ran the business on his own. Next to Aubrey is his wife, Mary, while their son, Fred, is in front. The woman to the right is labelled on the picture as an aunt. George V. Rand owned much of the land between Highland and Gaspereau avenues, bounded by the business properties along Main Street on the north and the buildings on Acadia Street on the south. For a time the area was known as "Rand's Field." Rand donated to the town the land needed for a street running up from Main Street to Acadia Street, proposing to call the road Rand Avenue, but the town fathers preferred the name Linden Avenue.

Rand children on Linden Avenue, c.1900

The children in this lovely, poignant picture are said to be those of Aubrey Valentine and Mary Rand. They are sharing what could be a glass of lemonade, through straws, in the yard of the Rand's Linden Avenue home. The girl, Marjorie Lydia, was born on November 8, 1897, but died just three years and two months later. Her brother, Fred, was born in 1894. A note in *The Acadian* on January 4, 1901, said that people were sympathizing deeply with the Rands on the severe illness of their little daughter. "As we go to press no hope is entertained of her recovery."

The next issue, on January 11, said that Marjorie, after being troubled for some weeks with whooping cough which developed into tubercular meningitis, "passed away early Saturday morning." Her death was a sad blow to the bereaved parents. "Little Marjorie was an exceptionally bright child, and with her winning ways made everyone love her." A large number of people assembled to show their sympathy, the service conducted by Baptist pastor Hugh R. Hatch being "of a most touching character." Besides Fred and Marjorie, there were three other children in the family: Theodore, born in 1900; Gilbert, born in 1902; and Aubrey, born in 1905.

Their parents had married on August 28, 1893, in the Baptist church in Canard. Mary had been Mary Lavinia Barnaby of Upper Dyke. Aubrey was described in the local newspaper as "our popular and rising young druggist and townsman." The church was full long before the ceremony started. Mary, described as being "pretty and charming," had her cousin, Mattie Barnaby, Halifax, as bridesmaid. Best man was John Jones, Wolfville. After the wedding, Aubrey and Mary drove to Kentville, where they boarded the 10:35 train for a honeymoon in Boston. "It is announced," *The Acadian* said, "that they will return to their home in Wolfville about the middle of September." Aubrey died in 1933, and Mary in 1956.

Rev. Kenneth Hind, rector, St. John's Church of England, c.1890s

In 1893, a notice appeared in the newspaper that K.C. Hind, son of Dr. Hind of Windsor, had been elected rector of the Parish of Horton. Hind, who had a Master of Arts, was inducted by the Lord Bishop of Nova Scotia on October 20, 1893. His church in east Wolfville was very old, having been consecrated in 1818. Hind served as rector until 1899. In this photograph he is shown sitting on the verandah of the Rand house, on Linden Avenue.

Picnic by ferry at Partridge Island, c.1890s

Picnics were a theme in the earliest days of Wolfville's history. *The Acadian* always carried stories about one picnic or another. Sometimes the picnics were major affairs with hundreds of people, and sometimes they were just a small group. At times, the picnics involved a ferry ride from Wolfville as far as Kingsport or Partridge Island, near Parrsboro. There were always good connections between Parrsboro and Wolfville, as Parrsboro was at one time a part of Kings County.

The temperance movement, very strong in the area, often held events across the Minas Basin. In September 1894 the Evangeline Division held its annual picnic in the form of an excursion on the steamer *Hiawatha*, with Parrsboro as the destination. Embarkation was at Horton Landing, Grand Pré. A light rain started to fall as the ferry prepared to leave, but the intrepid company "was not to be daunted with a few drops of rain," as *The Acadian* reported. Some boys cast off the moorings and the *Hiawatha* moved smoothly to the mouth of the Gaspereau River, where years before English ships lay waiting to carry the Acadians into exile. However, as the *Hiawatha* passed Boot Island, which lies to the northeast of Evangeline Beach, a steady drizzle set in, continuing while the picnic-goers passed Blomidon.

The clouds hung heavy over Partridge Island when the ferry arrived. Some of the people took teams of horses for the village, others took a hotel room on the island, and still others remained aboard the *Hiawatha* to eat their meal. By now the wind was blowing a gale and rain squalls obliterated Blomidon. A man from the village pitched a tent nearby, stocking it with liquor, but there were no takers among the temperance crowd. By six in the evening it was time to leave, though the night looked bad. The excursionists decided to take their chances, the skipper saying he would do his best. They set off: "The water is lumpy and the steamer wobbles and the rail is soon lined with victims." The *Hiawatha* made it safely to Boot Island and then to Horton Landing, where it docked, but it could go no farther, and the passengers had to remain on board all night. Younger people gathered at one end of the ship's saloon and giggled and chattered through most of the night. When morning came it was sunny. Before long there was hot tea and a good breakfast for all, and then the *Hiawatha* set sail for Wolfville, landing the party safely at the wharf. "The prevailing opinion is that it wasn't such a bad time after all," *The Acadian* concluded.

Stephen Woodworth Eaton: A Planter family and its roots, c.1897

Stephen Woodworth Eaton was a dental surgeon born in 1841 in Lower Canard. His parents were Leonard and Elizabeth Eaton. Leonard was the son of William Eaton, born in 1786; William was the son of Elisha Eaton, born in 1757 in Tolland, Connecticut, a son of David Eaton, who had thirteen children. Four of these children were born in Connecticut, and the rest in Cornwallis, after David moved as a Planter to take up lands left by the Acadians.

In this photograph, Stephen Woodworth Eaton is shown with his wife Elizabeth. Behind, left to right, are Rufus Sanford Eaton, born in 1875, who farmed near Canning; Leslie Emerson Eaton, born in 1877, who became a dentist in India and Wolfville; and Eugene Brayton Eaton, born in 1879, who also became a dentist in India and Wolfville. The girl in the front is Ethel Evelina Eaton, who married Alfred Little and died in 1919. Ethel's sister, Angie Adelia Eaton, the oldest, is not in the picture, having already left home. She married the Reverend Charles B. Freeman, one of their children being Olive Evangeline Freeman. In 1953 Olive married John George Diefenbaker, who became prime minister of Canada in 1957.

Evangeline Beach, Grand Pré.   Yours Sincerely

Recreation at Evangeline Beach, c.1907

The favourite summer destination for people from Wolfville was often Evangeline Beach, located east of Wolfville and across the Grand Pré dykes. At the end of the summer of 1895, *The Acadian* carried a story about a swimming tournament at Evangeline Beach. The newspaper said the beach presented a lively appearance the previous Saturday afternoon. Wolfville had turned out en masse, creating a big demand on the livery stables: "Every team that could be pressed into service was in use and a number of persons who would have liked to have been there were unable to procure a conveyance," the paper informed its readers. "Besides the attractions of the tournament the number of visitors was swelled by a mammoth picnic from Canard and Sheffield's Mills. It is estimated that over one thousand people were present. Long Island probably never saw such a crowd of people before."

This photograph shows what it might have been like to have been on the beach that day. *The Acadian* noted that while the day was not an especially pleasant one, the skies being overcast, the tide was well up to the banks. A raft for diving had been constructed and a number of boats were sailing beside the beach. As well, "The gasoline launch, with a party on board, presented a pretty appearance." The newspaper carried social notes from Evangeline Beach in its edition of July 7, 1899, noting that "the cottage occupied by Mr. Thomson, of the People's Bank, has been given the name of Dingwall, while Prof. Sawyer and family occupy Point Pleasant. Prof. Davis and wife, of Boston, who spent last summer at the Beach, have returned to Cottage D'Almaine. Quite an addition has been made to the northern end of the restaurant—the front considerably enlarged."

Evangeline Beach in the 1940s

This photograph shows the busy Evangeline Beach in the 1940s. Its success was the result of the efforts begun in 1895: a story in *The Acadian* in August of that year noted that the proprietors of Evangeline Beach were doing all in their power to make the area a pleasant resort. "The splendid beach, convenient bathing houses and restaurant, and the drive through beautiful and historic Grand Pré, make it a delightful means of enjoyment," the newspaper said. "Numbers of tourists and townspeople are every day conveyed to and fro, all of whom express themselves as delighted with the bathing facilities and excellent accommodation afforded by the genial and obliging managers, Messrs. Rockwell and Patriquin, to whom much credit is due for making this beautiful spot one of the finest watering places in the Province." *The Acadian* was referring to Frank P. Rockwell and Charles A. Patriquin, who were both busy with the life of the town, serving together on such organizations as the Board of Trade and the Town Improvement Association. Rockwell was very much involved in what is now called the hospitality industry, operating the Acadia Seminary Hotel in the summers in the ladies' seminary, and erecting the Acadia Villa Hotel at the corner of Linden Avenue and Acadia Street in 1901.

By the end of August of 1895 more than five thousand people had been to Evangeline Beach. Attractions included swimming, band concerts, boating and the restaurant, which featured ice cream, fruits and other refreshments. Advertisements for the beach gave the times for high tides for the coming week and promised five hours of bathing at each tide. Teams of horses carried visitors to the beach on a daily basis, and those interested in booking tickets were invited to contact Rockwell at the Wolfville Book Store. By the end of the century, the newspaper reported that "the merry-go-round will be put up shortly and will be run all summer. It is expected that the Wolfville band will play at the Beach on Friday, July 14th, and that the Wolfville or Hantsport band will be at the Beach once every fortnight during the summer." A hotel was built in 1900.

The Evangeline Beach property was sold in 1909 to W. Marshall Black, who publicized the resort and built additional cottages, as well as a large dance hall with a stage, later called the Starlight Room. Eventually there were twenty cottages, a stable for forty horses, picnic areas and tennis courts (Bishop).

Let's go to Watson's, c.1900s

In the late 1890s, Hugh Watson opened a candy store and ice cream parlour in Wolfville. According to an advertisement in *The Athenaeum* in December 1899, Watson's sold choice fruits and confectionery. Advertising in the same issue was E.B. Shaw's, next to Watson's, which sold custom-made boots and shoes. The photograph was in a photograph album owned by Lucretia Florence Nicholson and donated to the Esther Clark Wright Archives, Acadia University. The picture was entitled "Let's go to Watson's," which appears to be the building just behind the horse and buggy.

 The Athenaeum was still carrying ads for Watson's a quarter century later. In November 1925, the advertisement for Watson's Ice Cream Parlour read "fruits, confectionery, ice cream, sodas and college ices, hot drinks, light lunches and home-made candy for the winter months."

H. M. WATSON

DEALER IN

Choice Fruits and Confectionery, Ice Cream, Ice Cream Sodas and College Ices.

OYSTERS and HOT DRINKS
Served in Winter Months.

Private Ice Cream Parlors
Up Stairs.

MOVED OCT. 1

TO A. J. WOODMAN'S NEW BRICK BUILDING, - EAST OF POST OFFICE

John Frederic and Minnie Herbin in their library at home, c.1900

In this priceless photograph John Frederic Herbin reads in his library, while Minnie, also reading, looks up at the camera from a comfortable spot in a hammock. It could be said that Herbin was Wolfville's Renaissance man. He was a writer, outdoorsman, geologist, sportsman and merchant. He wrote a number of books, including histories, novels, poetry and even a guidebook for visitors to the Grand Pré area. He called himself the last of the Acadians, "the only descendant of the exiled people who lived in the Grand Pré of the Acadians," and was very sensitive to the ways in which the history of the Acadians was interpreted. Herbin thought Longfellow's portrayal of the Acadian way of life in Evangeline was accurate, and resented the fact that much of what had been written about the expulsion in 1755 appeared to be an attempt to show that the Acadians themselves were "largely to blame for the fate that befell them."

Herbin worked to preserve the memory of the Acadians, acquiring the land on which the national historic site now sits, promoting the idea of a park and erecting a stone cross, built from the stones of the old Acadian church. On Sunday, December 29, 1923, he left home at three in the afternoon to go duck hunting on the dykes. When he failed to return at nightfall his family became worried. As The Acadian reported the events, his son, Fred, went to investigate on returning from work "and found the body of his father in the Wickwire lane, not more than a hundred feet from Main Street, where he had apparently dropped and expired without a struggle."

Minnie Rounsefell Simpson, of Grand Pré, married John Herbin in 1896. John's father was a native of France and his mother a descendant of the Acadians, a part of the Robichaud family that settled on St. Mary's Bay, Digby County.

The Wolfville Shamrocks, county champions, 1907

This Edson Graham photograph shows the Wolfville Shamrocks, champions of the Kings County Junior Hockey League in 1907. In the back row are: Leonard Eaton, right wing; John Gould, rover; Jud Harris, centre; and Aubrey Dakin, left wing. Those in the middle row are Roland Gibbons, business manager; Frank Godfrey, captain and centre; and Lloyd Woodman, president and treasurer. In front are Harry Fraser, point; and Harry Sleep, goal.

For three years running the Shamrocks were champions of the Kings County Junior Hockey League. In the year this picture was taken, *The Acadian* reported that the team had lost a game in Yarmouth in February, but defeated the Yarmouth players in a return match a few days later, by a score of 12-5. Other games were noted during the winter, and by March the newspaper said that the third game of the championships had been played between Canning and the Shamrocks at the Evangeline Rink, built the year before. The Canning team arrived late, the game not starting until eight in the evening. From the start the Shamrocks had the advantage, and when the game ended, the newspaper said, the score was the Shamrocks 8, Canning 5. The Shamrocks were champions again.

Sally and Harry Starr and their dog, Starr's point, c.1911

For years, one of the best-known shops in Wolfville was the Sally Starr Gift Shop, located on the north side of Main Street in a building constructed in 1858 for tailor Joseph Weston. It was known as much for the teaching that went on in the shop as for what it sold; Sally Starr herself was a skilled craftswoman and weaver. Joseph Weston originally owned the shop until 1904 and carried on a merchant tailor business. Later, his adopted daughter, Katie, turned the store into a candy shop. James Fry, from the Wolfville Heritage Advisory Committee, writes in *The Advertiser* that Katie Weston loved nature and spent many hours gathering flowers, berries and mushrooms on the Beckwith, Wickwire and Grand Pré dykes, either selling or giving them to customers or friends. Architect Leslie R. Fairn owned the building from 1929 to 1969, and for a time it served as a plumber's shop for Edward J. Delaney.

Sally Starr, who was born Charlotte Evelyna, died in 1983; Harry, her brother, in 1990. Kirkconnell and Silver, in *Wolfville Historic Homes*, note that the Sally Starr shop had a good deal of the Old World atmosphere. They write that Sally's maternal grandparents, Samuel and Elizabeth Dupont Morse Prat, had lived in the building for a time. Sally and Harry were the children of Richard Sidney Starr and his wife, May Rosina. Sally's childhood was spent at Willowbank Farm, Starr's Point, which had passed down from Richard's father, C.R.H. Starr.

The Governor General, the Duke of Connaught, visits Wolfville in 1912

An event of major importance in Wolfville occurred in 1912, when the town received a vice-regal visit from the Duke and Duchess of Connaught, accompanied by the Princess Patricia. The photograph shows the car carrying the duke and duchess arriving at a reception stand built especially for the occasion on the Acadia campus. The duke was the son of Queen Victoria and brother of King Edward VII. He was governor general in Canada between 1911 and 1916.

The royal party arrived by train at the Wolfville station, with a guard of honour provided by the Boy Scouts (next photograph). A parade carrying the visitors wound its way through town, to Gaspereau Avenue, across Acadia Street, and to the university. The day was a beautiful one and the town was decked out with flags, arches and welcoming signs. At Acadia they were greeted by a party that included University President George B. Cutten, Mayor J.D. Chambers, and "the town councillors and ladies, and representatives from the Institutions, consisting of…the Deans, the Principals of the Seminary and Academy and ladies" (*Acadia Bulletin*). The governor general, in return, expressed interest in the university and asked questions about the history and conditions at Acadia. Immediately afterwards, the royal party took a drive, looking at the Gaspereau Valley from the Ridge, then visiting Grand Pré to see the old French willows, Evangeline Beach, Greenwich and Port Williams, Starr's Point, Canard, Upper Dyke and Kentville. The photograph was taken by Jack Stewart, who lived in Grand Pré and was killed in World War Two.

Boy Scouts on parade, 1912

These Boy Scouts march along Main Street in ceremonies to honour the visit of the Duke of Connaught in 1912. Wolfville was home to a Boy Scout troop just four years after the movement was founded by Lord Baden-Powell. In April 1911, the troop was formed when a group of boys met at the home of E. Percy Brown, who became one of Nova Scotia's best-known scout leaders (Davison, 1985). The scouts provided a guard of honour for the Duke of Connaught the next year. It was particularly appropriate that they did so, since the duke was a great supporter of the Scout movement and served as its president.

By 1913 the scouts were meeting in their own quarters, in a building donated by J.D. Chambers behind his store. By 1920 the Girl Guides were also meeting, organized by Mrs. Percy Brown and Jennie Tamplin. An article about the history of scouting in Wolfville, published in *The Advertiser*, Kentville, in 1971, says that from the beginning camping was a major part of scout and guide activities. Regular troop camping began at Black River Lake in 1912, while the first camp at Sunken Lake was held in 1920. Camping at Sunken Lake became an experience treasured in the memories of generations of Wolfville Boy Scouts and Girl Guides. Percy Brown obtained land for a permanent camp in 1921, and erected a long, wooden cookhouse the next year. Log cabins were built, canoes were acquired, and swimming and boating facilities established. Many young people, after growing too old for scouts, returned to the camp as junior leaders and introduced their children to the movement.

Wolfville girls and their sports teams, 1914 and 1925

Young women in Wolfville were not about to let the men play all of the sports. Reports of female hockey teams in action dot the pages of the local newspaper from early in the century, and these girls on a team in 1914 show the kind of attire they used to wear. One has on her jersey the letters WHC, which stood for the Wolfville Hockey Club. Unfortunately no names were put on the photograph, which is in the collection of the Randall House Museum. *Mud Creek* identifies the woman at the top left as Violet Sleep, who was the daughter of hardware merchant Lewis W. Sleep. Violet married Lawrence Williams, of Halifax, in a wedding at her home on Summer Street on June 8, 1921.

A little more than a decade after 1914, Wolfville High School teacher and coach Ella Jean Warren sits among her team members in this photograph of the WHS girls' basketball team. In the bottom row on the left is Gertrude Phinney, later a nationally recognized athlete. On the right is Virginia MacLean. Behind her, left, is Marion Eaton, and next to her Waittie Stackhouse. Behind are Helen Ingraham, left, and Edna Doyle, right, and on top is Annie Fitch. The coach, Ella Warren, was born in Prince Edward Island and taught in Wolfville between 1923 and 1926. She received her BA from Acadia the year before taking up her teaching position at Wolfville High. Later, she became Mrs. E. Wallace Archer and lived in Australia.

The 1925 Wolfville High School girls' basketball team

Wolfville in World War One, c.1916

This storefront recruiting office in Wolfville, set up to recruit young men for the Highland Brigade, shows the appeals being made to get them to sign up to fight in World War One. A number of Wolfville men answered the call; the first to be killed overseas was William Arthur Elderkin. In all, more than thirty of the town's young people gave their lives. They are remembered by the monument in their honour, which sits outside the post office.

The women in the community were generally expected to provide support from their hometown. They prepared food, knitted socks, collected clothing, raised money, worked with the Red Cross, corresponded and kept the homes for their loved ones overseas. They formed a club called the Give Service Girls, which raised money in a variety of ways for the war effort. Vernita Keddy Murphy, in *Chronicles of Another Era*, says they had a tea and lunchroom, and a music room, on Main Street: "The girls wore white bib aprons over their frocks and white kerchiefs on their heads," she writes. The Give Service Girls' president was Mary Black, daughter of W. Marshall Black, who had been Wolfville's mayor. Mary went on to become head of the provincial government's handcraft division and was Nova Scotia's only master weaver, and wrote a book still in use today, *A New Key to Weaving*.

olfville detachment D. Co. 219ᵗʰ Batt. Leaving for Aldershot Camp

Wolfville and Acadia go to war, 1916

The town of Wolfville and Acadia University united in a patriotic fervour to fight in World War One. Students and townspeople alike volunteered. The Man from Grand Pré, Robert Borden, was the prime minister leading the war effort. George B. Cutten, the university's president, played an active leadership role: he was made a captain in charge of a company formed by the university. Forty students volunteered. The first to enlist was Frederick C. Manning, who was a senior in the spring of 1916. He was also captain of the Officers' Training Corps and the valedictorian of his class.

The decision had been made to recruit a Highland Brigade in Nova Scotia, a feat accomplished within two weeks. The company shown in this panoramic photograph was part of the 219th, which was a brigade made up of men from Halifax and the western counties of Nova Scotia. M. Stuart Hunt, who wrote *Nova Scotia's Part in the Great War*, spoke of the historic recruiting tour made by Lieutenant Colonel Allison H. Borden and Captain Cutten, beginning in Lunenburg on February 26, 1916, and ending in Wolfville on March 12. Accompanied by a military band, they went by train, stopping at all of the South Shore towns on the Halifax and South Western Railway, as well as those on the DAR. "The extraordinary enthusiasm aroused by their speeches and by the martial strains of the band formed an epoch in each community." Recruits were taken from their home towns to Camp Aldershot, outside Kentville, on June 1.

In this Edson Graham photograph, actually two sides of a panoramic photo, Wolfville Detachment D Company, of the 219th Battalion, is formed at Wolfville station, about to leave for Aldershot. In the picture on the left, the local Boy Scout troop provides an honour guard, as one of the scouts plays a drum. The men are lined up with their duffel bags. On the right is the crowd at the station, including all of the school children, assembled in the sunshine for the momentous occasion.

That summer Aldershot was open to the public: eight thousand people from around the province took the railway to visit the camp. "Nothing," Hunt said, "revealed more clearly how tenderly the thought of the Province centred about the rows of white tents, where the flower of its manhood was encamped." There were brigades from all over the province at Aldershot, as well as the 97th, which was made up of men from the United States who had come to "share in the fight for the freedom of the world." On Friday, September 26, the men were ordered overseas. Leaves were cancelled, Hunt wrote, and an order was issued that no one was to have the privilege of seeing his home again. The men, who had counted on a chance to say farewell, were stunned: "The men were resolute to see their homes, many of which were in the vicinity of the Camp. Every effort was made to stop them. Cordons with fixed bayonets were placed around the station at Kentville. But all to no purpose. The majority simply rose and went. They hired motor cars, mounted horses, or even walked. For a moment there was a sense of alarm and humiliation, which quickly changed to confidence and pride as the men came streaming back, satisfied that they had seen their friends, and ready to do their duty in facing the foe."

The 219th sailed early in October, representing the finest sacrifice ever made from the western part of the province (Hunt). "Fisherman, farmer, lumberman, student, minister, lawyer, doctor drilled side by side in a spirit of comradeship seldom excelled." With them was Frederick C. Manning, who, on April 9, 1917, was in the battle of Vimy Ridge. He was struck by a machine gun bullet and lay on the battlefield in snow and sleet. He died in Boulogne, France, on April 14. More than thirty men from the town and more than sixty from the university died in the war. When the troops returned, Acadia was the only university in Canada which provided them with a year's free tuition.

Wolfville, George Cutten, and the great Halifax Explosion, 1917

Captain George B. Cutten, the university president, talks with student Bessie Lockhart in 1916. A year later Wolfville was called upon to assist the wounded after the Halifax Explosion of December 6, and Cutten threw himself into the job. In a letter he wrote two months later, he described the efforts made by Wolfville people in the aftermath of the explosion.

Cutten said that at nine o'clock on the morning of December 6, the Wolfville exchange was trying to get Halifax on the phone when all communication stopped. Thirty minutes later, word came from Truro about the explosion of the French munitions ship *Mont Blanc*, which had collided in Halifax Harbour with the Belgian relief ship *Imo*, leading to the deaths of over two thousand people. Ninety minutes later Wolfville was told that a special train would be coming into the station to pick up doctors and nurses, and by the time it pulled in medical people were ready at the station. Cutten himself was among them. Doctors George E. DeWitt, M.R. Elliot, and J.W. Allen were on the platform, in addition to the following nurses: Mrs. Grace Andrews, Mrs. Charles A. Patriquin, Miss Ethel Brown, Miss Jessie Parker, Miss Georgie Miner, Miss Nellie DeWitt, and Mrs. Greta Harris. From the university, Dr. Cutten was accompanied by Dr. W.L. Archibald and Dr. W.A. Coit, together with other citizens, among them H.E. Calkin, the druggist.

The train pulled out of the station. In Windsor, more doctors and nurses were picked up. At Windsor Junction they saw the Number 10 train from Halifax, loaded with wounded people and on its way to Truro. One of those on the train was Major C.E. Avery DeWitt, a doctor, who had been on his way to Halifax on the morning train from Wolfville when the explosion occurred. He had boarded the train carrying the wounded in order to provide medical assistance. At Windsor Junction his father, Dr. George DeWitt, and his sister, Nellie DeWitt, transferred to the Truro-bound train and worked on the wounded until it got to Truro. Major DeWitt had morphia and a hypodermic needle in his case, and they used sheets from the sleeping cars as bandages. "Undoubtedly many more in this train would have died from exposure and haemorrhage had not these doctors been with them," Cutten said.

The others continued on the train to Halifax, where they went to work helping the wounded. They were assigned to various places, including Camp Hill Hospital, the Imperial Oil Company building, and the Knights of Columbus Hall. That evening, Acadia seminary nurses Mary Rust and Florence Saunders arrived, and were assigned to work on the USS *Old Colony*, a ship from the United States pressed into service as a 150-bed hospital. They remained there for eleven days, until the *Old Colony* had to leave port and the patients were transferred. Over the next few days, the Red Cross Society in Wolfville gathered clothing and bandage material, sending large quantities to Halifax. As well, a number of refugees were given shelter and care in Wolfville. Wolfville helped in other ways: by February 6, the School for the Deaf of Halifax had reopened its doors in Wolfville, in spaces provided by Acadia University. Later, Dr. Cutten worked with the Halifax Relief Commission as director of rehabilitation.

Victory parade at the Wolfville Station, November 11, 1918

A Wolfville girl readies her decorated pony in front of the Wolfville train station for the big parade through town celebrating the end of the Great War. Decorated cars can be seen behind her. The story of the day from the perspective of the students at the university was told well by *The Athenaeum*, which said that at five-thirty in the morning on November 11, 1918, the college bell began ringing, waking the students at Horton Academy, Acadia Ladies Seminary and Acadia University. The students scrambled to get up, dressed quickly, and a half hour later, university president George B. Cutten led the entire student body in a service of thanksgiving at the assembly hall.

The announcement was made that classes were suspended for the day. After breakfast the student body gathered once again, in College Hall, to sing patriotic songs and listen to the professors, who addressed the students on behalf of each of the allied nations. At three that afternoon the whole student body lined up with the people of Wolfville at the train station for the grand street parade, which wound through the streets of town. In the evening there was a huge bonfire on the Acadia campus, a prominent feature of which was the burning of a large effigy of "Kaiser Bill," prepared for the occasion by the engineers. A large supply of skyrockets and other fireworks were set off, then games were played around the bonfire. The entire day, it was said, was a complete success in every way.

Yokohama Maid, Wolfville, N.S. May 9. 1918

GRAHAM PHOTO.

Yokohama Maid, at the Wolfville Opera House, May 1918

In 1911, the Wolfville Opera House was established in the building that later housed the Orpheum and Acadia theatres. The Opera House, owned by W. Marshall Black, could seat over five hundred, had steam heat, electric lights and a telephone. Its stage had moveable scenery and dressing rooms backstage, and a pianist accompanied the silent pictures (Davison, 1985). The big feature, however, was live theatre, something that has always caught the imagination of Wolfville.

This photograph above shows the production of *Yokohama Maid*, put on in the Opera House on Thursday evening, May 9, and Saturday afternoon, May 11, 1918. It was a large, rollicking production directed by Cora Pierce Richmond, a teacher of singing. Mrs. Richmond had come to Wolfville to teach music at the ladies' seminary, and in 1917 established her own studio in the town. She also had a studio in Truro. Music was by the Kentville Orchestra under the direction of Burpee Bishop. Those in the cast were Lewis G. Pick, John Gertridge, Lewis McNeil, R. St. Clair Hopgood, A.J. Mason, Evelyn Neily, Mildred Harvey, O. Marie Wilson, Marjorie Chute, and Gwen Rowe. There was also a chorus made up of men and women. The accompanists were Lewis McNeil and Miss Viola Bishop.

Rev. R.F. Dixon in his church, c.1920s

Glen Hancock writes about Rev. Richard Ferguson Dixon in his reminiscences about growing up in Wolfville, *My Real Name is Charley*. The first work he ever did for pay was for Dr. Dixon, when he picked potato bugs from his garden. "Dr. Dixon was the Anglican rector," he writes, "and he liked Black Horse Ale. I could tell by the empty bottles outside his back door." The Anglicans sometimes seemed less straight-laced than the Baptists.

Dr. Dixon had taken over St. John's from the Rev. Kenneth Hinds in 1899, serving as rector until 1931. In 1926, *The Acadian* said that no man in Wolfville was more generally respected than R.F. Dixon, who had so long been among them, the newspaper said, that he had become an authority on local affairs: "He is regarded by everybody as a friend and takes a very lively interest in all that affects the welfare of the community and its people." Dixon was born in England, arriving in Canada in 1873. He spent time in Ontario harvesting crops and working as a teacher before entering divinity school, after which he held parishes in Ontario before coming to Nova Scotia in 1894. In 1899 he was appointed to the Parish of Horton. He was a noted writer, contributing to church publications as well as to the *Montreal Star*, *Saturday Night*, *Canadian Magazine*, *The Standard*, and *The Canadian Bookman*. He was married to Bessie Geary, daughter of John Geary, who built both roads and railways in Ontario, and who had an important part in putting down the Mackenzie Rebellion of 1837.

Hockey on the Wolfville dykes, c.1930s

Wolfville boys play a game of pick-up hockey on a pond below Acadia University, using boots to mark the goal. In the background are University Hall and the War Memorial Gymnasium. It is said that the first game of hockey in Wolfville was played on a patch of good ice north of Main Street; Edmund Crawley, who wrote about his memories of Wolfville, said that the game was called hurley then. Johnson's Hollow was apparently also a good place to skate—and on the dykes one could skate all the way from below Main Street to the edge of the dyke.

Hockey fascinated the townspeople of Wolfville. By mid-century, people were following the fortunes of the Wolfville Falcons, whose goalie in the 1960s was Dave Graham, also a member of the varsity team at Acadia. Graham taught science at Wolfville High School and went on to be vice-principal, later becoming headmaster of a private school in St. Andrew's, New Brunswick. Young people from Wolfville often gathered at the rink, calling themselves "rink rats" and looking for jobs clearing the ice during Falcons or Acadia Axemen games. Money could even be made from the sport: A.V. Rand had a factory for making hockey sticks in a building he had set up in cooperation with Roy Jodrey, located just west of the railway station. It burned on September 13, 1923, with a loss of valuable machinery and the materials for the season's hockey sticks. The players in the picture are identified only as Otto '34, John '37, Don '35, Vern '36, Crafty Taylor, '36, and Dave.

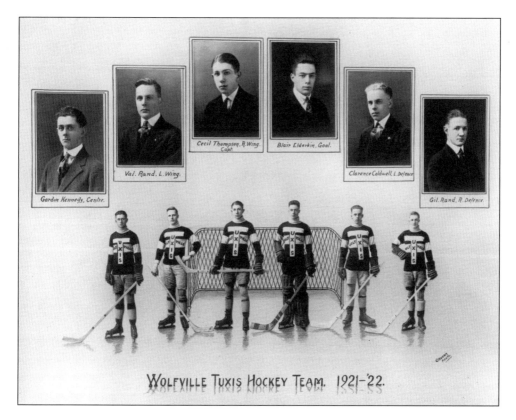

WOLFVILLE TUXIS HOCKEY TEAM. 1921-'22.

The Wolfville Tuxis hockey team, c.1922

The Tuxis movement was associated with the Boy Scouts and stood for Clean Speech, Clean Sport and Clean Habits. The first game played by the Tuxis boys was held in January 1920, when the Canning Scouts and Tuxis Boys visited to play the Wolfville Tuxis Boys. With the Scout band in attendance, Wolfville defeated the Canning team by a score of 10 to 4. The band played for an hour after the game.

The names under the photographs of the boys are, left to right, Gordon Kennedy, centre; Val Rand, left wing; Cecil Thompson, right wing; Blair Elderkin, goal; Clarence Coldwell, left defence; and Gil Rand, right defence.

Visiting Nova Scotia. — Nine to a car.

Tourists visit Wolfville, c.1920s

Edson Graham stepped out of his studio and took this photograph of a car with suitcases strapped to the outside. He labelled it "Visiting Nova Scotia—Nine to a car." Behind the car, to the left of the telephone pole, the Edson Graham studio can be seen, with a display of snapshots in the window.

The building to the right is the one that today houses the Kipawo Arts Centre, though it now looks much different. The *Wolfville House Inventory* says that it was built around 1914, its original owners being George and Florence Coldwell. Between 1903 and 1906 there had been a livery stable on the site, owned by William and Abbie Balcom. At the time this photograph was taken, the building was part of the town's electrical generating system, and close inspection of the photograph shows a series of electric wires running to the top. During the 1920s, when water was low at Roy Jodrey and Charles Wright's power station on the Gaspereau River, the old town system was sometimes called back into action.

Gertrude Phinney, Canadian track and field star, c.1920s

One of the outstanding athletes from Wolfville High School and Acadia University in the 1920s was Gertrude Phinney, who set Canadian records in the sprints, hurdles and broad jump. After the Halifax explosion in 1917, doctors advised Gertrude's father, Horton W. Phinney, to move his family out of the city. He looked for a home in Wolfville, finally settling on the house built by shipbuilder Rufus Burgess (now the Blomidon Inn). Eventually, Phinney, who was at one time mayor of Wolfville, exchanged that house for one on Acadia Street, so that the children did not have so far to walk to school. At Wolfville High School in the mid-twenties, Gertrude starred in basketball. This photograph shows her sitting on a tree stump at Kedge Lodge, now part of Kejimkujik National Park. Gertrude's family owned the lodge for many years.

Gertrude continued her athletic triumphs as a student at both Dalhousie and Acadia universities. Between 1927 and 1929 she was the Canadian champion in the 60-, 100-, and 220-yard dashes, and in the hurdles and the broad jump. She held Canadian records set in the sprints, winning forty-five prizes and trophies for her athletic prowess. Gertrude was invited to join the Canadian Olympic team and to compete in national and international events, but could not accept those invitations because her father understood from experts that the strenuous effort required was not good for women. In 1965 she was inducted into the Nova Scotia Sport Hall of Fame; a story written in the *Chronicle Herald* that year says that the Toronto press of the time had called her the "little, demure miss" who was "the most promising runner Canada has for the next Olympics." She won the first gold athletic D ever given by Dalhousie and won a gold A from Acadia. She competed on the women's basketball teams at both Acadia and Dalhousie, and was the captain of the women's tumblers team at Acadia.

Gertrude married F.B. Young, had a career as a teacher of home economics in the Annapolis Valley, and now lives in Wolfville. Her second husband was Thomas Beattie. Her children are Bette, Fred, Harold, Carol and Rick.

The Nova Scotia Tennis Tournament, Wolfville, August 1927

Tennis was a major sport in the town of Wolfville during the 1920s, with a great many players from both town and university playing at a competitive level. In 1927 the provincial tennis championships were held for the first time in Wolfville, on the seven tennis courts that formed a part of the Acadia Athletic Field near the dykes, below the university. Among those competing in mixed doubles were Dr. Leslie Eaton and Gertrude Phinney, listed on the back as occupying the far court in this picture taken by Edson Graham. Eaton, who had been one of the organizers of the tournament, and Phinney, who would shortly be a national track and field champion, defeated a couple from North Sydney but were knocked out of the tournament by a pair from the South End Tennis Club in Halifax.

Players from across Nova Scotia were enthusiastic about the reception they received in Wolfville. As *The Acadian* noted, all visiting players and friends were grateful for the way in which they had been entertained and were appreciative "of the beautiful environment of the tennis courts, and especially of the excellent arrangement as provided by the University authorities in connection with Whitman Hall, Dining room, and Memorial Gymnasium." The players used the gymnasium as a clubhouse and made good use of the swimming pool and showers. The tournament's success led to a suggestion that Wolfville "be made the Wimbledon of Nova Scotia and have the Provincial tournament here every year." As soon as the provincial championships were over, the Maritime championships were held at the same venue.

Dr. Leslie E. Eaton and family, c.1926

Dr. Leslie Emerson Eaton sits on the steps of his Gaspereau Avenue home, surrounded by his children, shortly after the death of his wife, Minetta. Eaton was born in Canning in 1877, attended Kings County Academy in Kentville, and went on to study at Acadia, where he was a star with the university track team, graduating in 1903. In the same class was Minetta Vaughan Crandall. In 1905 Leslie received his doctorate of dental surgery from the University of Pennsylvania, and in October married Minetta, before moving to Madras, India. In India Leslie joined his brother Eugene, who had a dental practice there. Dentistry was something of a family trait: Leslie and Eugene's father, Stephen, had been a dentist, and Eugene's sons John and Karl both became dentists. They too practised in India before opening offices in Kings County.

When the Eatons returned from India in 1920, Leslie and Eugene opened Eaton Brothers, Dentists, in the Eaton Block, formerly the McKenna Block, on Main Street. Leslie became heavily involved in the life of the town, serving on Town Council, as chairman of the school board and as a member of the Acadia University Board of Governors. He still found time to hunt, fish (*The Acadian* reported in June of 1926 that he had caught three salmon below the power dam on the Gaspereau River) and compete in championship tennis tournaments. Minetta too was active. She had been born in 1880 in Tatamagouche, graduated from Horton Academy and Acadia, was principal of the Chester Public School and taught at Acadia Seminary before her marriage. On returning from India, she was regent of the Sir Robert Borden Chapter of the IODE, a member of the executive of the Victorian Order of Nurses, and was active with the Acadia Alumni and with the Wolfville Baptist Church.

Minetta contracted influenza in April 1926, dying five days later. The Halifax *Morning Chronicle* reported that, with two of her children at Acadia and Leslie on the board of governors, the university cancelled its classes during the service, so that students and faculty could attend the funeral. In this photograph Leslie is shown with Barbara, left; Elizabeth, centre; and Gerald, right. Barbara was an English teacher for many years, Elizabeth trained as a dietitian and ran the university dining hall, and Gerald was a chemist who worked in the United States.

Wolfville High, Valley League Champions in 1929

Edson Graham took this portrait of the Wolfville High School football team in 1929, when the boys were champions of the Annapolis Valley League. It was a good year for the school, as the hockey team also won the championships, with many of the same players. The school's vice principal, R.W. Johnson, coached both sports.

Captain of both teams was William Oliver, son of Clifford and Dorothy (Moore) Oliver, who went on to graduate with a Bachelor of Divinity from Acadia, to serve as pastor of the Cornwallis Street Baptist Church in Halifax from 1937 to 1962, and eventually to be recognized with honorary doctorates from both Acadia and the University of Kings College. Shown in the picture are, left to right, back row: Kenneth Whitman, John Eaton, William Oliver, Lloyd MacPherson, Lloyd Shaw, Vic Duncanson, Maurice Hennigar, and T. Baird; middle row: Rex Porter, John Roach, Arnold Tedford, Vice Principal R.W. Johnson, A. Duncanson, Keith Warren, and H. MacLeod. In the front are William Lockhart, Ron Forbes, Ronald Coldwell, and R. Lightfoot.

The Wolfville Business Girls' Club, c.1930s

In October 1930, a group of twenty young women from Wolfville met to establish the Wolfville Girls' Club. They gathered at the home of Jean Stewart, whose idea it was to start the club. Maxine Williams was chosen as president, Jean Stewart as vice-president, and Sabra Wetmore as secretary-treasurer. They decided to call themselves the Odds and Ends Club, but soon changed the name to the Wolfville Business Girls' Club. There would be meetings once a week and dues would be five cents at each meeting.

The idea of the club was to perform services for the community. A month after the club formed, members were busy packing Christmas boxes for the needy. A history of the club, presented at an anniversary dinner held in 1972, said that "during the first years the club was very social—there were molasses candy parties, pyjama parties, skating and swimming parties, Valentine and Hallowe'en parties, sleigh rides, corn boils, drama productions and of course, Christmas parties....In 1932 a Hallowe'en party (with men yet!) was held in the Temperance Hall and the best costume prizes were won by Olive Greenough and Lovett Bishop." The history noted that during those years the very charming girls were whisked to the altar with regularity and the club put on a number of wedding showers. There were serious times, too: in February 1933 the club was addressed on the issues of the day by George C. Nowlan, who was then member of the provincial legislative assembly for the area.

This picture shows the Wolfville Business Girls' Club and its members. From information on the back of the photograph, we can identify them as follows: back row, left to right: Esther McIntosh, Marion Whitman, Olive Greenough, Francis Olford, Blanche Angus, Naomi VanZoost, Jean Stewart, Della Phinney, Marion Whitman, and Dorothy Stevens; middle row: Beatrice Baker, Ross Rand, Doris Regan, Daisy Coldwell, Pinky Coldwell, Bessie Coldwell, Jean Murphy Youden, Hope Redden, Virginia Tufts, and Catherine Beveridge; front row: Phyllis Barteaux, P. Fitzgerald, Helen Young, and Dorothy Burgher. (The name Marion Whitman appears twice, meaning either that there were two Marion Whitmans, or that one was misidentified.)

Freeman S. Crowell, Wolfville's long-time police chief, c.1930s

Even policemen in a quiet town like Wolfville needed a break now and then. This rare photograph shows Freeman Crowell on a camping trip; Crowell is identified on the photograph as being in the foreground, cooking. There had been a need for a police force long before Crowell's time. A celebrated murder case occurred in town in 1879, when Albert DeWolf, who had studied medicine in Scotland and then spent two years in Halifax, returned to Wolfville and found his wife unwilling to resume their marriage. He killed her, hid in the woods behind Acadia, was captured, then hanged himself in the Kentville jail before he could be brought to trial. Usually, however, wrongdoings in the town had to do with petty thievery, drunkenness, and disturbances in the streets of the town. In 1893, the year Wolfville was incorporated, *The Acadian* called for the services of a policeman. The newspaper thought there was a large amount of unnecessary noise and rowdyism during the evenings on the town streets, and offered its columns for a discussion of the matter. The next year James Toye was appointed the town's first policeman.

In 1903, when Wolfville was again without a policeman, its advertisement for one was answered by Freeman S. Crowell, a native of Lawrencetown, Halifax County. He had worked in the brickyards at Avonport and later on a farm in Canard. Vernita Keddy was eleven when she moved to Wolfville in 1916, and the presence of a policeman was one of the things she found different about her new home. He had a navy blue uniform with brass buttons, she writes in *Chronicles of Another Era*, and he seemed severe, but she soon found him friendly. "I lived in Wolfville for thirty-five years," Vernita says, "and Freeman Crowell was the only town policeman for all of those years. The town people thought of him as a member of the family." One of Crowell's jobs was to be at the station when trains came in. Sometimes his duties to the town conflicted with his responsibilities to the railway. For example, some passengers travelled by clinging between the cars or even by standing on the cowcatcher. Crowell had to run them off the train, but he always chased these "gentlemen of the road" in such a direction "as would enable them to board the train again as it was leaving town" (Gibson, 1973).

On July 7, 1941, Chief Crowell booked off sick. Over the next ten days, friends visited him at his Prospect Street home and reported him cheerful and anxious to get back to work. He died suddenly on July 17, ending a police career that spanned thirty-seven years. His job was eventually filled by Alex Kendrick, who served for thirty-four years, from 1945 until 1979.

The Wolfville Fire Department, 1938

The year 1938 was just one of many years in which the Wolfville Fire Department was called upon to fight serious fires in the town of Wolfville. The year began with a fire that started on New Year's Eve, when the building housing the Rand store burned, and continued with two fires in the Westcott building, which housed, among other businesses, Hutchinson's Taxi and F.C. Bishop's. Electrician Roy Pulsifer lost his life in the Rand fire. He and his partner E.C. Harrington had rented space in the building for six years; their store carried radios and other electrical supplies. A new brick structure, first called the Rand Block, then the Brownell Block, was built later that year as a replacement. Despite that loss, the fire department was competent and efficient. When fire broke out in the west Main Street home of Mrs. H.H. Marshall in June, fire fighters arrived to find the interior of the building "ablaze," according to the newspaper, but soon put it out.

From the community's inception, fires were a constant threat and an unfortunate occurrence in a village like Wolfville, where so many buildings were of wood frame construction. *The Acadian* agitated for a volunteer fire department soon after the newspaper's founding. In August 1884, it complained that Wolfville had no fire protection of any kind and that it was a hard matter to find even a ladder. A month later a spectacular fire destroyed the Wolfville Knitting Factory, which only four years before had received raves in *The Nova Scotian*, which said it was "producing excellent goods," making hose for men, women and children. It was owned by William Charles Archibald, but lately it had gone out of business and had been

occupied by A.C. Redden for storing pianos, organs and sewing machines. *The Acadian* said the fire was the work of an incendiary, but it certainly provided ammunition for its campaign. The paper suggested a "Hook Ladder and Axe Company," and said, "we feel confident that there are any number of young men who would be glad to organize a Volunteer Fire Co. if they got any encouragement from property holders and those who should take action on the matter."

Early in 1890, that action was taken. A fire hall was to be constructed on Main Street, east of Gaspereau Avenue, and officers were quickly elected. Chosen president was Everett W. Sawyer, son of the Acadia president, a Harvard graduate who later would be principal of Horton Academy and a town councillor. Merchant Burpee Witter was the vice-president.

This photograph was taken by Edson Graham in July 1938. The firemen are posed with their trucks in front of the duck pond. Fire Chief C.A. Brown is shown fifth from the left. The firemen are, left to right: Clarence Coldwell, Harry VanZoost, Horace Jackson, Frank Murphy, C.A. Brown (chief), Edward Fraser, Carl Angus (vice-fire chief), Val Rand, Stanley Murphy, Ross Walsh, Vernon Brown, Ralph Spencer, Gilbert Tanner, Clark Cook, Dennis Lake, Dan Rogers, Robert Rogers, Russell Whitman, John Murphy, Harry Farris, Fred Herbin, Alex Stevens, Willard Stewart, Allison Carey, Harold Spencer, Delancy Gesner, Percy Cook, Howard Whidden, Frank Dakin, and Dick Coldwell. Even this number did not represent all members of the department, as several members were absent when the picture was taken. The famous LaFrance fire engine is on the left. The picture appeared on the front page of *The Acadian* on July 21, 1938.

Rosamond DeWolfe Archibald, campaigner for better English, c.1940s

Rosamond Archibald, born in Truro in 1882, made news across Canada with her campaign for better English. She had been both the university librarian and a teacher of English at Horton Academy, and then head of the English department at the Acadia seminary. In 1921, while at the seminary, she wrote *The King's English Drill*, a book which was based on the innovative idea that the best way to teach people to speak correctly was not through the memorization of formal rules of grammar, but rather by speaking correctly. To that end, the book sets up a series of drills whereby students would become used to speaking English in the proper manner.

The Acadian editorialized about her success: "The agitation set in motion more than a year ago by Miss Rosamond Archibald, to promote a more correct use of the English language, has already produced surprising results. Miss Archibald recently returned from an extended trip, in which she went as far west as Toronto, and was much gratified by the evidences of appreciation which were everywhere manifested towards her work." The newspaper said that the campaign was providing good publicity for Wolfville as the headquarters for "Better English." It said that in her introductions at various meetings she was referred to as "coming from a town widely known and highly respected."

Some evidence of the widespread appeal of Rosamond Archibald's work can be seen in the fact that a contest called Better English Week was held at the Acadia Ladies Seminary in May 1924, involving the seminary, the Acadia Collegiate Academy, Wolfville High School and contestants from four other provinces and two American states. Rosamond Archibald, who lived on Hillside Avenue in a house called Treetops, was one of the founding members of the Wolfville Historical Society. A plaque hanging in the Randall House Museum describes her as "a Founder of the Society and an Active Promoter of its objectives." She died in May 1953.

The LaFrance fire engine at work, November 26, 1940

Fire broke out at nine-thirty in the morning in the Acadia Villa Hotel, at the corner of Linden Avenue and Acadia Street, on November 26, 1940. Plumber's blowtorches, used to thaw out frozen pipes, had ignited the building. The *Acadia Bulletin* wrote that the flames "spread with appalling rapidity and soon attained such spectacular proportions that classes in the neighbouring university buildings were deserted as students (and faculty) raced off down Acadia Street." Many of the students helped by removing hotel furnishings. By noon the roof and walls caved in, one of the tall chimneys came down, and the portico and verandah collapsed. The only reminder of the hotel today is a three-storey structure on Acadia Street, which was originally a twenty-room addition to the hotel, designed by Leslie Fairn and put up in 1919.

The 1923 LaFrance fire engine is shown mopping up after the fire was extinguished. There was excitement in the town as it arrived in Wolfville on Saturday, May 17, 1924, having been built in Toronto. It immediately passed a series of pumping tests designed by the machine's underwriters and the town manager, G.S. Stairs. Assigned to operate it were firemen Frank Murphy, Stanley Murphy, William Lynch, George Stevens, and Ralph Farris. Until recently, the LaFrance was on display at the Wolfville fire hall, but when the fire department needed the room for expansion, the LaFrance was taken to the Biggs Farm in Grand Pré, where it is today awaiting restoration.

The Wolfville High School orchestra, c.1928

Few young people who went through the Wolfville Schools could avoid music, which was important both in the school and in the town. By 1924, Wolfville High School had an orchestra, and many of the students who played in it and in the school's cadet band kept an association with music throughout their lives. *The Acadian* of December 4, 1924, reported that Wolfville High School principal Basil C. Silver had organized an orchestra and that its first public performance was in Bligh's Theatre, Berwick, on November 27, raising $72 for Berwick school programs. The newspaper said that this was the first school orchestra in the province, but Silver, who was principal from 1921 to 1940, wrote the newspaper a week later to say that Wolfville High was one of a very few schools having an orchestra. In 1928 it became the first high school orchestra to play live over radio station CHNS: its first on-air performance was broadcast from the Phinney Music House in Halifax, and the second from the penthouse of the Lord Nelson Hotel, South Park Street, Halifax. Included on the program were marches, waltzes, overtures, a grand opera selection, and a medley.

B.C. Silver kept notes for a history of music in Kings County. He wrote in those notes, now at the Nova Scotia Archives and Records Management, that the orchestra gave public concerts from a bandstand on Main Street in Wolfville, and that the band eventually merged with the cadet band organized by O. Rex Porter, who can be seen in the orchestra holding a cornet. There was also a bandstand on the school grounds, just to the right of the Munro School.

The photograph above is of the orchestra as it was ready to play for Radio Station CHNS. In it were, back row, left to right: Harold Perry and John Eaton, flute; Glen Porter, piccolo; Leon Shaw, clarinet; Vernon Brown, baritone; Ronald Smith, clarinet; Gordon Wheelock and Marshall Hennigar, cornets; middle row: Rose Cohen, Ron Peck, and Marguerite Fowler, violin; Lloyd Shaw, clarinet; Florence Jodrey, Bernard Hennigar, and Helen Young, violin; front row: Sidney Wheelock, cornet; Margaret Fullerton and Helen Perry, violin; Lloyd MacPherson, Hilda Peck, and Ruth Ingraham, violin; Rex Porter, cornet; and Jessie Bishop, piano. The boys in the front are: Soley Roop with the cornet, and Keith Forbes with the cello. Principal and orchestra conductor Basil C. Silver is standing at the right.

The Wolfville High School Cadet Band, c.1946

In 1910, Wolfville School Principal Robie W. Ford said in his report to Town Council that he would be pleased to organize a Boy's Cadet Corps at the school. That began an association with cadets that lasted for more than half a century. Some of the boys who participated drilled as a part of the corps, which won awards for its precision drilling, and some joined the school band, formed in the fall of 1936 by O. Rex Porter. Its first performance, shown next, came during the royal coronation exercises held at the school the next May. The band became the Cadet Corps Band #268 in 1942.

Porter was the musical director of the band, recruiting the players, helping to select the instruments on which the boys focused, teaching them the basics of reading music, and conducting the band practices after school. He taught the cadets to march, to look after their uniforms, to keep their instruments polished, and to be ready for inspections. He prepared the band for parades, concerts and the Remembrance Day services in front of the post office, which were often memorable for cold weather, in which lips would freeze to mouthpieces. In 1950 the band came first in the Halifax Music Festival, competing against bands from Sydney, Liverpool and Yarmouth. The cadet band was a school ritual that continued to the 1960s, when it was changed to a bugle band.

According to the information on the picture, the band members are identified diagonally from top to bottom, meaning that the player at the top left is John Sproul, with Merritt Gibson below him, then Dean Gertridge, and at the bottom, Lyall Swansburg. At the top of the next diagonal is Sam Stanford, with Paul Harris, George Kinnie, then Larry Machum below. The next diagonal has Harold Parker, with David Ross below him, then Roger Erskine behind the drum. Rex Porter is in the centre; behind him is Maurice Frank, to his left is Bill Parker, and just below (next to David Ross) is Dave Richards. The next diagonal, running from top to bottom, has Hugh Fairn, Eric Murphy, Doug Spidle and Arthur Murray, while the outside diagonal has, top right to bottom, Garth Bishop, Ronald Coldwell, Tony Erskine and Ray Swansburg. The picture was taken on the front steps of University Hall.

Wolfville celebrates the Coronation, 1937

King George V died on January 20, 1936. His successor, Edward VIII, fell in love and abdicated the throne, leaving it for his brother. King George VI was crowned on May 12, 1937, the town of Wolfville rising to the occasion. Because of the time difference between Nova Scotia and England, townspeople got up early `to listen to the radio broadcast of the coronation ceremony in Westminster Abbey. For those who didn't have radios, the Rotary Club and the Orpheum Theatre sponsored a public broadcast at the theatre, where a radio had been installed, attracting a good crowd. Next, at 11:30 in the morning, in the Masonic Hall lodge rooms in the Eaton Block on Main Street, a public meeting was held where a portrait of King George VI was unveiled. Dr. Ronald Longley presided over the ceremonies, J.D. Chambers did the unveiling and a prayer was offered by Ingraham B. Oakes. Dr. J.H. MacDonald gave an address, during which he said the new king was the embodiment of our constitutional form of government.

In the afternoon, a large crowd gathered at the school grounds, the ceremony under the direction of Principal B.C. Silver. As the *Wolfville Acadian* told the story, "Promptly at 1:30 the children marched onto the grounds from their rooms and took their places facing the Munro

building. At the same time a procession formed of the school band, color guards from the Boy Scouts and Girl Guides, twelve standard bearers and twelve girls in white bearing the medals on purple cushions...[who] marched down Highland Avenue and Main Street, returning to the school grounds by way of Linden Avenue." Prayers and speeches were offered, the school chorus sang selections, former principal Robie W. Ford read an address by the Governor-General, and a letter from the King was read by George C. Nowlan. The first photograph captures the events of the day: the band has reassembled in front of the school with the dignitaries either standing behind or sitting on the sides. The smallest children are in the right foreground on their little chairs, while others are sitting on benches in the centre. The standard bearers and the girls in white have broken up into groups and are passing out medals, while the public is gathered around the edges of the school grounds. The second picture shows the ceremonies at the front of the Munro school, with B.C. Silver speaking. To his left is Dr. Malcolm R. Elliott, long-time Wolfville physician, and to Dr. Elliott's left is Robie W. Ford. On the chair in the front is architect Leslie R. Fairn, while the man visible just above his hands is school inspector Seymour Gordon.

The Bachelors with Miss Apple Blossom, c.1937

A group of Wolfville boys who called themselves the Bachelors carry a young Miss Apple Blossom in the apple blossom festival parade in 1937. The girl is nine-year-old Jean Cochrane, daughter of Mr. and Mrs. D. Ross Cochrane. Eleven years later Jean was the grown-up Queen Annapolisa. In this photograph, Jean is being carried by Fred Sleep, holding the float at the front on Jean's left, while next to him is Doug Roach. Jean was born in Wolfville in 1928 and attended Wolfville High, then graduated from Acadia in 1951. The Queen in 1937 was Wolfville's "Babsie" Harris, daughter of J.D. Harris, Wolfville insurance broker and town councillor. The newspaper described Babsie as tall, graceful and blonde. She was also captain of the champion Maritime Intercollegiate girls' basketball team at Acadia. Years later, in 1987, when Babsie Harris was long married and was Babsie Harris Young, she looked back at the 1937 festival and remembered that federal cabinet minister J.L. Ilsley, himself a Valley boy, had crowned her queen. Wendy Elliott, in *The Advertiser*, said he used a duplicate of the crown used at the coronation, just a month before.

The very first festival was held in June 1933. Five thousand people gathered at Grand Pré for the closing ceremonies. It was a grand first festival: the weather was perfect, the blossoms profuse, and the activities attended by people from across the province. Apple blossoms came so quickly after the snows of winter. People had talked about a festival for some time and it was in 1933 that a committee headed by Frank Burns and Reg Caldwell, of Kentville, organized the first one. It opened with a program of folk singing and folk dancing directed by B.C. Silver, Wolfville's school principal, and Daisy Foster of Halifax, and involved two thousand school children from all over the Annapolis Valley. It continued with an apple blossom pageant on Friday night portraying the history of the apple through the ages, a show that included a cast of seventy and a real horse. That over, the Cornwallis Inn in Kentville was the site of a festival dance. There was a grand street parade the next morning; a baseball game between Yarmouth and a Valley team, which was made up of its best players; an evening performance in the Kentville Arena by the Massinet choir of Montreal; and the next afternoon another pageant and the closing at Grand Pré. A girl named Mary Armour, of Middleton, was the first Queen Annapolisa, crowned at the Dominion Experimental Farm in Kentville.

Charles A. Patriquin, c.1940s

Charles A. Patriquin was the son of James G. and Mildred (Pick) Patriquin. James established a harness-making business in Wolfville in 1863. Charles was born in 1864 and lived until 1947, making an indelible impression on Wolfville. In this photograph Patriquin, a noted naturalist, is demonstrating taxidermy to a group of Boy Scouts. He was many things in his life. At eighteen, he took over his father's harness making shop. He married Sarah Craig of Cambridge, Kings County, helped to establish Evangeline Beach as a summer resort area, and was a council member of the town of Wolfville. He and his son Graham were the last owners of the house near the duck pond that became the Randall House Museum.

Patriquin was instrumental in having the area below his house made into a park and duck pond (the town bought the land for the park from E.C. Randall in 1912). Patriquin was a friend of Mayor J.D. Chambers, and the two of them, with the assistance of town superintendent Aubrey Dakin, had the end of the creek closed off and grass put around the edges. Charles then made arrangements with local farmers to lend ducks to the pond. His son Graham once said that "a generation of Wolfville-nurtured kids carried memories of feeding the ducks to virtually every corner of the world." Esther Clark Wright wrote in *Blomidon Rose* that "there was never a kindlier spirit nor a greater lover of children and youth than this old man who tilled his garden on the slope above the duck pond, and, as long as he lived, delighted to see the youngsters playing there."

Edson Graham, Wolfville's foremost photographer, c.1940s

Edson Graham took over as manager of W.W. Robson's photographic studio in 1904. Born in Colchester County, he became a photographer while spending his early years in the United States, doing photography in Massachusetts and New Hampshire. He returned to Truro in 1903 and came to Wolfville the next year, living from 1913 to 1944 in the house at 5 Acadia Street, built in 1894 by storeowners Charles and Augusta Strong. When Graham retired in 1945 the *Halifax Herald* said his departure from the studio marked the passing of a landmark in local history.

Over the years Graham, as the newspaper put it, took the photograph of nearly every Acadia student and Horton Academy student, as well as of the hundreds of groups on campus. Many of the photographs were published in the Acadia yearbooks. In addition to his portrait work, he had time to take many landscape photographs; the newspaper said "in the early days of the tourist trade the Graham photographs of the Annapolis Valley and environs attracted numerous tourists and found their way all over the continent" as popular postcards. Graham was also very much involved in the life of Wolfville, serving at different times as president of the board of trade, president of the Rotary Club, a town councillor, an officer with the Wolfville Historical Society when it was formed in 1941, and a supporter of the local Boy Scout organization.

Graham's studio was taken over by a Liverpool photographic studio owner, R.B. Macaulay. Graham's photographs are now a part of the historic photograph collection of Tony Kalkman, Kentville. Edson Graham is shown in this photograph, fittingly, working with his camera. His wife, Irene, died in 1942, and Edson himself died in 1956.

Rhoda Wright and Alex Colville, c.1940s

This is the family of Rhoda Wright and artist Alex Colville. The children are, left to right, John, born in 1946; Graham, born in 1944; Ann, born in 1949; and Charles, born in 1948. Alex is reading the funnies from the *New York Herald Tribune* to the children while Rhoda watches from behind. She studied Fine Arts at Mount Allison University, where she met Alex Colville, today one of Canada's finest internationally-known artists. Colville grew up in Amherst and also attended Mount Allison, like Rhoda taking the Fine Arts program. They married in 1942. He was soon to go to war, serving as a war artist, recording war's horrors in a series of moving paintings. When he returned he taught at Mount Allison for seventeen years, moving to Wolfville in the 1970s. He was chancellor of Acadia University from 1980 to 1991.

Rhoda's parents were Charles H. and Annie Louise Eaton Wright. Charles was a legendary Wolfville builder, born in Canard in 1881. He was responsible for numerous structures in Wolfville, among them the Baptist Church, the Royal Bank, War Memorial Gymnasium and the United Church. In July 1929 he was in the process of building Kings County Academy in Kentville when, on the way back from Windsor, his car was hit on a crossing by the DAR express passenger train. It was a tragedy that stunned Wolfville, visitors reporting that on the night the news became known, the streets of the town were deserted. Charles Wright was killed, along with his daughter Jean, 15, his son Graham, 10, as well as his sister-in-law and his father-in-law. It was his partner and friend Roy Jodrey who, out of respect for Charles, completed the building of the school in Kentville.

The Colvilles lived until recently in the stucco house on Main Street built by Rhoda's father for her mother as the family home. That house was constructed in 1920 after Charles H. Wright and Kentville architect Graham Johnson travelled to New England to study building styles. The Colvilles now occupy a home they built near the stucco house, the main house still in the family. The picture was taken by a family friend, the late Lionel Naylor.

Highland Avenue, showing the home of ornithologist Robie Tufts, c.1940s

The house just above the rooftop on the left of this photograph belonged to Robie W. Tufts. It was an Andrew Cobb-designed home, which Tufts had built and into which he moved in January 1921. In a wood-panelled study at the back of the house, with a fire crackling in the fireplace and his dog at his feet, Tufts inspired generations of Wolfville youth with a love of the outdoors, and especially of birds. He taught them the varieties of birds in the area, how to observe them, their particular habits, how to keep records of sightings and even how to stuff and mount the ones found dead.

It was in the same study that Robie Tufts wrote his seminal book *The Birds of Nova Scotia* from thousands of index card entries he had made over the years of birds seen on his rounds as Federal Migratory Birds Officer, or on field trips with the young people he was instructing. In the basement was a caged area where birds ranging from saw whet owls to finches could recover from injuries; some of these had the run of the house and could be seen flying about. Many of the young people who studied birds with Robie Tufts went on to careers in the natural sciences; one was Wolfville native W. Earl Godfrey, who became Curator of Ornithology at the National Museum of Canada and who wrote *The Birds of Canada*.

Tufts was the son of legendary Acadia professor John Freeman Tufts, who was born in 1843 and who died in February 1921. Robie Tufts' first wife was Evelyn S. Tufts, who wrote for the *Halifax Herald*, and who was the first woman elected to the Parliamentary Press Gallery board of directors in Ottawa. His second wife was Lillian Thompson. His daughter, Virginia, was the wife of Canadian diplomat J.H. Thurrott, and later was married to Allison Pickett, who spent a career developing methods of controlling apple pests without resorting to pesticides. Robie Tufts wrote a long-running column in a Halifax newspaper, entitled *Woods, Water and Sky*, where he passed on his knowledge of the outdoors to countless readers. Born in 1884, he lived to be almost a hundred, driving fast convertibles even in his nineties. A memorial to Robie Tufts is located today near the old Wolfville train station, now the town library; it celebrates the chimney swifts that swoop down the chimney of the old Acadia Dairy. The dairy was on this site; all that remains is the brick chimney, kept as a part of the memorial.

Mona Parsons, Wolfville heroine in World War Two

The Acadian reprinted a story from Toronto's *Evening Telegram* on June 14, 1945, datelined "Somewhere in Germany." In that story, Allan Kent wrote that when Mona Parsons was studying dramatic art at a Canadian university twenty years before, she could not have imagined that some day she would be trudging barefoot across Germany, a fugitive from the Gestapo and a life sentence, acting the part of the half-witted aunt of a beautiful Dutch countess. It was a story reminiscent of another Wolfville girl, Gladys Vaughan, who during World War One led 2,300 frightened people in small boats across a river to safety in Poland.

Mona Parsons was born in Middleton in 1901, the daughter of Colonel and Mrs. Norval A. Parsons. Her family moved to Wolfville when she was ten. She attended the Wolfville schools and graduated from Acadia, then studied drama and nursing in the United States. Allan Kent wrote that she married a Dutch businessman named Willem Leonhardt, moving to the Netherlands. When she hid two members of a downed British bomber crew in her attic, she was arrested by the Gestapo and sentenced to death, a sentence later commuted to life in prison. The judge had been impressed by her courage and dignity as the sentence was read. She was jailed in Amsterdam and then transferred to a German prison, where she was kept from March 1942 to September 1944, then moved to another prison camp when allied bombing came close. She and a twenty-three-year-old Dutch countess managed to escape, spending the next three weeks walking toward the border, having many close calls but eventually crossing into Holland.

In a book written about Mona Parsons, Andria Hill says that the first soldier Mona saw after crossing the border into Holland was a Canadian who was distrustful of Mona, given the fact that she was filthy and dressed in shabby clothes, until she said she was from a little town called Wolfville. It turned out that he was from Halifax, and that she had just met up with the North Nova Scotia Highlanders. Even so, her story had to be confirmed. Captain Robbins Elliott, in Oldenburg, Germany, met Mona several days later and wrote his father in Wolfville to say she was alive. Elliott's father was Dr. Malcolm R. Elliott, who had been Mona's doctor when she was growing up in Wolfville. Robbins Elliott lives in Wolfville today; his daughter is Wendy Elliott, who has written many historical pieces about the town in *The Advertiser*. His sister is Shirley Elliott, also a Wolfville resident and long-time legislative librarian for the Nova Scotia Legislative Assembly. Mona Parsons spent the last of her life in Wolfville, moving to a turreted Queen Anne-style house on west Main Street. She died in 1976.

The end of World War Two, 1945

The huge headlines in the newspaper the girl is reading say, "Victory in Europe." She is sitting on the curb in front of the Wolfville post office; the picture was taken by customs officer Jack Marriott, whose office was on the top floor. The girls next to her are also reading about the end of the war, while the boys on the bench have newspapers, but one of them is absorbed in the comics. Victory flags are strung from the light standards. The students are waiting for the V-E Day parade, which came along a short while later, passing in front of the post office. Marriott was outdoors by this time, snapping the cadets and band as they marched by. The Scouts followed the cadets. David Sheppard provided the photographs.

Jack Marriott described the scene in his diary, noting that the king had proclaimed the day a public holiday, that it was cool, but that hot sun beat down: "Such an air of holiday that it seemed like Sunday, students free too for one day in the middle of their exams thronging the streets and reading the morning papers. I take a snap from the office window of the flags and the people loitering, old J.D. Harris standing in the sidewalk with the Halifax paper pulling in the breeze." Marriott could see students reading the newspapers: "I recognize three girls below, Anna Muggah, Deane McCain and Joyce Lockhart sitting on the grass. From the open window I call 'Anna.' Up and down the street she looks, wondering. I call again. Joyce sees me and tells her. I call out to turn the paper to V I C T O R Y. She does and I get another snap, flags waving over their heads.

The Wolfville High School cadet band marches in the victory parade, 1945

Mud Creek says that Wolfville was ready for victory in May 1945: "Flags flew, the siren sounded, church bells rang, car horns tooted and the V-E day parade was accompanied by fireworks and a bonfire on Raymond Field." Among those who died in the war were Wolfville men Cyril G. Cavanagh, Kenneth W. Eagles, Bernard W. Fullerton, F.R.W.R. Gow, Samuel R. Kenny, Leo M. Regan, Donald M. Smith, J. Beverley Starr, Alfred G. Stevens, and Jack Stewart. The book says that among the heroes were Max Forsythe-Smith, who won the Military Cross; David Waterbury, QC, who won the Distinguished Flying Cross; and Keith Forbes, who won the Distinguished Service Cross. *Those Waiting Dreams,* a moving tribute to those who served in the wars, was written by Robbins Elliott of Wolfville and published in 1999.

Charlotte Coombs and K.D.C. Haley, 1945

The bride in this 1945 photograph was Charlotte Coombs, daughter of Wolfville stationmaster Chester G.C. Coombs. Charlotte was born in 1915 in the apartment over the train station. The town library, which now occupies the old building, has a meeting room upstairs named in her honour. She attended Wolfville High School, graduated from Acadia with a degree in education, and eventually taught in Port Williams, staying with Lalia Chase. She was teaching at a private school in Toronto when she got a telephone call from Kenneth David Cann Haley, whom she had known seven years before while at Acadia. As the story is told by her daughter, Susan, Haley called Charlotte in Toronto and asked her to marry him. "Yes," Charlotte said. "Pardon me, who is this speaking?"

David Haley was born in Saint John, also in 1915, the son of W. Kenneth Haley, who with his brother Rupert owned a lumber mill which had been in the family for several generations. The family moved to California when Kenneth and Rupert moved the Haley Brothers mill to Santa Monica, where it specialized in doors and sashes; it is still in business. David Haley's father and grandfather had both graduated from Acadia, so, although David studied for a year at the University of California, his father insisted that he and his brother return to attend Acadia. That is where he met Charlotte. He graduated from Acadia, served in the U.S. Army, married Charlotte in 1945, then earned his PhD from Stanford University.

David Haley taught mathematics at Acadia University for many years, in the summers teaching at Stanford, where he had the honour of being the only visiting professor with tenure. He was a masterful teacher, making mathematics understandable even to the weakest students, his character leaving both an indelible impression and a collection of stories told over and over again through the years. One of the classic Haley stories has to do with a mathematics class in University Hall, where the concept of infinity was being impressed upon undergraduates. Haley demonstrated with a piece of chalk, drawing a line across the board, along the wall, on the door and up the hall. The students sat quietly. After a time, one looked tentatively out the door, but there was no Dr. Haley in sight. He had disappeared.

One sunny day class was underway when a student, looking out the ground floor window, noticed a boy who should have been in the class walking by University Hall. He pointed this out to Dr. Haley, who flung open the window, yelling to the students, "after him, men," leading them all out through the window. They surrounded the student and dragged him back, stuffing him inside. At that moment Dr. Watson Kirkconnell, the gentle, cerebral president of the university, happened to be strolling by. "Get your man?" he politely asked the students. Then there is the story of the girl who came late into the class, asking if it were English Bible. "Yes, *yes*, it is," said Dr. Haley. "Come right in." He quickly erased the board and taught the class as if the statistical notations were like the Biblical hand, writing on the wall. When the girl finally caught on she made a hasty exit, but later joined the Acadia Dramatic Society, with which Dr. Haley worked tirelessly as faculty advisor.

Schoolgirls run the gauntlet in front of the post office, c.1945

This photograph of two girls passing the post office and attracting the attention of the young men loitering in front was taken by Jack Marriott. At about the same time as he became customs officer, Marriott became involved with photography, eventually taking hundreds of portraits of people, many of them students from Acadia University.

Marriott, a friend of the E. Sidney Crawley family, had come to Kings County from England in 1921, buying the Planters' Barracks near Port Williams and hoping to grow and sell apples. When the apple industry collapsed he attempted to survive in a number of ways, including raising chinchillas and boarding American tourists. He was also a composer of music, an amateur artist, and a diarist, whose journals cover fifty years. In 1939 he was given the position of collector of customs. Marriott died in 1986, just two years short of a hundred years old.

**George C. Nowlan,
Wolfville lawyer
and Canadian cabinet
minister, c.1958**

George Clyde Nowlan was
born on August 14, 1898. In
1911, his family moved to
Wolfville from Havelock,
near Clare, in southwestern
Nova Scotia. They bought a
farm almost opposite Kent
Lodge, on the western edge
of town, George entering
grade eight in the Wolfville
school. By 1915, he was
enrolled at Acadia, and by
1917, his country at war, he
had enlisted in the Canadian
army. By 1919, he was back
at Acadia and turning
towards the study of law. In
1920, he was speaking on
behalf of the Conservative
candidate in the provincial
election. In her book *George
Nowlan: Maritime Conservative in National Politics*, historian Margaret Conrad says that
despite the fact that the Conservatives made a poor showing in the election, "Nowlan had
publicly identified himself as a Conservative and had impressed party notables with his poten-
tial as a platform speaker."

Nowlan graduated from Dalhousie Law School in 1922 and by 1923 had married a
Wolfville girl, originally from Canard, named Miriam Chisholm. He had also married the
world of politics: by the time of his wedding he had been named the Conservative candidate in
the next provincial election. He won office in 1925. At the same time he threw himself into
work in Wolfville, from his law office over the Orpheum Theatre. He was involved in the
board of trade and the Masons, and active in the university's alumni association. By 1933, he
had been defeated at the provincial level, and turned his attentions to his law practice and
political organizing. It was not until 1948 that the opportunity came for him to run again, this
time winning for the federal Conservatives in a by-election. He stumbled slightly in the federal
election called the next year, but won in a by-election after the election was declared void. He
became minister of internal revenue under John Diefenbaker, then minister of finance in 1962.

In this photograph George Nowlan is shown during a visit to Acadia in October 1958. He
is speaking to a weekly assembly of students and faculty in University Hall, after which he was
entertained at a reception in the Student Union Building. His wife, Miriam, told *The
Athenaeum* at the time that "Mr. Nowlan has given his life to politics, and it has not been a
wasted life." He died in 1965.

Chapter 7

Grand Pré
and Countryside

Beginning in 1755, the Acadians were sent from their lands around the Minas Basin and their farms destroyed. For five years the Acadian lands lay idle, while government officials worked on the idea of inviting settlers from New England to come and live in the areas the Acadians had been forced to leave. Proclamations were posted, offering land to New England farmers, the final act of a drama that completely changed the face and history of Grand Pré and the countryside around the shores of the Minas Basin.

Men representing their fellow farmers in Connecticut came to Nova Scotia in 1759 to check out the lands for themselves. It was springtime. "The orchards were in their earliest budding," writes A.W.H. Eaton, "the dykes were beginning to grow green, the rich uplands were waiting for the plow, and here and there was still standing some lonely barn, or perhaps house, that had escaped burning at the sad time when its owner was taken away." The men were very pleased with what they saw. The governor of Nova Scotia was requested to set aside grants of land in Horton and Cornwallis, the names decided upon at that time. That was done at a meeting on May 21, 1759, with the land in Horton to be divided among two hundred families, and that in Cornwallis between one hundred and fifty.

The chief surveyor for Nova Scotia was Charles Morris. In 1760 he mapped out the lands the New England settlers would occupy, also setting up town plots in both Horton and Cornwallis. The idea was that each Planter family would have a mixture of farmland, woodland, and dykelands, plus a place in the town plot for a house. Each town plot was laid out with houses in a grid, with spaces set aside for parades, or open spaces, to be used by the New Englanders for town meetings. There were also spaces for schools and churches. The Horton town plot was quite large, with three public parade areas near the centre, a burial ground on the southwest corner, and room for two hundred homes, each sitting on a piece of land measuring 250 by 100 feet.

Families began arriving in the spring of 1760. After a rough, three-week voyage from Connecticut, six ships rounded Cape Blomidon in May with the first contingent of families to settle the township of Horton. The main body of settlers arrived in twenty-two ships on June 4. Those destined for Cornwallis went ashore near what is now Starr's Point, those for Horton at Horton Landing near the mouth of the Gaspereau River—the same place the Acadians had been sent from five years before. Draws were made for land, each share consisting of over five hundred acres.

As the families arrived, Fort Montague was erected near Horton Landing to give shelter to the settlers and to provide protection. Debra Anne McNabb notes that the first houses built that summer were near the fort, and that the proprietors began building the settlement quickly. A bridge across the lower Gaspereau River, a ferry link to Cornwallis, and a grist mill and sawmill were built. Distribution of land was fairly rapid, so that by 1763 almost seven hundred people lived in Horton, in 122 families. The settlers owned 99 horses, 159 oxen, 302 cows, 402 young cattle, 369 sheep and 162 pigs, and were raising significant quantities of wheat, rye, barley, corn and potatoes. By 1770 virtually all lands were allocated. The town plot for the settlers was located on cleared upland just south of Horton Landing, on a bend of the river (McNabb).

Planter descendant Esther Clark Wright did much to bring Planter history to its important place in the overall story of this country. Both she and Ronald S. Longley, Acadia history professor and university vice-president, wrote extensively about Planter beginnings. In *Blomidon Rose*, which takes its title from a line in Longfellow's poem *Evangeline*, Wright remarks upon the courage and fortitude of the Planter women, who set out in crowded sloops with their children, their worldly goods and sheep and cattle, to travel to an unknown land. As they settled in their new land, they proved diligent in making the items needed for survival.

Wright quotes the granddaughter of a Planter, Rachel Bishop, who in 1808 wrote that there was not much money, and people raised everything they needed on their own farms: "We had plenty of good hard wood for the cutting, and a nice fire it made on the long winter evenings. We raised our own meat and grain and made our own cloth and sugar and molasses from the sap of the maple tree, and cider, for we had no graft apples then, and we had to make cider of them. We made our candles and soap and linen thread, and as we had no matches we kept the fire alive all night by 'raking' it or covering it with ashes."

Wright notes that there was a store where things could be bought, but what the farmers had to sell was cheap, and what they had to buy, dear. Elizabeth Mancke's study of women and the economy in eighteenth-century Horton provides a list of what was sold in Planter times. Hardware items such as barrels, seeds, hammers, jack knives, cod hooks, clapboard, glass

The village of Grand Pré, 1884

In 1884, E. Sidney Crawley took this classic photograph of the village of Grand Pré, looking down toward the crossroads.

panes, horse whips, oil, paint, putty, rope, saddles, shingles, shovels, pokers and wire were sold in 1793 at a store said to have been kept by Edward DeWolf at Horton Landing. Housewares sold included bottles, bowls, brushes, candles, wine glasses, tea pots, stone jars, soap, coffee pots, tin cups, dishes, frying pans, mirrors, pitchers, razors, and snuff boxes. Foods sold included wine, wheat, tea, spices, butter, sugar, salt, rum, rice, cod, coffee, maple sugar, mustard, mutton, pork and raisins, and dry goods ran to things like bed ticking, broadcloth, satin, muslin, linen, flannel, corduroy, chintz and calico.

The Planters established themselves in the Acadian lands, ready to make a contribution that continues to this day. "In subduing the tides, in carving farms out of the forests," says Wright, "the New England Planters and their wives made their Horton, their Cornwallis, their Falmouth, communities of which all speak with pride and respect, communities which have sent out men and women who have made worthwhile contributions to the world's endeavour and the well-being of its peoples."

The name "Horton" applied to so many different localities that it is useful to sort out what is actually meant by it. Horton itself was the grant of land given to the Planters that stretched from the mouth of the Gaspereau River to the west of what is now Kentville, bounded on the north by the Cornwallis River. Cornwallis was roughly equal in size and began on the other side of that river. Horton Landing was by the mouth of the Gaspereau River, where the Planters came ashore. Horton Township—Horton Town Plot—was the site laid out for a town, fronting on Horton Landing and on the rise just south of it, in what is Grand Pré. Lower Horton began more or less from the middle of what is now Grand Pré and included the easterly part of Wolfville, while Upper Horton is central and western Wolfville. Horton Corner was the name given to what is now Kentville.

Road in Grand Pré , c.1910s

On the back of this postcard from a photograph by Edson Graham is printed the message: "It is such a road as this that charms the eye of the lover of the picturesque when he travels in Nova Scotia." Grand Pré may not be the only spectacularly beautiful part of what has been called Nova Scotia's Garden County, but given the fact that it is—as John Frederic Herbin called it—a "land of legend," it is perhaps the most famous of the destinations for visitors to Kings County. Recognition of the fact that it lies at the heart of Acadian history came with its designation as a National Historic Site. It is also a Provincial Heritage Conservation District and a Federal Rural Historic District, the first area so designated in Canada, in recognition of its historical and architectural significance.

In 1935, the Dominion Atlantic Railway published a lovely guide to its "Land of Evangeline Route," saying that by 1720 Grand Pré had become a prosperous country, with fine orchards and gardens, herds of black-horned cattle and flocks of sheep. It quoted the English governor of Port Royal as saying that the farms in Grand Pré were the finest in the country, noting that both Louisbourg and Annapolis sent their "smart little vessels to trade for these supplies, paying in gold which the Grand Pré farmer hoarded in the chimney or buried in the garden." The railway called the Land of Evangeline the "most alluring and soul-satisfying summer vacation country in America."

Longfellow's celebrated poem *Evangeline* spoke of it: "Distant, secluded, still, the little village of Grand Pré lay in the fruitful valley." A.W.H. Eaton, in his 1910 *History of Kings County*, wrote of the shimmering dykelands, the calm Minas Basin's surface of matchless turquoise blue, and a "panorama of unusually varied beauty." Eaton described the area historically designated as Grand Pré as including the country between Long Island on the north, Gaspereau River on the south, Horton Landing on the east, and Wolfville on the west.

Grand Pré from Harris Hill, c.1890s

This old photograph from the Notman Archives shows, in the distance, the mouth of the Gaspereau River. In the Nova Scotia Archives and Records Management, the photograph is entitled "Evangeline's House." The scene is pastoral, with a man holding a scythe, his son nearby, while in front of them are houses and barns, and, up on the hill, the church. The people living in these houses seem not far removed from the original Planters.

On June 4, 1760, twenty-two ships rounded Cape Blomidon and dropped anchor in the water at the top of this photograph. Ronald Longley's paper for the Nova Scotia Historical Society in 1960 said the ships were escorted by a brig of war and carried an average of fifty passengers apiece, in addition to stock and equipment. A group of the settlers had landed at Cornwallis, at Starr's Point, while the others disembarked at Horton Landing, seen in the distance in this picture. Their first homes were tents and other temporary shelters, Longley said. One of the first things they did was to hold town meetings, where land was divided into lots and then drawn for. Most heads of families were given five hundred acres, Longley said, each lot containing a town lot, and portions of marshland, upland and woodland.

A Planter house in Grand Pré, home of Perry Borden, c.1870s

This New England Planter house sat at the southeast corner of the crossroads of the village of Grand Pré, south of what is now Grand Pré National Historic Site. This house, built by the Planters, was identified on photographs in the 1930s as the oldest existing house in Grand Pré. It was the house of Perry Borden Jr., grandfather of Sir Robert Laird Borden, Canadian Prime Minister between 1911 and 1920. The house is no longer there.

Perry Borden Jr. was the son of the first Perry Borden, born in Rhode Island in 1738. His mother was Mary Ells. Perry Borden Sr. had lived on his father Samuel's lands in Cornwallis, later moving to Grand Pré. A history written by W.C. Milner—former *Sackville Post* publisher, Wolfville resident, and the man in charge of the Maritime Provinces section of the National Archives, Ottawa—said the house was a favourable type of farm house in use in New England before 1800: "Its leading feature was its fireplaces—two in the bedrooms and a cavernous one in the kitchen. They formed parts of one chimney, which crowded the staircase into a narrow winding one….The fireplaces had to be fed, and a woodpile probably containing fifty or sixty cords was to be seen in the spring in the yard between the house and the barn."

Perry Borden Jr. was born in 1773. He married Lavinia Fuller, a girl from Horton, the couple producing four boys and two girls. One, Andrew, was the father of Sir Robert, while his brother Jonathan was the father of Sir Frederick Borden. Both are described elsewhere in this book. The picture shows a white-bearded man with a dog on a leash, a woman standing beside him, and a younger woman standing to the right of the gateway to the house. The house is similar in age, though not in design, to the Jeremiah Calkin house in Grand Pré owned by Elizabeth and Ed Goodstein, who provided this photograph. Their house, built before 1768, was moved to a site several hundred metres east of the Perry Borden house from its original location above the old Covenanter Church.

The Old French Willows, at Grand Pré, c.1900s

Three horses and wagons carry visitors to the old French willows, at Grand Pré. A man leans on the fence talking with a couple in the rig on the left, while in the centre, beside a stile which goes over the fence, a two-horse team pulls a driver and three women dressed in their summer best. A sign on a post in the ground in the centre of the picture is labeled French Willows.

The willows, planted by the Acadians close to what became the old DAR railway station, and in what is now Grand Pré National Historic Site, were often visited in the 1800s by residents and tourists. An article in the *Halifax Herald* in 1898 had this to say: "Near the former station are the old French willows, whose pictures, along with other Evangeline scenes, are found on souvenir china, etc. Here, too, the hallowed waters of Evangeline's well are sipped by the romantically inclined tourist." Thomas Chandler Haliburton spoke of the willows as far back as 1829, in his history of the province, when he called scattered groups of willows "the never failing appendages of an Acadian settlement."

John Frederic Herbin's *History of Grand Pré*, first published in 1898, also makes reference to the willows, calling them living testimony of the Acadian occupation: "All over Minas stand these immense trees, marking the sites of roads or houses before 1755. No other memorials save the old dykes and an occasional apple tree, tell of the hapless race whose country this was, and whose only happiness was here. The willow is extremely tenacious of life. A green limb broken from a tree and thrust into the earth will take root and grow. In this respect it is a fitting memorial of the people who set them out; a foreign growth that has become indigenous. The tree was brought from France at an early date."

Remnants of the old trees in the picture above, some of the ancient limbs propped up with supports, can be seen today at the edge of Grand Pré National Historic Site.

Longfellow's Evangeline, Acadian heroine, c.1890s

Henry Wadsworth Longfellow's *Evangeline*, published in 1847, has lent an atmosphere of "peculiar romance" to the area around the Minas Basin. A.W.H. Eaton's *History of Kings County* said in 1910 that no modern narrative poem had done so much to excite interest in a special locality as the famous poem, "which perpetuates the loves and sorrows of the simple French peasant folk who in the 18th century were rudely torn from thrifty homes in a favoured province, and dragged forcibly into suffering exile in other colonies."

There was controversy over the poem, a controversy which was parallel to that over the expulsion of the Acadians itself. John Frederic Herbin, whose mother was Acadian, thought the poem was a remarkably correct page of history. A French missionary and Acadian descendant named Louis N. Beaudry visited Grand Pré and in 1882 engaged in a correspondence with Longfellow, in which he asked the poet if he had ever been to Grand Pré, and how he had obtained the facts which formed the basis for the story. Longfellow, as reported in *The Acadian* of April 3, 1885, wrote Beaudry and said that he had never been to Grand Pré. Said Longfellow: "The poem of *Evangeline* is so far historical only as it is founded on the dispersion of the Acadians. The story itself of a maiden separated from her lover and, after life-long wanderings, finding him dying in a hospital, is a legend, or tradition. The name Evangeline is of my own invention, as are all the details of the poem." Longfellow told Beaudry that he was prevented by illness from writing more; he died the next month.

G.P. Bible, who in 1906 published a book on the Acadians as the historical basis for the poem, said that he thought it had been based on the real life story, told to Longfellow, of an Acadian girl named Emmaline Labiche, even though the poem had represented a divergence from the facts. Provincial Archivist C. Bruce Fergusson wrote in 1951 that Longfellow had likely been inspired by a story told him through his friend Nathaniel Hawthorne in 1838, and that he relied on Thomas Chandler Haliburton's two-volume *History of Nova Scotia* for the background to the poem. In 1903, a monumental history of Nova Scotia entitled *Markland*, by Queens County writer, geologist, lawyer and minister R.R. McLeod (who is buried in the same graveyard as Longfellow), considered the poem and said it was taken to be true by the great majority of its readers, and that it therefore placed British subjects in the attitude of defence or apology. McLeod thought the poem would not have been weakened if Longfellow had given "a few lines to the causes that led up to this expulsion."

The Acadian blacksmith shop, Grand Pré, c.1890s

A.L. Hardy took the photograph of this ramshackle old blacksmith shop, with two people standing in the doorway and a young girl by the pole, a wagon to the right and almost behind the shop. This photograph was published in Philadelphia in 1906 in *An Historical Sketch of The Acadians, Their Deportation and Wanderings*, by G.P. Bible. A similar picture, clearly taken at the same time but without the people, was published in *Through Evangeline's Country*, by Jeannette A. Grant, in 1894. The information with the photograph in the book states that the blacksmith shop is on the site of the one used by the Acadians in Grand Pré. The blacksmith shop in Grand Pré is a part of the lore of the area, even appearing in Longfellow's celebrated, if fictional, poem *Evangeline*. Margaret Graham wrote in the *Halifax Herald*, in 1898, that near Evangeline's old well "were unearthed some blacksmith's tools from the forge of Basil, the blacksmith. At least tradition says that this was the site of Basil's smithy, and since no one can prove that these prized relics were not once in the possession of the poet's Basil, I know of nothing to prevent any tourist from accepting what tradition sayeth."

Closer to earth, a note in *The Acadian* in 1893 mentioned Mr. Ogilvie, Horton Landing's "genial blacksmith," who was "rapidly showing himself a thorough workman, and is getting a good share of the work of the place. His reputation as an excellent horse-shoer is quickly spreading." Nearby, we are told in *Kings County Vignettes*, J.L. Brown was running a blacksmith shop near the Wolfville train station in 1888, and Ned Mahaney had a shop at the harbour, in a red building torn down in the 1940s.

Lighthouse at Horton Bluff, near William Hall's birthplace, c.1900s

In 1851 a lighthouse was built at Horton Bluff, east of Grand Pré at the edge of the Avon River. A.W.H. Eaton's *History of Kings County* described it as a square, white building, standing ninety-five feet above high water, with a fixed white light. One of the early keepers was Captain James Lockhart, who travelled six miles twice a day to tend the light. This later lighthouse, built around 1883, is somewhat more refined. The picture shows a man in a horse and wagon, a woman at the fence gate talking, another man sitting in the doorway of the lighthouse, and, up the tower, by the light itself, a woman watching the scene below. With the roses by the back door, the picket fence and the neat appearance of the building, it is clear that this lighthouse was well cared for. Wendy Elliott, in *The Advertiser*, says that for many years the light was tended by Mrs. Charles Rathbone, whose family had been in charge of the lighthouse. The Rathbones were still looking after the light in 1940. Its last keeper was Bill Crosby, who came to the job in 1962. A new light was built in 1984 and is still in operation today; however, on Wednesday, October 14, 1987, the workings of the light were taken over by computer, and the Horton Bluff lighthouse was manned no more.

The lighthouse stands close to Hantsport, at the mouth of the Avon River. Not far from this spot Canadian Victoria Cross winner William Hall was born, on April 25, 1829. Hall was the son of Jacob and Lucinda Hall, who had settled there during the War of 1812. He received his Victoria Cross, the first Nova Scotian to do so, after bravery during a battle known as the Relief of Lucknow, which put down a mutiny among native troops in India in 1857. Hall served in the Royal Navy until 1876, as recorded in a 2003 article on Hall by retired army colonel John Boileau in the Halifax *Sunday Herald*, and retired to his small farm near Horton Bluff. He said, "I want to spend my days in the old place, the land of my birth." Hall died on August 25, 1904, was buried in Lochartville, and later reburied in Hantsport. A memorial was placed over his grave and his medal is kept in the Nova Scotia Museum.

REMAINS OF OLD FRENCH DYKE, GRAND PRÉ NS.

An old French dyke, Grand Pré, c.1920s

When the French settlers arrived in Acadia they were already familiar with building dykes. They came to the Minas area from Port Royal and in all likelihood immediately began to apply their skills in constructing dykes. Poet and merchant John Frederic Herbin told of how the men and boys built dykes to "shut out the turbulent tides," reclaiming vast stretches of meadowlands. Their dykes were simple but required, as Marjory Whitelaw says in her history of the Wellington Dyke, great patience and years of heavy manual labour.

As Whitelaw explains it, the Acadians first built dykes along the river banks in order to confine the water, and then built dykes across rivers, "along with a sluice, or aboiteau, to control the outflow of river water." The aboiteaux allowed the fresh water to leave the rivers but prevented salt water from entering. "Their achievement," she writes, "is almost unimaginable today…visualize a long line of men with spades and shovels, very simple tools, slithering in mud with the animals, mud so thick and gluey that the horses had to wear wooden mud shoes."

Eaton's *History of Kings County* said that the Acadian dyke builders brought their art with them from the Netherlands, and that there were no other provincial workmen as skilful as the Acadian French. He said it was the broad, fertile, dyked marshes, left unoccupied by the expulsion of the Acadians, which attracted the New England Planters. This photograph of the old French dyke in Grand Pré was taken by Edson Graham, probably in the 1920s.

THE MOUTH OF THE GASPEREAU RIVER. LAND OF EVANGELINE. GRAHAM PHOTO.

The elm tree at Horton Landing, by the mouth of the Gaspereau, c.1900s

Kentville photographer A.L. Hardy took this photograph of the mouth of the Gaspereau River where it empties into the Minas Basin. This is a legendary site in Canada, the place from which the Acadians were sent into exile and at which the Planters arrived. Moored in these waters, just to the left and off the land on the right, known as Oak Island, were the ships on which the Acadians were placed. The tiny strip of land at the top left of the picture is Boot Island.

There is a 1931 letter in the Nova Scotia Archives and Records Management in Halifax from W.S. Hamilton, Larchmont, New York, to former provincial archivist Bruce Fergusson. In it, Hamilton writes that the elm tree in this picture stands at the head of what is left of a wharf at Horton Landing, and is approximately the place from which the Acadians embarked in 1755, and also where the New England settlers landed in 1760. "Tradition, which I believe is authentic, based on what my father has told me, is that this tree was brought as a sapling from New England, and planted in 1760 to mark the location where the settlers landed," he wrote. He said the tree had noticeably deteriorated since 1931 and was apparently dying. "It would seem that such an historic tree should be marked with a stone and tablet before it dies completely."

The date of the tree was given differently in an article published in *The Advertiser*, in 2001. L. Ross Potter wrote that in 1845 a fifteen-year-old boy named Stephen MacIntosh often went fishing from the wharf at Horton Landing with a neighbour named George Hamilton, who was born in 1810 and died in 1895, and was possibly an ancestor of the W.S. Hamilton above. Because of a lack of shade at the Landing, Stephen dug up a young elm tree and planted it at the site. When an old man, he would sometimes drive down to Horton Landing to relive the old days and to comment on how much the tree had grown. He died in 1925, at the age of ninety-five. The tree is thought to have survived through the Dutch elm disease epidemic because of its isolation. It is still there, its photograph in the Esther Clark Wright Archives, Acadia University. One of Canada's well-known paintings is Alex Colville's *Elm Tree at Horton Landing*, painted in 1956. It is a portrait of the tree showing its strength despite the ravages of time, and is owned by the Art Gallery of Ontario.

The old Covenanter church in Grand Pré, c.1888 and 1917

This church in Grand Pré is one of the most recognized in Nova Scotia, and is the oldest Presbyterian church building in Canada. It is known as the Covenanter church because its minister from 1833 to 1840 was Rev. William Sommerville, a Covenanter—or reformed Presbyterian—who was in opposition to the Baptist practice of immersion at baptism and to the use of hymns not sanctioned by the scriptures. The church was built between 1804 and 1811 in the New England meeting-house style, under the direction of Rev. George Gilmore. Gilmore was born in Ireland but moved to Philadelphia and then New England, having to flee to Nova Scotia at the beginning of the American Revolution because he was hated as a Tory. As Eaton tells us in his *History of Kings County*, Gilmore was given poor land near Windsor but in 1788, moved to better in Horton, where he became pastor of the congregation there. He worked to build this church, dying at the age of eighty-eight, just as it was completed.

Calling the church "the Covenanter Church" upset Watson Kirkconnell, a scholar and president of Acadia University for many years.

Kirkconnell wrote explanatory notes to *The Diary of Deacon Elihu Woodworth*, who helped build the church, in which he said it was "an irony of history" that the term "Covenanter" was used. Kirkconnell explains that Rev. William Sommerville's thoughts ran counter to those of the Baptists in a number of areas, particularly in terms of the disagreement over baptism by immersion: Sommerville believed that immersion and baptism were opposites. Others, like Eldon Hay of Mount Allison University, feel Kirkconnell was too harsh in his assessment of Sommerville, pointing out that the minister grew to understand and work well with his congregation, and that the differences over baptism were resolved.

The church sits on the hill south of the Grand Pré corner. A side note is that it was Sommerville's son, Robert, who built the Presbyterian church on Prospect Street in Wolfville, which was later moved to the town's Main Street and is pictured elsewhere in this book.

Prime Minister Robert Laird Borden's home in Grand Pré, c.1900s

The house in this photograph is labelled the Sir Robert Borden Place, Grand Pré. Built by Sir Robert's father Andrew, it still stands near old Highway One in Grand Pré, south of the centre of the little village. It was the home of Borden, Prime Minister of Canada from 1911 to 1920, the Nova Scotian who led Canada during World War One, and who won for Canada a measure of independence from Britain unheard of before the war. Bruce Hutchinson's classic book, *Mr. Prime Minister*, says of Borden's predecessor, Sir Wilfred Laurier, that he had genius while Borden had common sense. Borden's qualities were "exactly what the nation needed in the dark days ahead."

Robert Borden was born in Grand Pré on June 26, 1854, in what is known historically as the Edward and Sophia MacLatchy house, still standing to the right of the Covenanter Church. When he was four his family moved to the house shown in this picture, at the intersection of the road leading to the village. His parents were Andrew and Eunice Laird Borden. Andrew was the son of Perry Borden, stationmaster in Grand Pré for the new Western and Annapolis Railway, whose home is described earlier in this chapter. Robert went to Acacia Villa School, the private school situated on the rise of land above Horton Landing. One day in the spring of 1869, the assistant master of the school, James H. Hamilton, had an argument with the headmaster and departed. Robert—just shy of fifteen—was asked to take his place. He taught there for the next three years, some of his students being boys older than himself. In 1873, according to historian Robert Craig Brown, the same James Hamilton, by now the headmaster of a school in New Jersey, invited Robert to be his assistant headmaster. Robert took the job for a year, returning to Nova Scotia to study law with the firm whose leading partner was Sir Robert Weatherbe, profiled in Chapter six. Borden was called to the bar in 1878 and established a partnership with Charles Hibbert Tupper, the son of Sir Charles Tupper. He was first elected to the House of Commons in 1897.

The Acacia Villa School, Grand Pré, c.1910s

In 1852, Joseph R. Hea founded the Acacia Villa School in Grand Pré. Hea was born in New Brunswick and taught at Mount Allison between 1843 and 1852, at which time he decided to open his own school. He chose a site in Horton Township. Dr. Ronald S. Longley, Acadia professor and administrator, who wrote a history of the school, said it was "to meet the needs of those who wished to send their sons to a boarding school where there was strict discipline, careful supervision and organized study hours."

The school was successful, lasting from 1852 to 1920. Its most famous graduate was Sir Robert Borden, Prime Minister of Canada from 1911 to 1920, who, on hearing in Halifax of his landslide victory over Sir Wilfred Laurier, headed immediately for Grand Pré in order to digest his shocking victory. Borden had been both a student and a teacher at Acacia Villa. Other graduates included Isaac Walton Killam and Lloyd E. Shaw. When Hea moved on to become president of the University of New Brunswick in 1860, he sold the school to A.M. Patterson, a native of Aylesford, who had also taught at Mount Allison. The school, which had two buildings under Hea, grew under Patterson in 1891 with a new dormitory, assembly hall, and classroom structure, and in 1900 with a building housing a library, reading room, music room and hospital.

In the December 22, 1889 issue of *The Acadian*, there was an article on the closing of the school for Christmas holidays. "From the beginning of the term the school has had thirty-five boarders, a lot of bright, clean, intelligent, manly little fellows, always ready for work or play, as true boys should be, and scarcely a day lost by sickness by any one of them during the term. Principal and teachers report one of the most harmonious and profitable terms in the history of the school, and looking at the happy, smiling faces of the boys as they presented Mr. Patterson with a fine large easy chair, a Xmas box from the boys of '99, and a kindly appreciative address, one could easily believe the truth of this report...." The member of parliament for Halifax, Benjamin Russell, gave the address at this time, putting emphasis on thoroughness in school and in life's work, saying it was better to strive for the complete mastery of a few things rather than a "mere smattering of many, as is too much the case now in our public schools." But the public schools were getting better all the time, leading to a decline in private schools. In 1920 the school closed its doors. The glass negative photograph was taken by Frank Harris, who lived in Hortonville, while he was a teenager.

Village of Gaspereau, c.1884

The Acadian of April 17, 1885, just a year after this photograph was taken by E. Sidney Crawley, reported that the village of Gaspereau had a grist mill, a saw mill, a carding mill, a shingle mill, a barrel factory, two tanneries, a cider mill and other industries, in addition to some of the best farms in the province: "Its people ought to be prosperous." Harry Bruce, in his biography of Roy Jodrey, says of Gaspereau that it looked faintly as though it belonged to a Rhine valley. He says an atmosphere of great age and memory lingered among its white wooden houses, which were closer together than buildings in most Nova Scotia towns, "and they huddle in an intimate clump near the site of the old millpond."

A Natural History of Kings County describes the Gaspereau Valley this way: "In the eastern portion of the County, the Wolfville Ridge is separated from the Southern Upland by the Gaspereau Valley. This secluded valley is very picturesque with its small farms and stony, shallow river winding towards the Minas Basin." Eaton's *History of Kings County* called the view of the famous Gaspereau Valley "lovely beyond words to describe." Through the Gaspereau Valley, he said, ran the gradually widening stream known as the Gaspereau River, from the mouth of which in 1755 vessels carried the Acadians into exile. In *Blomidon Rose*, Esther Clark Wright described looking at Gaspereau from the Wolfville Ridge, saying that she and her friends "enjoyed as ever the lovely little valley, so self-contained, so perfect, with its neat rows of apple trees and its snug homes, its meadows and its winding stream."

IN THE ACADIAN LAND.

Gaspereau River, above Grand, Pre.

The Gaspereau River, c.1900s

The Gaspereau River is one of the five rivers draining into the Minas Basin. It has its origins in what geologists call the Southern Uplands, the range of hills providing the southern wall of the Annapolis Valley. The 1992 *Natural History of Kings County* notes that the Gaspereau has the largest drainage basin in the county, a series of twelve major lakes, eight dams, and five hydro stations. It was this river which inspired men to dream of making electricity for the town of Wolfville, eventually brought to fruition by Roy Jodrey and Charles H. Wright in 1920. In the early 1900s, it was home to nine operating sawmills running from Salmontail Brook to White Rock.

The Gaspereau runs sixteen kilometres from its headwaters through the Gaspereau Valley to Melanson, where it becomes tidal for the next six and a half kilometers. Wolfville people knew the Gaspereau River for a variety of reasons beyond its commercial possibilities. For some, it was the pretty little river visible from the Stile, running through the village of Gaspereau. Others knew it as the best place to dip smelt, each net full of the silvery fish so delicious if cleaned immediately and fried in a cast iron pan. In the first part of the last century many excellent salmon were taken from its waters. The river was also home to the spring runs of the gaspereaux, bonier than smelt but just as plentiful, caught by dipping buckets or nets into the water. Esther Clark Wright ate them fried, baked, or broiled, or even cold, between slices of bread and butter, and they were "luscious and life-giving." And, she said, it was because the fish chose the river that the Acadians decided it would be a good place to settle, building their dykes and homes by its mouth in Grand Pré. More recently young people used the river for a tubing festival, where inflated inner tubes carried them along. Still others use the watershed for swimming, canoeing, and for family cottages. This postcard was sent by a girl in Acadia Ladies Seminary in 1907.

On the Gaspereau, near Wolfville, N.S.   GRAHAM Photo.

Covered bridge across the Gaspereau River, c.1940s.

At thirty-five minutes past noon on Tuesday, January 19, 1952, dynamite blew up this bridge across the Gaspereau River between Hortonville and Avonport. The bridge had been erected in 1876 and was one of the most photographed sites in all of Nova Scotia, but by 1952 its structure had become twisted by three quarters of a century of storms. Despite efforts to save it, the decision was made that it had to be replaced, so government engineers stripped off the planking, set the charges, and sent what was left of it into the Gaspereau River, at the time filled with the highest tides of the year. The tide slowly took the debris out to the basin.

Watching was a crowd of people, Highways Minister Merrill Rawding, and local legislative assembly members D.D. Sutton and W.H. Pipe. There was also a man named Horace West, from Cornwallis. The Halifax *Chronicle Herald* said that his father, Adolphus West, a shipwright, had made and put in place the massive ship's knees which still kept the top cross members attached to the sides. It said they appeared as fresh and strong as when they were placed there nearly eight decades before.

The first covered bridge had been built at the site around 1812. Burpee R. Bishop, of Kentville, was quoted in the *Herald* as saying that records of the municipal sessions for the county in 1819 noted that "repairs were made on the covered bridge at Lower Horton during the year." In 1839, January storms had taken out all four of the Gaspereau River bridges; the replacement on this site lasted until 1872, when a new covered bridge was put up. It soon burned and "in 1876 it was replaced by the sturdy structure so familiar to present day motorists from all parts of North America." Since this was the main route from Halifax through the valley, traffic had to be rerouted through the village of Gaspereau. Within twenty-four hours a new, temporary Bailey bridge was in place.

A close-up of Blomidon, with ferry and schooner, c.1900s

The fabled home of Glooscap is seen from the approaches to what is now Blomidon Provincial Park. A schooner is tied up at the wharf below, while the ferry *Evangeline* moves into dock. The tide is high. At low tide there is a rocky beach along the bottom of the cliffs, where people still find amethyst. It was here that Isaac Chipman—the professor from Acadia whose energy built the first College Hall—spent the last three hours of his life. Longfellow's *Evangeline* spoke of it: "away to the northward, Blomidon rose." Esther Clark Wright followed that famous line of poetry and called her 1957 book about the Minas Basin countryside *Blomidon Rose*. For her, Blomidon was a never-ending delight. She said people love Blomidon not because of its height or grandeur, but because it "has a part in making us what we are."

Wolfville people have always been drawn to Blomidon, often travelling there by boat. Donald R. Munro was quite a man about town in the late 1800s, an athlete, builder of yachts, and manager of the town's electrical generation plant. One Monday afternoon at the end of August, 1884, he and a party of four gentlemen, six ladies and three children set out from Wolfville on his new yacht, bound for the area near that shown in this picture. According to *The Acadian*, the plan was that he would sail to Pereau, leave part of the company there, and return to Wolfville on the same tide. Stiff breezes carried the yacht past Starr's Point, and Pereau appeared in view. All hands on board were in ecstasies, the baby was in hysterics, the bottle was passed around, and the merry crowd cracked jokes. The bottle, the pro-temperance newspaper noted, was a nursing bottle.

The newspaper said that in the midst of the merriment and as the yacht careened gaily up the harbour there was a crash, a harsh grating sound, a shriek, a groan, a giggle, and a soft swear word. The boat was aground. Even the baby stopped crying and became interested in the situation. Munro had the ladies hanging on the rigging trying to get the boat off, but the tide kept going out and soon the flats were completely bare. Those on the boat were stuck in the mud fifteen miles from home with nothing to eat or drink save what was in the baby's bottle. A small boat from shore put out in the channel and collected one of the men, who secured lodgings for the night and fetched a horse team to take the ladies off the boat, the men remaining behind to dig a trench for the boat in anticipation of the next tide. The next morning the boat was still stuck, so a team drove the party home to Wolfville. No mention was made of what became of the boat.

The Starr family and Willowbank Farm, Starr's Point, c.1904

This panoramic photograph of Willowbank Farm was taken around 1904 from the roof of the big barn on the property. It shows magnificent apple orchards, the Grand Pré dykes, lower Wolfville, the Wolfville wharf, and the Wolfville lighthouse. Willowbank Farm got its name, according to the WINS history of Port Williams, from the French willows which once lined the nearby riverbank. Originally, it was the James Allison homestead, but it was bought by Richard Starr at a Sheriff's sale in 1868. After Richard, his son, Charles (C.R.H. Starr), owned the property, followed by Charles' son, Richard. C.R.H. Starr is profiled in this book with the photograph of his daughter, Evelyn Starr. His son Richard lived there until 1915. E.D. Haliburton, writing in *The Acadian* in October 1924, said of Willowbank that it was a beauty spot which the public had long been allowed to use as a park and picnic ground. He said its situation was delightful, with avenues of apple trees, its tip covered with spruce, the "bold outline of Blomidon away on the left," and "serene and beautiful Wolfville across the Cornwallis River on the right."

The Starr family figured prominently in the history of the area. The second photograph, of the house at Willowbank, shows Richard Starr standing by the fence, Mrs. Starr in the chair, Lide Chipman beside her, and little Richard Sidney Starr sitting on the grass. Richard Sidney Starr was the father of both Sally Starr and Harry Starr. He married May Rosina Prat, the daughter of Wolfville stationmaster Samuel Prat; the story of May Rosina and her sisters is told in Chapter six. Harry Starr provided much historical material about the Starr and Prat families to the Esther Clark Archives and to the Nova Scotia Archives and Records Management in Halifax.

The family descended from New England Planter Samuel Starr, who came to the township of Cornwallis from Connecticut.

The Planters' Barracks—
Acadiacroft, c.1920s

On September 12, 1778, a letter to government officials in Halifax said that, as of that day, the troop barracks had been finished. Designed to house soldiers who would ward off enemies of the Planter settlers, the barracks consisted of two rooms, with a good fireplace, bunks for twenty men in each room, and space in the loft for sixteen more (Port Williams Women's Institute). The barracks was located near the original Cornwallis Town Plot. Local troops were established in the barracks, along with the Loyalist regiment called the King's Orange Rangers.

The structure was sold as a private home not long afterward. The first owner was ship owner and judge John Whidden, who named it Acaciacroft. His son David was the customs officer who kept his office in a small building near Acaciacroft. In recent years the house was occupied by another customs officer, Jack Marriott, who had his office first in Port Williams and then in Wolfville, in the big stone post office. Marriott, whose full name was Henry John Burton Marriott, was born in Lewisham, England, in 1888. He became a clerk with the Bank of England in 1906 and married Leila Frederica Talbot in 1912. He got to know the sons of Wolfville's E. Sidney Crawley when they were stationed there as soldiers and decided to emigrate to Canada, buying the Planters' Barracks in 1921. In fact, young Edmund Crawley, mentioned elsewhere in this history, married Leila's sister. In the photograph, Marriott family and friends can be seen on the lawn of the Planters' Barracks after a game of croquet, Leila being seated to the left on the wicker lounge. Today, the house is owned by Allen and Jennie Sheito and is a provincial heritage property.

Wellman Hall at the Port Williams dock, c.1890s

A number of the vessels that moved in and out of the Wolfville and Port Williams port facilities were built in the Parrsboro area. Shown here is *Wellman Hall*, built in 1892 by Silas F. Knowlton of Advocate, and described in the records as a schooner of 136 tons. In 1895, *The Acadian* notes the ship's arrival in Wolfville from New York, with a load of hard coal for the Wolfville Coal Company.

The *Wellman Hall* is sitting on the bottom at low tide in Port Williams. When the tide goes out in the Cornwallis River, all of the water disappears and ships rest on the bottom. Later, when the docks were rebuilt, fancier cribwork was constructed on which the ships would sit. Esther Clark Wright had a story in *Blomidon Rose* about the sea captain from London, England, who brought his ship into port and swore loudly when he realized that his ship had to sit on a muddy ledge when the tide was out. He vowed never to return, but others did, and often.

The General Store in Port Williams, c. late 1920s

The general store in this picture belonged to George A. Chase, nephew of W.H. Chase, one of Port Williams' most famous entrepreneurs and the millionaire king of the apple industry in Nova Scotia. According to Harry Bruce, when W.H. Chase's son decided to go into medicine rather than into apple speculating, Chase decided to pass on his business wisdom to his nephew George. George was something of a gambler; once, while waiting for his wife to join him in New York in order to board a steamer for Italy, he had taken "a flyer in potato futures. He made a fast profit sufficient to pay for their Italian holiday twice over" (Bruce). George Chase had a hand in developing Port Williams into one of the world's least likely salt water ports, setting up the port as the place from which to ship apples and other produce to England: "One year, they took nearly half a million barrels of apples back down the river and out to Fundy and the sea." Using Port Williams not only saved valley orchard growers millions of dollars in shipping and rail charges, it enabled George Chase to build for himself a substantial import-export empire.

W.H. Chase himself had started his career in Port Williams, working in his father's general store in 1867, when he was fifteen. The Port Williams Women's Institute history says that the first store in Port Williams had belonged to David Clark, and that the Chases had taken it over around 1867. It apparently had competition. The first Wolfville newspaper with the name *Acadian*, which went by the grand name of *The Acadian and General Provincial Advertiser*, said in its issue of Saturday, January 16, 1869, that O.H. Newcomb wished to inform the inhabitants of Cornwallis that he had opened his new store at Port Williams, "where he will keep constantly on hand" groceries of all kinds of the best quality, cottons, domestic and fancy hardware items, plus "a good assortment of Ladies' and Gents' rubber chains, Bog Oak earrings, brooches" and more. In 1894 a hardware store had been built next to the Chase grocery store, which had passed on to other owners. George Chase purchased both stores in 1919.

Acacia Grove, the home of Charles Ramage Prescott, Starr's Point, c.1930s

The man who has been called the father of the apple industry in the Annapolis Valley, Charles Ramage Prescott, built this Georgian house in Cornwallis Town Plot, near Starr's Point, in about 1814. Eaton's *History of Kings County* calls Prescott the man who exerted the greatest influence on the early history of the apple industry. Born in Halifax in 1772, Prescott was married twice, the first time to Hannah Whidden in Cornwallis, and the second to Maria Hammell in Halifax. He was first a very successful merchant in Halifax, but failing health forced him to move to Cornwallis some time between 1811 and 1814. There he "bought land and built a fine colonial brick house, which is still standing. His place he called 'Acacia Grove'" (Eaton). The house had twenty-two rooms and was made of local clay bricks, the foundations set with stone imported from Scotland.

Prescott was forty when he moved to Kings County. In *Valley Gold*, Anne Hutten notes that once in Cornwallis, it was to horticulture that Prescott turned with a real passion; "Like many country gentlemen of his day, he kept stables for horses and cattle, as well as a piggery; but the big attraction of the estate was found in its extensive gardens and hothouse." There were local and exotic flowers, pear trees from France, nut trees, cherries, peaches and plums. There were also more than one hundred new varieties of apples. "Charles Prescott established what amounted to a precursor of today's government experimental stations," writes Hutten. He brought in apples from Britain, New England and Quebec, testing them for suitability to the valley climate. To Prescott goes the credit for introducing the Gravenstein, one of Canada's most popular apples. Since Prescott often invited farmers to Acacia Grove to study grafting, by the time he died every farmer in the province had at least one Gravenstein tree (Hutten).

Prescott died in 1859, at the age of eighty-eight. Over the years, the house suffered the ravages of age. By the 1930s it was almost a ruin, with cattle on the lawn, floors torn up, and plaster and windows broken. When Mary Allison Prescott, a great-granddaughter of Charles Ramage Prescott, saw the house in 1930 while on a tour of the Maritimes, she bought it for $1,800 and had it restored. Today, Prescott House is a museum, part of the Nova Scotia Museum system.

Pair of oxen with teamster, Grand Pré, c.1930s

The man in this picture is Joe Parsons, shown with a boy on his wagon heading towards the dykelands in Grand Pré. Joe lived near Horton Landing, and worked on a farm. Glen Hancock writes of seeing him in the summertime passing through town on his way to the dykes, calling him a character: "His yoke of oxen, their horns adorned with old felt hats, pulled a hay wagon on which Joe sat, colourfully attired in winter long johns and lumberman's rubbers, even in July." Hancock relates a story in which Joe Parsons, moving down Wolfville's Main Street with his oxen, was caught up in a civic parade and won the prize for most original float.

Main Street, Canning, c.1900s

A number of people are standing outside the stores watching the horse and buggy driven by a liveryman and containing passengers. Information with the picture does not identify the occasion. The memorial at the centre of the crossroads was at the time new; it was erected in memory of Harold Lothrop Borden, killed on July 16, 1900, while fighting in the Boer War. Harold was the son of Sir Frederick Borden, whose home, pictured next, was just down the main road as it disappears to the left.

The store on the left, which belonged to A.D. Payzant, sold dry goods and furniture. Canning was first called Apple Tree Landing because of an old apple tree that had stood from Acadian times, but in the mid-1800s its name was changed. Its first inhabitant was John Stewart, whose ship plied the waters of the Minas Basin. A.W.H. Eaton's history notes that shipbuilding grew up as an industry in the area, early shipyards belonging to men such as William Baxter, Ebenezer Bigelow, Joseph Northup, Edward Lockwood and Edward Pineo. However, its real growth as a town occurred after the Cornwallis area began growing potatoes following a disease affecting New England potatoes in the 1840s, with Canning being used to ship the crop to markets. Eaton writes of wagons from all over in Canning, loaded with potatoes, filling the streets from morning to night, and vessels lying at the wharves as many as eleven deep. In the 1880s, the community had a population four times larger than it does today. An axe factory operated there until the 1930s, and ships were constructed, the last a three masted schooner called the *Fieldwood*, launched in 1920 and lost off Sable Island in 1938 (Gibson, 1997).

In July 1866, Kings County's most destructive fire occurred. It destroyed the entire business section of the town, including ten stores. Within two years, the village was wholly rebuilt.

The Frederick Borden House, Canning, c.1900s

Children in the valley sometimes called this the gingerbread house, because of its design and colour. It was the home of Sir Frederick Borden, whom Eaton's *History of Kings County* calls the most distinguished householder in Canning. The house still stands, surrounded by trees and gardens.

Borden, a medical doctor, was elected to parliament as a Liberal in Ottawa in 1874, seven years after Confederation. He was defeated in 1882 but re-elected again in 1887, serving for many years in the cabinet of Prime Minister Wilfred Laurier as Minister of the Militia. Frederick Borden was born in Cornwallis on May 14, 1847 and graduated from King's College in Windsor. He took his medical degree at Harvard in 1868. Until his entry to federal politics he practised medicine in Canning, and it was he who sent seven thousand men and five thousand horses to South Africa during the Boer War.

Borden married Julia M. Clarke, of Canning; they had three children. When she died, he married Julia's sister, Bessie. He was the son of Jonathan and Maria Frances (Brown) Borden, Jonathan's brother Andrew being the father of Sir Robert Laird Borden of Grand Pré, Conservative prime minister of Canada from 1911 to 1920. Frederick and Robert's grandfather was Perry Borden Jr., whose father Perry was the son of the man—Samuel Borden—who had been hired by the Nova Scotia government to lay out lands for the other New England Planters in 1760. Samuel returned to New England but gave his grant in Cornwallis to the first Perry.

The house is lived in today by retired Acadia biology professor Merritt Gibson, author of *The Old Place: A Natural History of a Country Garden*.

Kentville, the shiretown, in the 1890s

Kentville is the seat of government in the county of Kings and its major commercial centre. This photograph, by Kentville photographer Amos L. Hardy, shows the town as it looked at the turn of the century. Visible on Academy Hill, at the top of the picture, is the school, built around 1870 and destroyed by fire in 1883, then rebuilt. Because it was a county academy, students from many parts of Kings County took their high school education there. Also visible is the railway, where the Dominion Atlantic Railway had its headquarters, and in the centre left is the Hotel Aberdeen (see next page).

When the townships of Horton and Cornwallis were established by the New England Planters, the area around Grand Pré was planned as the centre of Horton. Horton itself stretched west to what was known as Horton Corner. Just as the area around Wolfville became more important than Horton Town Plot, in Grand Pré, so too did Horton Corner, which became Kentville three decades after the Duke of Kent passed through the area in 1794. A hundred years before this picture was taken Horton Corner consisted of fourteen houses and a store, but by 1900 the town contained the courthouse, jailhouse, municipal building, fine houses, stores, and a substantial railway station.

A.W.H. Eaton said that Kentville was famous for the loveliness of its walks and drives, and for the beauty of its shade trees. He said that if you have passed through the town on one of the DAR's comfortable cars you would only have had a glimpse of "its broad level streets, delightfully shaded with trees of oak and maple, its pretty residences, surrounded by grounds that give evidence of the artistic taste of their owners in landscape gardening, its five good churches, its commodious, well-kept hotels, its ample-sized stores, its far famed orchards...."

The Hotel Aberdeen, Kentville, c.1890s

The Aberdeen was the primary hotel in Kentville after the railway took over from stagecoaches and the Kentville Hotel closed down. It was built by Daniel McLeod in 1892 on land next to the Windsor and Annapolis Railway station. The Union Bank branch, at left on the bottom floor of the hotel, was opened in March 1894. The Union Bank remained there until 1910, when it merged with the Royal Bank. For forty years, the Aberdeen was the town's leading hotel, "its spacious lawns shaded by stately trees where, in the summer, the town band played one evening a week. The railway platform became a board walk where crowds gathered to listen" (Nichols).

In December 1919, DAR general manager George E. Graham made the announcement that the Aberdeen had been added to the Dominion Atlantic Railway (DAR) system, which had already that year acquired the Pines, in Digby. *The Acadian,* of Wolfville, said the Aberdeen was splendidly situated and could be made very attractive. It would be renovated and refurnished from cellar to roof, the report said, with many of the rooms getting private baths. The cost of the hotel to the railway was close to $30,000. The outside was landscaped, gardens were planted, and the hotel was renamed the Cornwallis Inn. Eleven years later the hotel was gone, demolished by the DAR after it built the new Cornwallis Inn. That building still exists, serving now as shops, meeting rooms, offices and apartments. This excellent photograph by A.L. Hardy was taken not long after the hotel was built, as there are no lawns or permanent walkways yet in place. The sand to the left of the hotel was key to the founding of the town: Kentville owes its location to the enormous sand bank that narrowed the river and made a convenient place for a ford at low tide, and later a bridge. The sand covered most of the hotel property; the Western and Annapolis Railway began having it removed in 1892.

Bibliography

Acadia University. Alumni Directory 1989. Wolfville: Associated Alumni of Acadia University, 1989.

Acadia University. Alumni Directory 1995. Wolfville: Associated Alumni of Acadia University, 1995

Allison, David. *History of Nova Scotia*. Halifax: A.C. Bowen and Company, 1916.

Annual Reports, Town of Wolfville. Wolfville, various years, to 1923.

Armour, Charles A. and Lackey, Thomas. *Sailing Ships of the Maritimes: An Illustrated History of Shipping and Shipbuilding in the Maritime Provinces of Canada 1750-1925*. Toronto: McGraw Hill Ryerson Ltd., 1975.

Black, Mary. *New Key to Weaving: A Textbook of Hand Weaving for the Beginning Weaver* (1945). New York: MacMillan Publishing Co., Inc., 1957.

Bolles, Frank. *From Blomidon to Smoky*. Boston: Houghton Mifflin Company, 1894.

Borrett, William Coates. *Tales Retold Under the Old Town Clock*. Toronto: The Ryerson Press, 1957.

Bruce, Harry. *RA: The Story of R.A. Jodrey, Entrepreneur*. Toronto: McClelland and Stewart Inc., 1979.

Brown, Robert Craig. *Robert Laird Borden: A Biography. Volume 1: 1854-1914*. Toronto: Macmillan of Canada, 1975.

Buckner, P.A. and Frank, David, eds. *The Acadiensis Reader: Volume Two: Atlantic Canada After Confederation*. Fredericton: Acadiensis Press, 1985.

Burgess, Barry Hovey. *Burgess Genealogy, Kings County, Nova Scotia Branch*. New York: Chas. E. Fitchett, 1941.

Candow, James E. *The New England Planters in Nova Scotia*. Canada: Ministry of the Environment, 1986.

Chute, A.C. *Records of the Graduates of Acadia University 1843-1926*. Wolfville: Acadian Print, 1926.

Colwell, J.A. et al. "Wolfville Harbour." Wolfville: Prepared for the Geological Association of Canada and Mineralogical Association of Canada Joint Annual Meeting, Wolfville, May 1992.

Conrad, Margaret. "Apple Blossom Time in the Annapolis Valley, 1880-1957." *The Acadiensis Reader: Volume Two: Atlantic Canada After Confederation*. Eds. P.A. Buckner and David Frank. Fredericton: Acadiensis Press, 1985.

Conrad, Margaret. *George Nowlan: Maritime Conservative in National Politics*. Toronto: University of Toronto Press, 1986.

Conrad, Margaret, ed. *They Planted Well: New England Planters in Maritime Canada*. Fredericton, NB: Acadiensis Press, 1988.

Crawley, Edmund A. Comments on Some of Wolfville's Historic Houses. Unpublished letter in the Nova Scotia Archives and Records Management, 1967.

Cross, Leora Webster. "The Acadians and the New England Planters." Privately published.

Cuthbertson, Brian. *Wolfville and Grand Pré, Past and Present.* Halifax: Formac Publishing Company Limited, 1996.

Davidson, Heather. *A History of the Randall House.* Wolfville: Wolfville Historical Society, 1993.

Davison, James Doyle. *Alice of Grand Pré.* Wolfville: Privately published, 1981.

Davison, James Doyle. *Golden Jubilee, 1991: Fiftieth Anniversary of Wolfville Historical Society.* Wolfville: Wolfville Historical Society, 1991.

Davison, James Doyle. *What Mean These Stones? The Restoration of the Old Horton-Wolfville Burying-ground.* Wolfville: Heritage Advisory Committee, 1990.

Davison, James Doyle, ed. *Mud Creek: The Story of the Town of Wolfville, Nova Scotia.* Wolfville: Wolfville Historical Society, 1985.

Dominion Atlantic Railway. *The Land of Evangeline, Nova Scotia.* Kentville: Kentville Publishing Co. Ltd., 1935.

Eaton, Arthur Wentworth Hamilton. *The History of Kings County, Nova Scotia* (1910). Milton, Ont.: Global Heritage Press, 1999.

Eaton, Charles Ernest. *The Nova Scotia Eatons.* Privately published, 1979.

Eaton, Ernest L. "The Dykelands." *Nova Scotia Historical Quarterly.* (1980) 10.

Elliott, Robbins. *Those Waiting Dreams.* Wolfville: Gaspereau Press, 1999.

English, John. *Borden: His Life and World.* Toronto: McGraw-Hill Ryerson Limited, 1977.

Gibson, M. Allen. *Train Time: Nostalgic Glimpses of a Wolfville Boyhood During Which Train Watching was a Happy Pastime.* Windsor, NS: Lancelot Press, 1973.

Gibson, Merritt, ed. *A Natural History of Kings County.* Wolfville: Acadia University, 1992.

Gibson, Merritt. *The Old Place: A Natural History of a Country Garden.* Hantsport, N.S.: Lancelot Press Limited, 1997.

Grant, Jeannette A. *Through Evangeline's Country.* Boston: Joseph Knight Company, 1894.

Griffiths, Naomi E.S. *The Contexts of Acadian History, 1686-1784.* The 1988 Winthrop Pickard Bell Lectures in Maritime Studies. Montreal: McGill-Queen's University Press, 1992.

Griffiths, Naomi. "Longfellow's Evangeline: The Birth and Acceptance of a Legend." *The Acadiensis Reader: Volume Two: Atlantic Canada After Confederation.* Eds. P.A. Buckner, and David Frank. Fredericton: Acadiensis Press, 1985.

Haliburton, Gordon. *Horton Point: A History of Avonport.* Wolfville: Gaspereau Press, 1998.

Haliburton, Thomas C. *History of Nova Scotia in Two Volumes. Volume 2.* (1829). Bellville, Ont.: Mika Publishing, 1973.

Hancock, Glen. *My Real Name is Charley: Memoirs of a Grocer's Clerk.* Wolfville: Gaspereau Press, 2000.

Hay, Eldon. "Planter Politics in Covenanter Controversies." *Planter Links: Community and Culture in Colonial Nova Scotia.* Eds. Margaret Conrad and Barry Moody. Fredericton, NB: Acadiensis Press, 2001.

Herbin, John Frederic. *Jen of the Marshes.* Boston: The Cornhill Publishing Company 1921.

Herbin, John Frederic. *The History of Grand Pré: The Home of Longfellow's "Evangeline."* Saint John: Barnes and Company Ltd., 1898.

Hill, Andria. *Mona Parsons: From Privilege to Prison, from Nova Scotia to Nazi Europe.* Halifax: Nimbus Publishing Ltd., 2000.

Hunt, M. Stuart. *Nova Scotia's Part in the Great War.* Halifax: The Nova Scotia Veteran Publishing Co., Limited, 1920.

Hutchison, Bruce. *Mr. Prime Minister 1867-1964.* Don Mills: Longmans Canada Limited, 1964.

Hutten, Anne. *Valley Gold: The Story of the Apple Industry in Nova Scotia*. Halifax: Petheric Press Ltd., 1981.

Kalkman, Tony. *Along the Tracks of the Dominion Atlantic and the Halifax and Southwestern Railways*. Kentville, NS: privately published, 2000.

Kings County Historical Society. *Kings County Vignettes, Volumes 1–10*. Kentville: Community History, Kings County Historical Society, 1989-2000.

Kirkconnell, Watson. *Acadia's Fifth Quarter-Century, 1938-1963*. Wolfville: Governors of Acadia University, 1968.

Kirkconnell, Watson. *The Acadia Record 1838-1953*. Wolfville: Acadia University, 1953.

Kirkconnell, Watson, ed. *The Diary of Deacon Elihu Woodworth, 1835-1836*. Wolfville: Wolfville Historical Society, 1972.

Kirkconnell, Watson and B.C. Silver. *Wolfville Historic Homes and The Streets of Wolfville 1650-1970*. Commemorative issue containing both works. Hantsport: Lancelot Press, 1978.

Levy, George Edward. *The Baptists of the Maritime Provinces, 1753–1946*. Saint John: Barnes-Hopkins Limited, 1946.

Longfellow, Henry Wadsworth; introduction by Fergusson, C. Bruce. *Evangeline: A Souvenir of the Evangeline Country*. Halifax: H.H. Marshall Ltd., 1951.

Longfellow, Henry Wadsworth; introduction by Huntley, Joan. *Evangeline and the Evangeline Country*. Kentville: Dominion Atlantic Railway, undated.

Longley, Ronald Stewart. *Acadia University, 1838-1938*. Kentville, NS: Kentville Publishing Company, 1939.

Longley, Ronald Stewart. *The Wolfville United Baptist Church*. Wolfville: Published by the Baptist Church, 1953.

Margeson, Cathy. "Sawmills of Kings County." *Kings County Vignettes, Vol 8*. Kentville: Kings Historical Society, 1966.

Memorials of Acadia College and Horton Academy for the Half-Century 1828-1878. Montreal: Dawson Brothers, Publishers, 1881.

McLeod, R.R. *Markland or Nova Scotia: Its History, Natural Resources and Native Beauties*. Toronto: Markland Publishing Co., 1902.

McNabb, Debra Anne. "Land and Families in Horton Township, N.S. 1760-1830." Diss. UBC, 1986.

Milner, W.C. *The Basin of Minas and its early settlers*. Wolfville: reprinted from the *Wolfville Acadian*, undated.

Moody, Barry M. *The Acadians*. Toronto: Grolier Limited, 1981.

Moody, Barry M. "Esther Clark Goes to College." *Atlantis*, (20:1) 1995.

Moody, Barry M. *Give us an "A": An Acadia Album 1838-1988*. Wolfville: Acadia University, 1988.

Murdoch, Beamish. *A History of Nova Scotia or Acadie*. Halifax: James Barnes, Printer and Publisher, 1866.

Murphy, Vernita. *Chronicles of Another Era, Book One*. Privately Published, 1993.

Murphy, Vernita. *Chronicles of Another Era, Book Two*. Amherst: Acadian Printing, 1993.

Ness, Gary W. *Canadian Pacific's Dominion Atlantic Railway, Volume One*. Calgary: The British Railway Modellers of North America, undated.

Nichols, Mabel G. *The Devil's Half Acre*. Kentville: Kentville Centennial Committee, 1986.

O'Leary, Charles. "A Brief History of White Rock Mills." Publishing data unavailable.

Perkin, J.R.C. *Ordinary Magic: A Biographical Sketch of Alex Colville*. Hantsport, NS: Lancelot Press and Robert Pope Foundation, 1995.

Philpot, H.S. *The Province of Nova Scotia*. Ottawa: Department of the Interior, 1930.

Port Williams Women's Institute. *"The Port" Remembers: the History of Port Williams and its Century Homes*. Kentville, NS: Kentville Publishing Company, 1976.

Province of Nova Scotia. *Maritime Dykelands—the 350 Year Struggle*. Halifax: Department of of Government Services Publishing Division, 1987.

Robertson, Barbara R. *Sawpower: Making Lumber in the Sawmills of Nova Scotia*. Halifax, NS: Nimbus Publishing and the Nova Scotia Museum, 1986.

Rogers, Grace McLeod. *Stories of the Land of Evangeline*. Toronto: McClelland and Stewart, 1923.

Ross, Sally and Alphonse Deveau *The Acadians of Nova Scotia, Past and Present*. Halifax: Nimbus Publishing Ltd., 1992.

Russell, Burton. *Hurrah! Acadia*. Kentville, NS: Privately Published, 1986.

Saunders, Edward Manning. *History of the Baptists of the Maritime Provinces*. Halifax: Press of John Burgoyne, 1902.

Saunders, Kathleen. *Robert Borden*. No other publication data available.

Shaw, L.E. *My Life in the Brick Industry*. Privately published, 1955.

Town of Wolfville. *Wolfville House Inventory*. Unpublished. Binders At Town Office, Wolfville, and at the Randall House Museum.

Tufts, Robie W. *The Birds of Nova Scotia*. Halifax: Nova Scotia Museum, 1973.

Tufts, Robie W. *Looking Back*. Windsor, NS: Lancelot Press Ltd., 1975.

Whitelaw, Marjory. *The Wellington Dyke*. Halifax: Nimbus Publishing Ltd. and the Nova Scotia Museum, 1997.

Woodworth, John E. "Sketch of Journalism in Kings Co." *The Berwick Register*, September 11, 1929.

Wright, Esther Clark. *Blomidon Rose* (1957). Windsor, NS: Lancelot Press, 1977.

Wright, Esther Clark. *Planters and Pioneers: Nova Scotia, 1749 to 1775*. Hantsport, NS: Lancelot Press, 1978.

Young, Bertram. *My White Rock*. Wolfville: Gaspereau Press, 1999.

Newspapers and Journals Consulted

Acadia Bulletin. Wolfville, NS.
The Acadian. Wolfville, NS. Also called the Wolfville Acadian and *The Young Acadian*
The Acadian and General Provincial Advertiser. Wolfville, NS
The Acadian Orchardist. Wolfville, NS
The Advertiser. Kentville, NS
The Berwick Register. Berwick, NS
The Chronicle-Herald. Halifax, NS
The Evening Mail. Halifax, NS
The Halifax Herald. Halifax, NS
The Messenger and Visitor. Saint John, NB
The Morning Chronicle. Halifax, NS
The Morning Herald. Halifax, NS
The Nova Scotian and Weekly Chronicle. Halifax, NS
Nova Scotia Historical Quarterly. Halifax, NS
Nova Scotian. Halifax, NS
The Star and The New Star. Wolfville, NS
Windsor Tribune. Windsor, NS
Wolfville Acadian. Wolfville, NS

Image Sources

Bishop, Eileen: p. x

Butler, Ruth: p. 55

Colville, Rhoda and Alex: p. 231

Crawley, E. Sidney: p. 249

Eaton, Joan: pp. xii, 62, 75, 216

Esther Clark Wright Archives, Acadia University: pp. xiii, 13, 17, 18, 22, 23, 26, 35, 41, 45, 46, 48, 51, 68, 72, 73, 74, 76, 78, 79, 80, 81, 82, 85, 86, 87, 88 , 89, 90, 91, 92, 93, 94, 95, 96, 97, 98, 99, 100, 101, 102, 103, 107, 115, 118, 119, 126, 135, 137, 141, 143, 145, 149, 159, 167, 180, 181, 184, 187, 188, 189, 193, 194, 195, 203, 205, 206, 209, 214, 215, 232, 238, 248, 255, 257, 261, 266

Goodstein, Elizabeth : pp. 5, 162, 163, 169, 212, 213, 242, 244, 252, 264, 265

Haley, Susan: p. 236

Hill, Andria: p. 233

Kalkman, Tony : pp. 49, 59, 63, 157, 164, 192, 211

Kings County Museum: pp. 165, 171

The Nova Scotia Archives and Records Management: pp. ix; 14, 25, 30, 32, 34, 50, 54, 57, 58, 71, 104, 120, 152, 155, 160, 166, 182, 183, 190, 197, 240, 241, 245, 246, 247, 250, 259, 262

Pearman, Bill: p. 178

Peck, Warren: pp. 61, 109

Randall House Museum: pp. cover, title page, 2, 6, 7, 8, 9, 10, 11, 12, 15, 16, 19, 20, 21, 23, 24, 36, 37, 38, 39, 40, 42, 43, 44, 47, 52, 53, 60, 64, 83, 111, 112, 113, 114, 117, 121, 122, 123, 124, 125, 127, 129, 130, 132, 136, 147, 148, 150, 151, 156, 160, 162, 163, 166, 168, 170, 172, 174, 177, 179, 185, 186, 196, 198, 199, 200, 201, 202, 207, 208, 210, 217, 219, 220, 221, 223, 224, 226, 227, 228, 229, 230, 238, 243, 251, 252, 254